Marching, Fighting, Dying

Marching, Fighting, Dying

Experiences of Soldiers in the Peninsular War

Gareth Glover

Pen & Sword
MILITARY

AN IMPRINT OF PEN & SWORD BOOKS LTD.
YORKSHIRE - PHILADELPHIA

First published in Great Britain in 2021 by
PEN & SWORD MILITARY
An imprint of
Pen & Sword Books Ltd
Yorkshire – Philadelphia

Copyright © Gareth Glover 2021

ISBN 978 1 52676 022 7

The right of Gareth Glover to be identified as Author of this work has been asserted by him in accordance with the Copyright, Designs and Patents Act 1988.

A CIP catalogue record for this book is available from the British Library

All rights reserved. No part of this book may be reproduced or transmitted in any form or by any means, electronic or mechanical including photocopying, recording or by any information storage and retrieval system, without permission from the Publisher in writing.

Typeset in 10.5/13 Ehrhardt by Vman Infotech Pvt. Ltd.

Printed and bound by CPI Group (UK) Ltd, Croydon, CR0 4YY

Pen & Sword Books Ltd incorporates the imprints of Pen & Sword Archaeology, Atlas, Aviation, Battleground, Discovery, Family History, History, Maritime, Military, Naval, Politics, Social History, Transport, True Crime, Claymore Press,
Frontline Books, Praetorian Press, Seaforth Publishing and White Owl
For a complete list of Pen & Sword titles please contact

PEN & SWORD BOOKS LTD
47 Church Street, Barnsley, South Yorkshire, S70 2AS, England
E-mail: enquiries@pen-and-sword.co.uk
Website: www.pen-and-sword.co.uk

Or

PEN AND SWORD BOOKS
1950 Lawrence Rd, Havertown, PA 19083, USA
E-mail: Uspen-and-sword@casematepublishers.com
Website: www.penandswordbooks.com

Contents

List of Illustrations vii
Preface ix

Chapter 1: Storms, Sickness and Near Shipwrecks 1
Chapter 2: First Impressions 16
Chapter 3: Long Marches and Cold Nights 27
Chapter 4: Sun and Sickness 47
Chapter 5: Bad Food and Little of It 58
Chapter 6: The Allied Nations 74
Chapter 7: Thoughts on Portugal, Spain and France 86
Chapter 8: Billets and Cantonments 109
Chapter 9: Camp Life 128
Chapter 10: Corresponding with Home 138
Chapter 11: Discipline and Punishment 162
Chapter 12: The Enemy 178
Chapter 13: Girls, Women and Nuns 193
Chapter 14: The Experience of Battle 205
Chapter 15: Sieges 225
Chapter 16: Wounds and Hospitals 255
Chapter 17: The Ultimate Sacrifice 272

Conclusion 285
Bibliography 289
Index 293

List of Illustrations

1. Young officer and servant set out to join his regiment, from Rowlandson's *Johnny Newcome*.
2. On the march in the rains, by St Clair.
3. Muleteers near Irun, by Batty.
4. Light dragoon outpost, by William Wollen.
5. A young officer learns how to smoke and drink, from Rowlandson's *Johnny Newcome*.
6. Soldiers on the march, by Thomas Rowlandson.
7. 10th Hussars in camp at Morales, by Denis Dighton.
8. Cavalry stabling in a church.
9. Bivouac at Vilha Velha 1811, by St Clair.
10. Spanish camp in the Pyrenees, by Batty.
11. Officer on the Sick List, from Rowlandson's *Johnny Newcome*.
12. The troops advance – note the soldier stripping the dead in the foreground – from Rowlandson's *Johnny Newcome*.
13. Battle of Albuera, by William Wollen.
14. Marching the French prisoners into Salamanca, by Edward Orme.
15. Storming a fortress.
16. Collecting the dead after Talavera, by Lady Butler.

Preface

A huge number of books have been published over the last two centuries on Wellington's army during the seven-year campaign in the Iberian Peninsula. Some of these works have been ground-breaking, utilizing significant original archival research to produce in-depth analysis which challenges our preconceptions and long-held beliefs. Unfortunately, however, these are still quite rare, while far too many simply repackage and regurgitate the same tired old clichés and use the same tried and trusted published sources, bringing little more to our understanding.

Many of these volumes have understandably concentrated on the strategies used (both at high and low level), the political maelstrom the war engendered and, of course, in-depth analysis of all of the individual campaigns, battles and sieges. Alongside these, there have also been a plethora of titles dealing with the uniforms worn and equipment used by the different armies, the logistical problems encountered in feeding large armies in the peninsula and even the influence of sea power on the campaign.

One aspect regularly explored within such works, is the analysis of the life of an ordinary soldier during these extremely hard campaigns. Previous titles on this particular subject, include Charles Oman's *Wellington's Army 1809-14*,[1] Antony Brett-James' *Life in Wellington's Army*,[2] Colonel H.C.B. Rogers' *Wellington's Army*[3] and of course Edward Coss's *All for the King's Shilling: The British Soldier under Wellington 1808-1814*,[4] to the very latest, in Gavin Daly's *The British Soldier in the Peninsular War*.[5] Alongside these works, many general histories of the campaigns and specific regimental studies often dip their toe into this subject area, as part of their overview of the campaign, but are usually little more than derivatives of these major works. However, all of these worthy titles suffer from the same single major flaw and it is the specific intention of the present volume to right this serious error.

---

1. Published by Edward Arnold 1913.
2. Published by Allen & Unwin 1972.
3. Published by Ian Allan 1979.
4. Published by the University of Oklahoma Press 2010.
5. Published by Palgrave Macmillan 2013.

There is an erroneous belief that literacy rates in Britain were very low in the early decades of the nineteenth century. In fact, literacy rates in Britain between 1750 and the early 1800s remained pretty constant at some 53 per cent of the adult population, but this generalized figure hides the true picture. In fact, male literacy rates regularly hovered around 60 per cent, whilst women saw a slow rise from a low of 30 per cent up to 40 per cent during this period and the gender gap continued to shrink until the 1880s, when it finally closed with both genders seeing literacy rates into the high 80 per cents.[6]

It is also presumed that both the Army and Navy were generally filled from the very lowest strata of society and therefore literacy rates were markedly lower within the armed forces than in the general population. There may well be a grain of truth in this assertion, but it can be shown that literacy rates within the armed forces was not as low as many would have us believe. The notion that the Army was simply full of the dregs of society and that very few in the ranks were literate is not only an outdated assertion, but is demonstrably wrong, although it is still strongly believed by many to this day. In fact, only around 5 per cent of recruits failed to sign their form (marking with an X instead) or record a previous trade of any description, although the 'catch-all' profession of labourer, which accounted for around 40 per cent of recruits, would clearly include a large number of unskilled workers, particularly agricultural labourers, with a low educational and literacy attainment. However, as the war progressed and economic hardships bit harder, the number of recruits from trades, particularly weavers from the hard-hit textile trade (hand weavers in Stockport saw wages decline from 25 shillings per week in 1802 to only 10 shillings in 1811), grew very significantly and therefore the educational standards of the average recruit rose with it.[7]

A second, but significant, factor in the steady rise in levels of literacy in the Army was the rise of religious Nonconformism, believing in individual Bible study, which of course encouraged converts to become more literate. Many senior officers, including the Duke of Wellington, were initially wary of the steadily-increasing number of prayer meetings and Bible study groups which were sprouting up within the Army, based on the fear that these soldiers would be less inclined to fight. However, experience showed this to be a fallacy and

---

6. Figures sourced from *The Great Escape, the Industrial Revolution in Theory and History* by Gregory Clark on Researchgate.net.
7. For further information on this subject, the reader is recommended to read Edward Coss's *All For the King's Shilling*, pp. 59–75.

Wellington allowed them to continue, although it is undoubtedly true that officers were strongly discouraged from becoming involved.[8]

This steady increase in overall literacy levels becomes significant during the 23 years of global war that was fought from 1793 almost without intermission until 1815, because of the very significant rise in the number of letters, journals and memoirs available to the researcher. The volume of social correspondence noticeably increases with each year of the war, but not simply within the better-educated officer class and non-commissioned officers, who were required to be literate to carry out their role fully, including completing written returns. There is also an admittedly smaller, but rapidly increasing, volume of personal correspondence from ordinary rankers as the war progresses and more is undoubtedly yet to be unearthed, as all the available archives are still yet to be searched thoroughly.

Even while the war continued, a few sets of letters were published from individuals serving in the Army, whilst journal-keeping on campaign almost became the height of fashion for officers. This however was less common for non-commissioned officers and virtually unknown for those in the ranks.

However, after the 'Great War' – as the Napoleonic Wars were known to Victorian Britain – there grew an insatiable public hunger for reminiscences of soldiers who had fought in the war, which graphically described not only the valour and bravery of battle, but also the hardships of long marches under a broiling sun and the terrible living conditions and hunger that they had often endured. Indeed, the genre is not unknown in our own times, with a public fascination still obvious for memoirs of those who fought in both World Wars and more modern conflicts.

This encouraged many ex-soldiers to dust off their old journals written during the conflict, or they simply wrote down whatever they could vaguely recall of events which happened decades before. However, such a competitive market, with its constant demands for ever-greater revelations, forced them to seek to bring more excitement to their stories. Unfortunately, the experience of war for most people is truly stated as 'long periods of boredom punctuated by short moments of excitement'.[9] It therefore often forced them to look beyond their own often mundane experiences, utilizing stories and experiences shared around the campfires, simply plagiarized from other accounts and unfortunately in some cases completely invented. Indeed, commercial writers even went so far as to 'ghost write' completely fictitious accounts of the war, possibly with the aid

---

8. See the *Memoirs of Lieutenant Edward Watson 9th Foot*, Ken Trotman, 2017, for clear evidence of such practices.
9. From John H. Arnold's *History, A Very Short Introduction*.

of an old campaigner for that feel of authenticity and these have too often been accepted as factual accounts by unwary historians.[10] Indeed, the use of the term 'Adventures' in their titles should always cause the historian to check their claims thoroughly. These memoirs should therefore be treated as suspect and must be used with extreme caution, fully understanding that their trials and tribulations will be heightened for pathos and their descriptions of battles and sieges fully exploit the reader's eager desire to read of valour, bravery and derring-do.

For all of these reasons, these memoirs are not firm material on which to base the true understanding of the soldier's lot serving with Wellington's army in the Iberian Peninsula. The dreaded 'hindsight', over-embellishment, exaggeration and the overt influence of William Napier's beautifully described but extremely biased *History of the Peninsular War*[11] make their accounts far too suspect to be of real use in gauging what it was really like to be there.

Even journals, apparently written up daily but not published until many years after the war, were susceptible to reworking by their authors. This again has to be guarded against, but the dangers of some editing of entries is less marked in those the author has studied, with many such journals produced purely for the interest of their families and themselves in later life. They were clearly never meant to be published and have often only been brought into the public domain many decades or even centuries later by military historians, who have generally faithfully reproduced the originals verbatim. The libellous and disparaging descriptions of fellow officers, the highly critical comments regarding the leadership qualities of their senior officers and their open criticism of the actions and tactics of their commanding generals prove that they were never intended for public scrutiny.

However, without doubt, the best evidence available to historians are the original letters sent from individual soldiers to their loved ones and the replies they received. The letters can contain much rumour and supposition, but no other writings honestly show the hopes, beliefs and aspirations of individuals at any given moment better than these. Secure from any fear of a censor and often totally disregarding the danger of the letters falling into enemy hands, these letters allowed the correspondent to vent their spleen in anger and frustration or to discuss their cunning plans for gaining recognition and advancement and to extoll their own virtues, when no one else seemed to notice them. Much of what

---

10. Examples of this genre are the three volumes of memoirs purportedly written by *Ned Clinton; the Commissary*, in fact the work of Francis Glasse who was a half-pay captain in the 25th Foot, and *Charles O'Malley, the Irish Dragoon*, written by Charles Lever, an Irish novelist. There is also much doubt over *The Military Adventures of Charles O'Neil* as no evidence has been found of his existence in the muster rolls of the 28th Foot.
11. Published between 1828 and 1840.

they say about the war, future operations and the abilities of senior officers were clearly never meant to be discussed beyond the four walls of their family home and regular cautionary statements appear warning against breaking this rule, many a young officer finding his career prospects severely blighted by the publication of their letters home in the newspapers, which were regularly delivered to the Army with the post.

This, of course, was a time when every single aspect of life was contracted via copious paperwork – indeed life seems to have consisted for many of little more than reading and writing endless reams of correspondence. Everything was committed to paper in a society which was influenced, instructed and indeed was completely reliant on the written word to function at all. Postal services were therefore highly efficient for the age, although overseas mail was always very susceptible to the vagaries of the winds and the threat of capture by enemy ships. Indeed, the Post Office packets ran out of Falmouth regularly, once a week to Lisbon, while another sailed weekly for La Corunna (later in the war this changed to San Sebastian).[12] In perfect wind conditions this journey could be achieved in four to five days, but in stormy weather or contrary winds this same journey could last up to three or four weeks. What it provided, however, was the possibility of a very regular and pretty certain correspondence with home and it was used increasingly to keep in touch with family and friends, to conduct business whilst out of the country and to obtain much-needed supplies from Britain via parcel post.

All of this encouraged the regular two-way correspondence between members of the Army and family at home and it is this material, written for a private, trusted audience, full of their hopes, fears and the gossip of the Army at that precise moment, that is so vital to historians, enabling us to gauge their honest, unfiltered views on all aspects of military life and the operations they were involved in at the very moment it was happening.

It is for these reasons that the author has chosen to reappraise their impressions, of the countries and peoples they encountered, the trials and tribulations they endured while serving in the British Army in such a trying climate and their attitudes to every aspect of this 'alien' world, only using their letters and the journals that can be shown to be untainted by later amendment or manipulation. This decision purposely prohibits the use of any of the post-war memoirs that flourished so much in Victorian times, but are so badly tainted as serious historic documents. Readers knowledgeable on the Napoleonic Wars will therefore search in vain for excerpts from such household names as John Aitchison, James Anton, George Bell, Robert Blakeney, Henry Browne,

---

12. Arthur Hamilton Norway, *History of the Post Office Packet Service between the years 1793-1815*, London, 1895, p 8.

Edward Costello, Joseph Donaldson, George Gleig, George Hennel, James Hope, John Kincaid, William Lawrence, Jonathan Leach, Thomas Morris, David Robertson, August Schaumann, Moyle Sherer, George Simmons, Harry Smith, William Surtees, William Warre and William Wheeler. One later journal has, however, been utilized, this being the memoirs of Private John Morris Jones of the 39th Foot, for a limited number of passages where he deals with subjects rarely discussed in letters home.

Most of the correspondents utilized in this work will be completely unknown to the reader or at least little known, for far fewer of these much less exciting but far more historically significant letters and daily journals have been published, something that the present author continues to seek to rectify.

The views and attitudes they portray are fresh and uncensored, but more importantly they are untainted by hindsight, revision or any of the other dreadful alterations and amendments that can seriously tarnish, if not completely destroy, their value as historic documents. Some of their attitudes will be familiar and will back up preconceptions based on reading the memoirs, but at other times, their attitudes will surprise the reader and seriously challenge these preconceptions. All that can be said is that, this is the nearest we can ever hope to get to actually being there over 200 years ago and experiencing what they saw and endured.

Gareth Glover

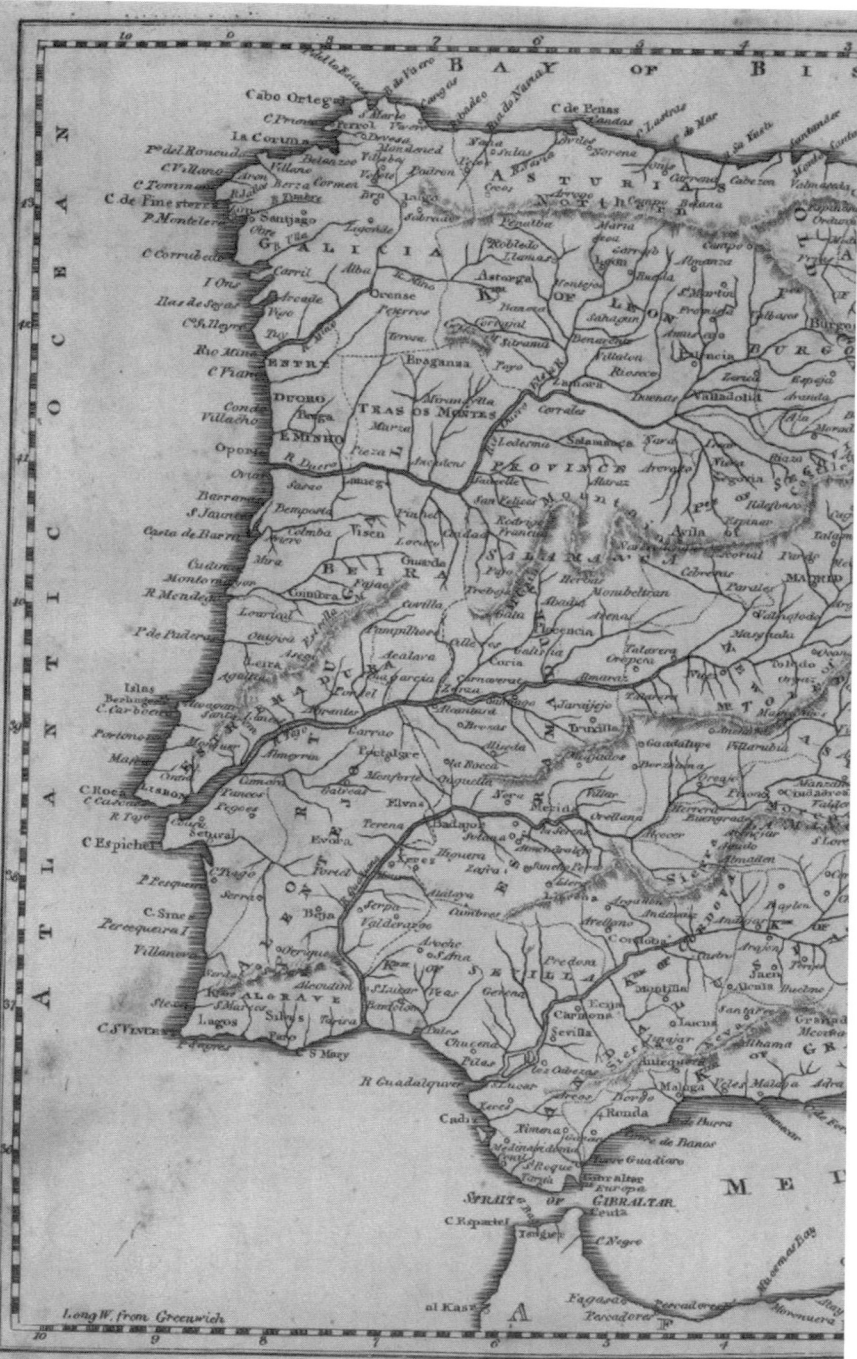

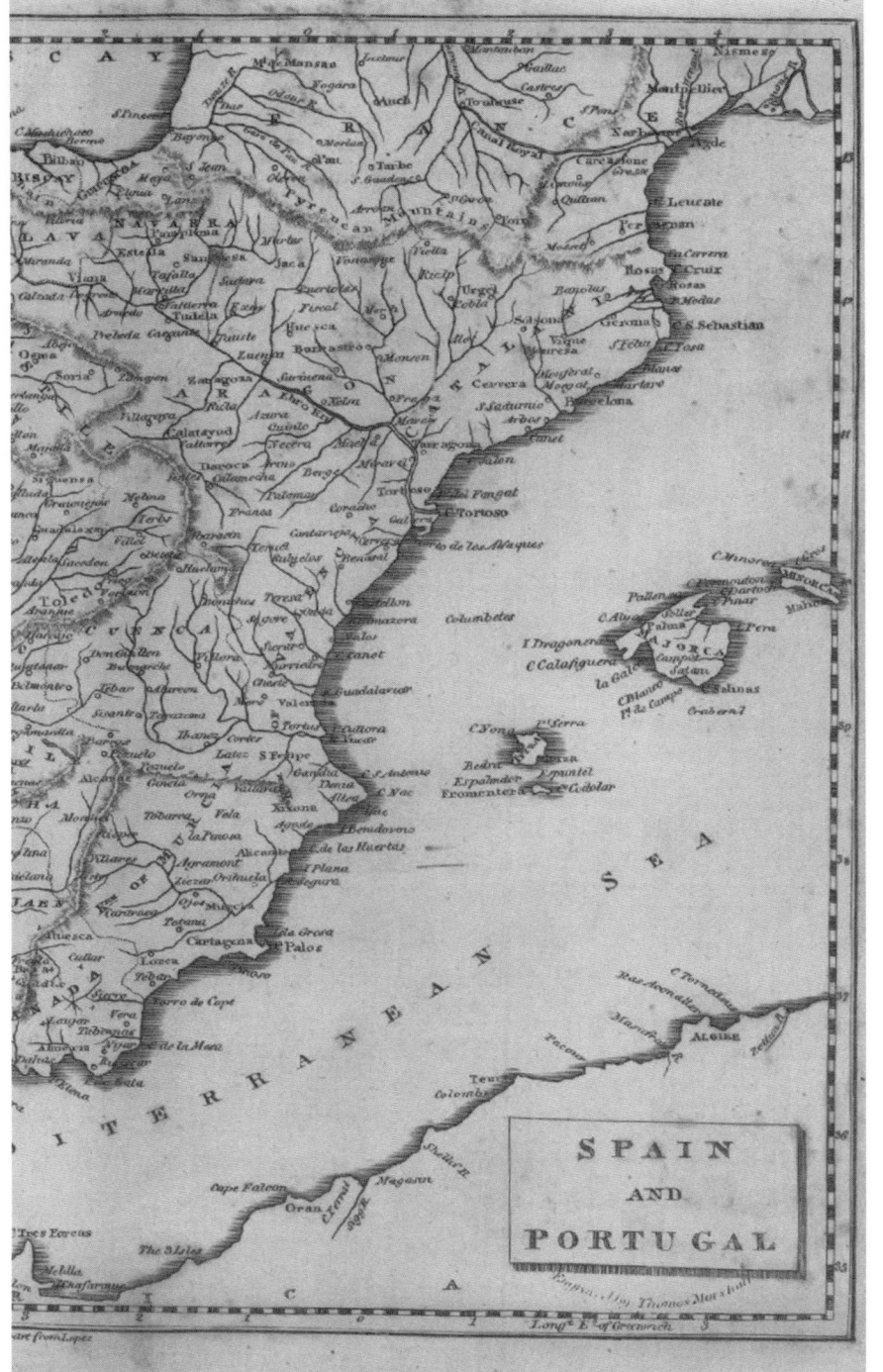

Chapter 1

Storms, Sickness and Near Shipwrecks

For most men, sailing with their regiment for foreign fields was often their first ever encounter with the sea and certainly of a prolonged sea voyage; unsurprisingly therefore, many wrote in detail of this alien world and of their adventures. Many young officers were also sent out to join their regiments to replace a fallen colleague, often accompanied by a reinforcement of men for the battalion on foreign service. When a large force was required to sail, the troops were often carried in Royal Navy vessels which had a number of their cannon removed to accommodate the soldiers (referred to as being armed '*en flute*') or on board fleets of hundreds of transport ships hired by the Board of Transport specifically for the occasion, all of which proceeded in a huge convoy for their protection. These small parties of recruits sent out to their regiments as replacements usually proceeded in transport ships, but as the war progressed it became clear that the danger of capture at sea was too great and the professionalism of their crews was not always what it should be; troops were therefore more often sent out on board warships, the transports being utilized for carrying supplies. Lieutenant George Ulrich Barlow of the 52nd Foot confirmed this change of policy in a letter home to reassure his family.

> Torbay, 13 February 1811
> You will I am sure, be rejoiced to know that instead of shipping us in Board transports, the government intends discontinuing this practise & for the future prefers sending out the troops in men of war, for which we have seen no unemployment. The dangers attending the former species of vessels & especially at this stormy season of the year, are well known to all, manned as they frequently are so badly & with such unskilful seamen. I could tell you stories about their experience, as astonishing as they are true. A part of our regiment were nearly lost off Portland Bill & the Master nearly carried them into Calais, mistaking it for Dungeness Point.

Private John Morris Jones of the 1st Battalion of the 39th Foot was ordered to sail with a detachment of troops to join his regiment in Malta in 1808. His first impressions of the ship were not good, but his description of the organisation of the troops on board is invaluable.

> We were embarked at Cowes on board the *William*, troop brig and ordered to proceed to Falmouth to join [a] convoy. Before leaving Cowes, two month's pay was advanced for each man, for the purpose of being laid out in [a] Russia duck frock and trowsers, two check shirts, tobacco, soup &c . . . We sailed from Falmouth on the 20 February [1808], under convoy of the *Antelope* man of war and a gun brig. There were certainly in this fleet not less than 40 sail in all, troop ships and merchantmen, principally the former. Our little brig was a slow sailing, clumsy old craft, formerly a South Shields collier; and altogether as unfitted for the use for which she was hired as it is possible to conceive. Besides which, the provisions she carried, (the grog alone excepted) were of the worst description; maggots in the biscuit, weevils in the flour, stinking suet. The oatmeal intended for porridge, or burgoo, as it is sometimes called, was as if it had been the sweepings of some storeroom of that article. The salt meat, especially the beef, was an indigestible nondescript substance, that when boiled four or five hours, had much the appearance of wetted lumps of dark coloured mahogany or logwood, stringy, sapless, salt and innutritious; the butter rancid grease and the cheese putrid and offensive in the extreme. In this old tub and to such food, we were in all probability, to be confined for several weeks. We had been at sea three days and were on the skirts of the Bay of Biscay, going before a fine stiff breeze, when the bad sailing qualities of our old craft became very evident, being the hindmost of the whole convoy; and unable to keep up, although we had what our skipper considered, as much canvas exposed to the wind as the brig could bear, or was consistent with safety. A signal from the man of war to crowd sail and close up for the night compelled him to shake out a few reefs; but still we were the only laggard.
>
> . . . The soldiers are divided into three watches. During the day everyone, man, woman and child, should there be any of the latter on board, are compelled to be on deck from eight o'clock in the morning, until dusk in the evening; excepting the sick, or when the weather is so very tempestuous that it is deemed dangerous for the whole to remain up; then in that case, two watches are ordered down, the other remaining on deck. In fact it would be next to impossible to cram the whole number between decks, unless they were to be packed as tightly as are the unfortunate negroes on board a slaver. For the berths, told off to every mess of six men, are not calculated to afford room for more than four. So that of necessity, two thirds only of the number on board

can find room below. During the night the watch on deck is relieved every four hours; and the noise occasioned thereby, that is in rousing up the heavy sleepers and the would be skulkers and in calling the roll, renders a nap of more than four hours' duration impossible. He must indeed, be a sound sleeper who can remain undisturbed amidst all this bustle and uproar. I should utterly fail were I to attempt to describe the compound of vile smells ascending from between decks. The breaths and exhalations proceeding from so many human bodies crowded below, added to the smells of pitch, tar and bilge water, from the depths of the hold baffles all description.

For an officer, the purchase of his 'sea stock' to ensure that he had a supply of decent food, rather than the ration 'slops' available during the passage, was vital. Indeed Cornet George Woodberry of the 18th Hussars listed the meagre provisions he purchased purely for his own voyage.

> Saturday 9 January 1812
> Laid in sea stock: 12 Live fowls, Lemons and Oranges [for punch], 2 Hams, 2 Cases Portable Soup, 3 Dried Tongues, 3 Quarts of Oats for porridge, 6 Half quarters of Loaves, 3 Dozen Sour Herrings, 3 Pound of Butter, 3 Dozen Bottles of Porter, 311 Pound of Tea, 3 Bottles of Brandy, 1 Pound of Coffee, 2 Bushels of Potatoes, 9 Pounds of Sugar, 2 Pounds of Cheese, 3 Pounds of Wax Candles, 30 pounds of Fresh meat, 3 Jars of Pickles, Milk, 6 Pounds of Rice for pudding.

Others, such as Robert Duffield Cocke, a clerk in the Pay Master's Department, were lucky enough to be able to procure a cabin on board the mail packet from Falmouth for a handsome fee[1] and was treated to spacious accommodation and excellent food. Falmouth was the packets' base simply because it was the furthest port to the west and therefore much less prone to becoming trapped by contrary winds.

> Lisbon 5 July 1811
> We all went in a boat to the packet where we staid [sic] till about 8 o'clock and then set sail, the packet is called the *Darlington*. It is possessed of every accommodation. It has a large cabin where we all messed and about 12 smaller ones to sleep in. We had the *quickest* passage I ever

---

1. The price of a passage out to Gibraltar, one way, was 35 guineas (nearly £2,000 in today's terms). Quoted in Norway, *History of the Post Office Packet Service*, p. 10.

heard of being only 4 days and a bit going over. We set off on Friday and got to Lisbon and anchored in the Tagus on Wednesday morning at 9 o'clock. It was impossible to have a pleasanter voyage for we fared most sumptuously always having three or 4 joints of the best meats and excellent soups. Captain Harvey is a very good fellow and made us all as comfortable as possible.

When a fleet left, there was often much pomp and ceremony as the warships passed each other, the scene further enhanced by the regimental bands formed on the quarterdecks to serenade the other troops as they passed. Band Master John Westcott of the 26th (Cameronian) Regiment described the scene as his regiment sailed from Jersey on 25 June 1811.

The fleet of transports having on board the 26th, 32nd and 77th Regiments under convoy of the *Alcmene* frigate sailed at day break with a favourable wind leaving on shore one major and several soldiers who had gone on shore the night before and could not join us, the sea being too rough for a boat to follow, during the latter part of the day the different bands of the fleet played on passing each other. The *Brixton* the headquarter ship of the 26th Regiment cheered their old companions the 32nd Regiment as their transports passed which was returned by the whole fleet in a grand style . . .

The vagaries of the wind and weather, however, could lead to days and even weeks of being trapped on board the transport ships without even leaving harbour, as the wind was constantly contrary. Although officers could take rooms ashore rather than stay on board, they found the wait equally frustrating and woe betide them if they missed the sailing gun announcing their departure. Even once at sea, poor weather and changes in the wind direction could force the ships back to harbour. Perhaps an excessive example, although not that uncommon, was that of Ensign George Ulrich Barlow of the 52nd Foot.

HMS Pompee, Torbay, 11 February 1811
   The morning subsequent to the date of my last, . . . we again put to sea & after beating about two days & nights the squadron has resumed its original station for the *fourth time* since it left Portsmouth. The whole of us are happy & comfortable enough it is true but are become heartily sick of these delays at a moment when we are so eagerly desirous of joining the armies. Westerly winds at this season of the year & on this coast constantly prevail so I fear much that we shall never clear the Channel or be detained at anchor for some time to come.

Being at sea for any length of time without employment can quickly become tedious, the days merging into one. Lieutenant William Swabey of the Royal Horse Artillery wrote unhappily:

> 1 August 1811
> This day passed with the usual sameness on board ship, it began however to get rough, and the wind blew from an unfavourable quarter.

Many found the process of gaining their 'sea legs' difficult, such as Lieutenant George Barlow, who, as he recorded in his letters, found it impossible to get over the intense feeling of nausea at all.

> *HMS Pompee* at sea off the Rame Head 1 February 1811
> By dint of constantly walking the deck & keeping in the air I have kept off the seasickness; It has affected me in a very slight degree, but neither so as to take away my appetite or spirits. In the wardroom however, some of my brother officers are in a deplorable state. Two or three have been stretched in their cots & bedding the whole of the last two days without stirring or eating a morsel & others are pale & as silent as the grave. Of this last sort you may suppose the number to be pretty considerable in a crew of 1,100 persons of all descriptions. I have just been visiting the lower deck as Officer of the Watch, but however was much surprised to find the soldiers in so much better a state than I could possibly have expected.

Others sailed with good prospects of a pleasant voyage only to find that the weather turned midway. The Bay of Biscay has always carried a reputation for stormy seas and Private Henry Willis of the 1st Life Guards was one of those who experienced them first hand.

> Belem, 13 December 1812
> My dear Sister,
> . . . I shall now give you a short account of our voyage since we left England. We embarked at Portsmouth on the 24th October for Lisbon and sailed the same day. We were obliged to anchor in Stokes Bay where we lay till the 8th of November. The wind proved favourable, we sailed until we came into the Bay of Biscay, the wind then proved unfavourable [&] we tossed up and down for three or four days and nights, expecting every minute to be our last. Thank God it proved to the contrary, the sea became calm [&] we sailed on till we came in sight of Lisbon.

Unsurprisingly, storms are a major theme of many depictions of the passage to Portugal or Spain. Lieutenant Henry Hough of the Royal Artillery wrote of his experiences in his diary.

> 23 March 1812
>
> When we found ourselves off Alderney, the wind blowing very fresh and a great deal of motion, saw the Cherbourg blockading squadron astern. Got cold roast mutton, biscuit and smoky tea, without milk for breakfast. About 11 o'clock spoke the *Thrasian* gun brig cruising, soon after which it began to rain and blow very hard. Reefed some of our sails but the wind was still favourable. About 1 o'clock we lost sight of land, going at this time nearly 8 knots an hour. There was a very great and sickly motion of the ship in the afternoon and with difficulty we managed to keep the dishes on table at dinner, continually getting the contents of your neighbour's plate into your lap.

The weather steadily worsened and on the Sunday Hough recalls that they apparently suffered a near-catastrophic loss.

> 29 March 1811 (Sunday)
>
> We lost all most all our crockery-ware this day by the ship's giving a sudden roll during our dinner hour and had not the officers of the gunroom volunteered their china, I fear we should have experienced great inconvenience the remainder of the passage.

William Swabey of the Royal Horse Artillery also found the stormy weather difficult to handle.

> 10 August 1811
>
> Today we were obliged to breakfast on deck, holding fast by the ropes and nothing would stand on the table at dinner. Every soul was sick except ourselves . . . so much so, that Burgoo was not cooked, the men had not stomach to eat it.

Ensign Charles Crowe of the 48th Foot recorded an amusing incident consequent of stormy weather in his journal, but as will be seen, the consequences became potentially very serious indeed.

> Sunday 16 November 1812
>
> Vander and I agreed to reverence the day, and a parade for divine service had been ordered. I was to have officiated as chaplain, but the

rain was too heavy to allow any but the sailors working the ship to remain on deck. The Master dined with us. When he left our cabin he foresaw a storm and gave orders accordingly. Late in the evening the hatchways were closed and covered over with tarred paulings [*sic*] and a most awful night ensued. The wind blew great guns, and the sea ran mountains high. Our ship pitched and tossed and reeled most furiously. Sleep was out of [the] question, especially after midnight, when the table broke from the lashings to the floor, and set at liberty all our trunks stowed beneath, which drove slap bang from side to side as the vessel rolled. Thus Cobbold and myself in the lower berths were alternately in dread of unwelcome intruders. I succeeded in catching hold of and securing my own trunk and was leaning forward to reach Vander's when Dr Rice, anxious about his case of instruments, dropped from the berth above, and caught my head between his thighs. At this very juncture, the ship lurched suddenly to larboard,[2] so that the doctor, being rather short, could but just reach the floor, and by clinging to his own berth, save himself from falling backward. Thus, I remained in a pillory without the possibility of withdrawing my head, to the great amusement of our opposite companions. Pinching and thumping availed me not, for the doctor could not budge a jot until the ship righted on its way to falling to starboard, which made the doctor scramble up to save his legs from the trunks, and thus set me free. All of us now could join the hearty laugh and joke the doctor's nimbleness in saving his shanks. Our glee was however, cut short, for as the ship was rising on a lofty wave and appeared to stand on end, a cross wave struck our stern, made every plank and timber quiver, smashed our dead lights, or storm window shutters, to atoms, and shipped much water.

Cobbold and I had now to change our operations, and were obliged as the vessel rolled to either side, to hold up our bed clothes to prevent the water washing into our berths, and were thus employed until the water by degrees found its way under the cabin door to the ship's waist. All this was bad enough, but in the hold, where men and horses were so closely stowed, the scene was horrible! Three fine horses were suffocated, and falling against those next to them, threw them down, and they by their plunging injured others. When the storm mitigated in the morning, so as to allow the hatchways to be partly opened and fresh air admitted some men fainted. As soon as practicable the dead horses

---

2. 'Larboard' was for centuries the naval term for the left, being replaced in the mid-nineteenth century by 'port' to avoid the obvious confusion with 'starboard'.

were drawn out of the hold and thrown overboard, but it was a very difficult undertaking to set the other poor fallen and frightened animals again on their legs, during the continued rolling of the vessel. Other ships also threw their dead horses, the most crowded had, consequently, more casualties.

Lieutenant Frederick Philips of the 15th Hussars recorded that on occasions even the ship's Master could be unnerved by the extreme weather and that physical injuries were not uncommon.

> Corunna 11 November 1808
> On Sunday morning about 3 o'clock the wind changed and began to blow most violently. Our ship rolled so amazingly that the Master of the vessel said that he did not expect the masts would have stood, everything was in an uproar in the cabin and all over the deck, several of the men were thrown down and cut their legs very badly . . .

Even Robert Duffield Cooke, sailing in luxury on the Lisbon packet, found the weather too much for him initially, although things did improve markedly as he admits in his continued comments of 5 July 1811 regarding his berth.

> It was only a pity we could not enjoy the good things, but we were so sick the first 2 days we could neither walk stand eat or drink. In fact, we could do nothing but puke which we certainly did, fine sport for the sailors. The third day we got a little better and the fourth we eat [*sic*] enough to make up for all the others, we had such famous meals on board the packet that I verily believe it has spoiled us for the Lisbon slops.

However, the vagaries of the constantly changing sea are encapsulated in Band Master Westcott's diary.

> 26 June 1811
> Spoke to a Spanish brig bound to Corunna in the morning, entered the Bay of Biscay with a gentle breeze in the evening, passed several Spanish ships through the day.
> 29th Becalmed in the bay from the evening of the 27th to the evening of the 29th, during this calm the officers paid visits from ship to ship.
> 1 of July Fresh breezes wind perfectly fair, fleet all in sight.
> 3 Some gales in the morning. [At] night drew near the coast of Portugal. The transport rocked very much from the heavy swell of the sea.

Storms, Sickness and Near Shipwrecks 9

Life at sea could always be very dangerous for the uninitiated, even at the most innocuous moments. Lieutenant William Swabey recorded an unfortunate accident which befell an artilleryman.

> 2 August 1811 off Falmouth
> As the *Trusty*, Captain Macdonald's transport, was bringing to, a Bombardier Cochrane, being on the anchor, unfortunately fell over and was drowned. He swam for some time, but the ship being under weigh, a boat could not be lowered with sufficient expedition. This poor fellow's fate is the more to be lamented as he had recently purchased his discharge, but on hearing the troop was for service, immediately joined us again; as a soldier, he is a great loss.

Fogs were of course a real danger, while constant rain was also a serious problem for ships crammed with troops, as George Barlow recorded in a letter home.

> *HMS Pompee*, Torbay, 11 February 1811
> During this last trip, two of our squadron parted company in a thick fog & the remainder steering as they thought for the Berry Head, when the atmosphere became a little clear found themselves making for the Eddystone,[3] so you see we were completely out of our reckoning & were obliged to stand off & on the whole of last night, not being able to reach the bay before dark. Independent of all this lingering work, I am afraid that the troops will become sickly by so long a continuance on board a ship, crowded together with rainy weather & seas which prevent the lower deck ports from being open, which is the more necessary as 600 men alone sleep in that part of the vessel.

Being near the English coast there was an opportunity to still write home regularly, as Barlow explained.

> I have written five or six letters to you since we first came to this anchorage. I know not whether you receive them regularly; a man comes off every day from shore, to whom they are intrusted, but whether this is executed faithfully & punctually I cannot ascertain.

---

3. Berry Head is near Torbay in Devon and approaching this would put the ship close to shore in the lee of the land. Eddystone Rocks are 30 miles to the west, off Plymouth, leaving the ship fully exposed to the heavy seas.

Meeting ships at sea was also taken advantage of to send off post when the opportunity arose. Captain James Gubbins of the 13th Light Dragoons readily took the opportunity to hastily write a few lines to reassure his sister of his safety.

> Friday 17 May 1811
> All well and a fine breeze, pleasant prospect, a vessel from Lisbon to England and a moment to say, God Bless you all a thousand and a thousand times. We expect to be in Lisbon in five or six days. I am [berthed?] with the captain and a pleasant party but my heart and best hopes are with you.
> My kindest and most affectionate love to my father & recollect me to dear Jane. Adieu, a thousand hugs and kisses, your affectionate brother, James Gubbins

The danger of being taken by an enemy privateer were also a constant concern, the sight of an unknown sail often causing preparations to be made for defending themselves. Robert Duffield Cooke was secure, however, safe in the knowledge that his sleek packet could outrun almost any privateer.

> Lisbon 6 July 1811
> During the time we were on board the packet we were chased 2 or 3 times by different ships but we sailed so fast they could not catch us. One ship followed 2 days and a night but was obliged to give up at last.

For those travelling on the slower, much more vulnerable and lightly armed transport ships, it was a much greater concern, as shown in Cornet George Woodberry's diary entry, despite the distractions of porpoises, owls and women!

> Saturday [23] January 1813
> Wind still continues very fair, saw the Lisbon packet sail through the fleet. An owl was found roosting on one of the masts this morning but was frightened away before a gun could be loaded. Two women aboard very ill, one brought on deck in a very fainting state, gave her some brandy and my oatmeal. One of them tried tonight to throw themselves over the edge. Great tumult! This night an American privateer chased us and we to windward of the fleet, but we sailed too fast for her, we saw large shoals of porpoises jumping out of the sea, round the vessel. Some on board who wished to be considered knowing, said it predestinates hard weather, but the weather still remains as it did. During the night, we passed Cape Ortegal on the coast of Spain.

> The fleet is very much dispersed. Hope to God, none of our transports are taken by the French or the Yankies, several suspicious vessels have been seen this evening.

The greatest fear of all for them, however, was the threat of the ship springing a major leak or being wrecked, a not-uncommon danger in the age of sail. Indeed, large numbers of troops were lost throughout the war by such tragic events. Most of our eyewitnesses were lucky enough not to encounter such a disaster, when the chances of survival were often very small indeed. However Private John Morris Jones recorded his misadventures in just such a near disaster, between 11 and 12 o'clock in the forenoon of 24 February 1808.

> Just as the steward was about to serve out the grog, one of our men . . . having occasion to go down the fore hatchway for something or other, discovered that the vessel had sprung a leak. In a moment all was alarm and confusion. The skipper above, was incredulous. His doubts however, were soon removed, when on descending the fore hatchway, he had startling proof of the truth of our state, by being convinced that what we had before asserted was nothing more than the water we occasionally shipped when a wave would break over us, was in reality as the man had reported. At this time the water was nearly as high as the orlop deck, or cable tier; and on sounding, it was found that we had upwards of five feet of water in the well. I was in my berth ill of seasickness, where I had lain nearly two days; but the fright occasioned by the reported danger, was an instantaneous, a complete and a lasting cure. Slipping on my nether garment only and not losing time to search for shoes, jacket, or any other portion of clothing, I sprang up the main hatchway and mechanically attached myself to the party then commencing to work the starboard pump, which was on the lee side of the vessel. It was soon ascertained where the leak was situate[d] . . . A signal of distress was made as soon as one of our four rusty and ill mounted carronades could be got ready; and a flag, for the same purpose, hoisted half-mast high. As soon as the *Antelope* got within hail and had learnt our condition, the skipper was ordered to keep the pumps agoing, to use every other available means of keeping the brig afloat and to make the best of his way to Gibraltar . . . No boat could have lived a moment amidst the tremendous waves that rolled around us, threatening every moment to engulph [sic] us for ever. In the meantime the wind was increasing; but the weather in other respects, was clear and fine for the time of year.

. . . In the first alarm, grog, dinner, all had been forgotten. Before evening the leak had so far increased, that it was found impossible to get at the provisions, all were under water; and therefore no refreshment could be had; and to add to our distress in this respect, the remains of the fresh water in the scuttle butt had, from the continued washing of the waves over us, become nearly as brine as the surrounding ocean; and as to getting a supply from the hold, that was entirely out of the question. It would have been madness to have attempted it, for by this time the water casks were beginning to get loose.

When I saw the sun setting I considered that it was the last time my eyes would ever greet it. Night now rapidly closed around us, increasing the horrors of our situation. Before it came quite dark the *Antelope* came within hail, nearer it was not safe to approach, who ordered us to fire a gun as often as practicable during the night to indicate our whereabouts. This duty devolved on our serjeant, our captain's heroic wife supplying our gunner with a red hot poker, which she continued to heat by maintaining a little fire in the cabin stove grate; her husband, who ought from his position to have shewn us an example of fortitude, had from fright I conceive, become a worthless cypher, an imbecile. Only once during this night of danger was his voice heard . . .

In arranging and posting the men for the work of pumping and baling during the night, I was removed with the others that had been employed at the whip and stationed at the weather pump. Here we were obliged to lash ourselves by the first rope each could lay hold of, in order to secure ourselves from being washed overboard; the sea frequently making a complete breach over us. In the early part of the afternoon, my cap had been blown far away to leeward. Conceive me bareheaded, barefoot, with nought on save a check shirt, and my Russia duck trowsers; constantly wetted by sea water; my right foot painful to a great degree from having been crushed and wounded by the brake or handle of the pump; the horrors of our helpless condition; my thoughts at times wandering to the home of my childhood, the quiet glens and lofty hills of old Cambria, but instantly recalled to the awful eternity staring us in the face; conceive all this and much more than I have language to express and all will fall far short to describe the agonised feelings experienced during that dreadful night . . .

About midnight the pump at which I was employed became choked and useless. How was this dreadful misfortune to be remedied? We had no ship's carpenter on board; a culpable oversight or neglect on the part of those whose duty it was to have seen to this. One of our men,

James Garnish, who had served an apprenticeship to the business of a joiner and house carpenter and who afterwards declared that he knew no more of a pump than did a pump of him, undertook to repair it. For this purpose it was necessary to lift the pump trees on deck. It was found on examination, that the valves were worn out. Leather for the purpose of replacing them could not be got at. The soles of two or three pairs of our men's new shoes supplied the material. During more than an hour which was occupied in this necessary repair, the leak gained on us frightfully. When the pump trees were replaced, a number of top coats tightly wedged between the deck planks and the pump sufficed to keep it tolerably steady. The rest that we had had the advantage of enabled us to recommence our labour with renewed energy. Not long after this the other pump became useless from the same cause, was repaired in the same manner and with equal success. In fact this man, Garnish, under divine providence, was the cause of our being enabled to escape a watery grave. By this time a great part of the ballast in the hold had been washed to leeward; and the brig headed dangerously to that side, her deck forming a considerable angle with the horizon, the water casks and every other buoyant article below, floating about and the lower berths on the lee side completely under water. All the canvas we had exposed to the wind during the night were the jib, the foresail, close reefed storm stay sail.

Shortly after the appearance of the morning star, the joyful news was passed among us that the wind had shifted a few points, and was indicating a cessation of the intense force it had so long maintained. Hope now began to beam where despair had so long reigned. By nine o'clock the gale had settled down to a gentle breeze; still the agitation of the immense waves was exceedingly great.

At 10 the commodore sent his long boat with his carpenter and crew to examine if it were possible to keep us afloat. He reported that the brig was sinking. Long before this time, owing to our prolonged labour and the want of refreshment of any kind, the spells at the pumps had become exceedingly brief and exhausting; in fact, five minutes was the utmost extent of a spell. The long boats from most of the troop ships were now ordered to crowd about us and take us off; but on no account to take more than four or five in each. At this time it was 'save yourselves who can'. The quarter deck became strewn with the officer's baggage; but we were ordered to take nothing but what we stood in, neither arms, accoutrements, nor knapsacks . . . In less than 20 minutes after leaving her, the *William* sank beneath the waves of the Bay of Biscay.

Lieutenant George Young of the 38th Foot wrote home rejoicing his safe arrival at Pasajes in Spain after severe weather.

> Arcangues, February 1814
>
> I sailed on the 27th of November and landed at Passages [*sic*] on the 17th of December after experiencing very severe weather and in danger of being lost at sea. We put into St. Andero [Santander] with our foremast and main topmast carried away and otherwise very much injured.

Thankfully, most succeeded in reaching the Iberian coast safely and the joyful description of the relief of the soldiers on their arrival in the mouth of the River Tagus is palpable in the diary entry of Band Master Westcott.

> 4 July 1811
>
> Fine with a slite [*sic*] breeze from the north, came in sight of land about five o'clock in the morning, a Portuguese pilot came on board, several fishing boats came alongside. Sailed passed [St] Julian Castle, said to be one of the largest castles in the country.[4] On entering the River Tagus, we passed a rock, to the right, which has a battery on it. The regiment cheered on passing Belem Castle which is situated on the left side the Tagus, and nearly about five miles from the castle of Lisbon which city it may be counted a part, as its buildings continue to Lisbon, a great depot is kept at Belem for the sick or rather convalescents of the army, and also all women having children are left at Belem and receive provisions at the expense of government not being permitted by Lord Wellington to follow the army . . . We anchored off the Commercial Square at *Lisbon* about four o'clock in the afternoon, a vast number of vessels of all nations were laying in the Tagus with the different flags flying, but particularly the Americans, who's vessels were all dressed off with colours in consequence of this being the day that America declared its Independence, from Great Britain, there appeared to be about two hundred American vessels in the river, several Portuguese men of war, were laying in the river, some not finished, with the three allied nations flags flying, the Portuguese on the main, British on the fore and Spanish, on the mizzen. Several British line of battle ships were also in the river, the *Barfleur* of 90 guns, was the admiral's ship, a number of

---

4. Wellington made Forte de Sao Juliao da Barra at Cascais his embarkation point behind the lines of Torres Vedras if all had failed.

boats came along side with the most delicious fruit of every kind that Portugal produced, which was very acceptable to us after the voyage and remarkable cheap.

It is clear that the naval world was a source of great fascination for many soldiers, often being their first experience of a sea voyage. However, the sameness of each day for those not engaged in the working of the ship soon became monotonous once they were over the miseries of seasickness. It was also a world full of dangers and mysteries and these often come across in their letters, but few were unhappy to see the end of the journey as their ships sailed into the mouth of the Tagus and the foreign adventures that lay ahead.

Chapter 2

First Impressions

For many, the arrival of their ship at the mouth of the River Tagus was their first experience of a foreign land, as access to much of the continent of Europe had been closed to Britons almost without intermission since 1793.[1] The shimmering blue waters, the whitewashed towns hugging the shoreline with magnificent mountains forming a picturesque backdrop and the discordant, incomprehensible chatter of the locals, all made the scene both enchanting and intriguing. Once ashore, however, the chimerical façade was quickly removed, as the reality of life in Portugal and the daily challenges it presented were revealed. Many of these young soldiers were keen to write home to advise of their safe arrival and to excitedly impart their immediate impressions, but the shock of encountering such an alien country is often palpable. Ensign John Lucie Blackman of the Coldstream Guards wrote home from on board the *Royalist* transport as they arrived in the Tagus on Saturday, 14 March 1812.

> We entered the Tagus yesterday about midday and of course we were all amazingly struck with the beauty and novelty of the prospect; we all expected to disembark that day or early this morning . . .

The response of Captain William Bragge of the 3rd Dragoons was also very typical on his arrival in the Tagus on 29 August 1811.

> The entrance to Lisbon is truly grand and beautiful, it being built on seven hills rising from the water's edge and every building retaining its original colour of white.

However, his enchantment did not last long as he continued:

> Here ends the beauty of Lisbon, for on setting your foot on land, you are almost overcome with the stench, every filth being thrown into the

---

1. A small window of opportunity to visit all of Europe did occur during the Peace of Amiens from 1802–3, but when war broke out again, many visitors were trapped abroad, under arrest as 'detenus' until the end of the war.

street and there left until it pleases God to wash the town with a shower of rain ... The inhabitants all have an unhealthy appearance, an immense proportion of them blind and objects of the most distressing kind are met with in every corner ...

Dreading to enter any house the first night, I gladly accepted a bed on the floor of an Englishman's house, where two other officers were accommodated in the same way. I accordingly turned in and then underwent the severest penance, fleas & bugs can inflict ... Rheumatism and diarheas [*sic*] are the usual complaints of the country but I trust [I will survive] by living temperately, wearing flannels and avoiding fruit to escape two disorders which have already carried off numbers.

Lieutenant William Swabey concurred in his diary, when writing regarding how beautiful Lisbon appeared from on board the ships.

21 August [1811]
Lisbon opened on our view standing majestically on a declivity of a hill like an amphitheatre, its appearance was grand, every building, of which there were many fine ones, appearing to advantage.

However, his view of the city also altered dramatically once he had landed two days later.

As to Lisbon, the part which was built after the last great earthquake[2] by the Marquis de Pombal, ... might be called fine, were the streets clean. The other parts, ... are filthy in the extreme, the stench so great that, in spite of manners on first arriving, one must hold one's nose and the streets are so intricate that it is extremely difficult to find one's way ... The people are indolent and filthy to a degree scarcely credible, and though there are wells and springs in almost every direction, they have no method of getting the water by pipes into their houses, but must send for it in casks and they even hawk it about the streets as we do mackerel ... their cookery consists of a vile jumble of oil and onions,

---

2. The Lisbon Earthquake took place on 1 November 1755, at around 09:40 in the morning, and was followed by a tsunami and fires which caused the near-total destruction of the city. Geologists estimate that the earthquake approached a magnitude of 9 on the Richter scale, with an epicentre in the Atlantic Ocean about 200km west-southwest of Cape St. Vincent. Estimates place the death toll in Lisbon alone at 90,000 people, making it one of the most destructive earthquakes in history.

very unpleasant to an English stomach; they however, almost compensate for it by the fruit . . .

Captain Edwin Griffiths of the 15th Hussars wrote much the same in his diary on his first arrival on 2 February 1813.

> Lisbon itself appears to uncommon advantage from the water . . . the whole of white stone, leads you to suppose that you are approaching one of the most magnificent cities in the world.
>
> Five minutes on shore though is sufficient to convince you of your error. You then see that the buildings are unfinished or clumsy; that the houses will still less bear a close inspection, that the streets are narrow & filthy, that a different stench assails you in each of them, while idleness & poverty stare you in the face at every corner you turn.

Band Master John Westcott of the 26th Foot wrote of the difficulties the men experienced on arrival in Lisbon. The troops were landed at Commercial Square (Praça do Comércio), which was far too difficult to pronounce for the average British soldier. As a large equestrian statue of King Jose I stands on a huge plinth in its centre, the square soon became known to the soldiers as '*Black Horse Square*'. However, Westcott also saw a number of positives in the city.

> 5 July 1811
>
> The brigade landed at the Commercial Square, Lisbon, and marched to their different quarters in the city. The 26th Regiment occupied St Paulisto Convent, the 32nd Regiment the castle, and the 77th Regiment St Dominic's Convent, the soldiers were neither provided with blankets, or straw & consequently laying in the cold passages of convents, for a proportionate part of the friars still continued in the convents and of course occupied their original apartments, the soldiers being confined to the cold passages could not undress themselves at night . . .
>
> The Commercial Square is painted yellow, the back streets are [however] very dirty, though not so dirty as formerly, and has a very disagreeable smell from their frying sardeenias [*sic*] a fish if not the pilchard, very much like it, which they appear very fond of, they fry them in oil, which is rather disagreeable to a stranger not used with their manner of cookery, they have a number of these fish houses in all the back streets for the accommodation of the inhabitants. Each house will contain a number of families (like Edinburgh) the stairs are generally of stone and of course free to the whole inhabitants of the house, though each storey contains a separate family, the stairs being

a thoroughfare to the whole, no particular family will take it upon themselves to keep them clean, consequently they remain in a dirty miserable state from one year to the other.

. . . all the streets of Lisbon are crowded with friars of the different orders, who's dress are cloaks of different colours, some of them brown and others black, with a cord round their middle, which keep the cloak closed, the top part of their head are shaved. A great number of friars travel this city begging for the church, they parade through the streets with a silk flag accompanied with a couple of men playing the bagpipes, and beating the drum, every person must respect those religious beggars. The police of this city are very regular and well kept up, everything being remarkable quiet at all hours through the night, they consist of two thousand men, including four troops of cavalry . . . Everything was uncommonly dear in consequence of the war excepting fruit which was very cheap and plentiful, particularly figs, grapes, oranges, pomegranates, chestnuts and the prickly pear, the British [notes] not taken, only at the exchange houses where they gave eighteen shillings for the pound note.

The women of Lisbon are worthy of remark being always uncommonly clean dressed, though not grand. No city in Europe appears to be better furnished with women than Lisbon, any person inclined to the fair sex can be accommodated as quick in this city as any in Europe, though, like all other large places not at all times with safety. Though to give the Lisbon fair ones their due, they generally (of all ranks) paid the utmost respect to the British soldiers, perhaps considering them more generous than their own. I now only speak of a certain class of ladies, which every large city abounds with.

Cornet George Woodberry describes in his journal how, having just landed, he wandered through Lisbon seeking a good dinner, but having no idea where to go or how to ask.

Lisbon, Wednesday 3 February [1813]
The tolling of the bells woke me this morning about six o'clock, I was awakened by a view of Lisbon which appeared fully as if by magic. Many boats brought us fruit, bread and edibles. The strange aspect of the Portuguese, their dress and their ways, meant that for a while I couldn't believe my senses. Thank God [I] landed safe at last after 14 days being tossed about. I had every eye on me as I came on shore at eleven o'clock at Black Horse Square. I then kept walking on not knowing where to go, at last I met Hesse who had soon followed me on shore, our uniforms did bring many curious looks and we then took a turn

through all the principal streets and so on until a time when fatigue made us think of our comfort. Seeing a name written at a hotel and hoping to find a compatriot there, we went in and we were not disappointed in our expectation and afterwards went to a hotel kept by a Mrs Benson, an Irish woman, got a good dinner.

Being stationed at Luz, just a few miles outside Lisbon, George and his fellow officers often took the opportunity to visit the city, but they soon discovered that going on a carnival day was not such a good idea.

Luz, Monday 1 March [1813]
Rode with Smith to Lisbon, the people all mad, throwing water, oranges, flowers, nuts and every kind of nuisance at each other, we got a pail of water over us, and Smith turned to insult the people who had made the attack, when a suave damsel threw the contents of a certain vase at him which unfortunately missed. I got him to understand that he looked like nothing on earth, and we sneaked out of town as quickly as possible, but not before having served as a target for ripe oranges, coffee and peas: and were covered with so much flour that we looked like two millers. Many I saw sporting masks and curious dresses, I think they say their carnival commences this day. I was very glad when I got out of the town. I laid in a good stock of tea, sugar, coffee, hams and tongues, to take up the country, so did Smith.

Ensign Charles Crowe of the 48th Foot wrote of his early experiences in Lisbon in his journal on 25 November 1812, not all of which were unpleasant; however, travelling the streets at night was not for the faint-hearted.

I will not attempt a history of Lisbon but as a passing soldier, merely state that I found it much smaller, more poverty stricken, and by far more filthy, than I expected. Its extent I thought somewhat larger than Dublin. The dockyard was a burlesque on the name, all its stores consisted of five small anchors, a small quantity of cordage and the frame of a frigate on the stocks, in the same state as when the English first entered Portugal . . .

The declivity of the city is from north to south, consequently the transverse streets are generally on a level, and these are filthy beyond the apprehension of an Englishman!! It is no easy task to cross them by day, and rashness by night, as we found on our return from the river to the doctor's lodgings. In our progress we heard the vile shouts 'Agua Ni' 'water is coming', which they are obliged to call thrice and show a light. But the shout and light were on our side of the street, and as these execrable deluges are thrown from the attic or fifth storey, we could not identify the exact house from whence the nuisance was coming, and our only recourse was to ensconce ourselves in the recess of some doorway, and escaped tolerably well. Had the light been on the opposite side, we could have bolted away at once. In Lisbon there are no underground sewers, no water closets of any kind; a large bucket with a board laid on the top receives the slops etc etc of all the house, and at night is poured from the attic into the street.

Cornet Charles Madden of the 4th Dragoons actually landed at Belem, but found time to visit Lisbon. It is fair to say that he was generally impressed once he overlooked the dirt.

28 April 1809
Rode into Lisbon; an ill-paved, filthy, irregular-built city, many of the streets are so steep and ill-paved as scarce to be passable on horseback. The eye is met everywhere by some dismal convent or chapel. The lower part of the town that is next the Tagus is principally inhabited by shopkeepers and the middle-class of people. As the hill rises from the river the houses improve and bear more the appearance of wealth, and form at a distance a grand appearance as most of the houses of the rich in Portugal are decorated with paintings without. There are two streets in the lower part of the town better paved and evener than the rest, called Gold and Silver street, from the number of jeweller's shops in them, where may be bought jewellery of a good quality at a reasonable rate, and gold trinkets of a better quality than in most other countries. Most of the men wear large cloaks and cocked hats and are in general dressed slovenly and dirty.
. . . The people, in general, have a dark, sallow, unhealthy look. You will see as you pass along the streets numbers of lazy wretches lying asleep in the sun, following one another with scarcely any cloaths [*sic*] on them; the lower class scarce ever wear shoes or stockings except when they go to Mass, when all classes put on their best cloaths and the upper classes display all their jewels and trinkets. Smoking and taking snuff is a general custom among the Portuguese.

Like many who had only witnessed the austere proceedings of the Church of England, the profusion of priests, monks and nuns and the use of religious statuary in such a fervently Catholic country was quite a shock to him.

The various hideous and ridiculous dresses of the different priests, monks and friars catch one's attention everywhere; one half of the people seem to be of the religious order. The only carriages which are made use of in Lisbon are small two-wheeled carriages like gigs, drawn by mules, and drove by a man riding one of them. Mules are principally used for riding and draught by the upper classes.

The dangers of being out at night were, however, always a major talking-point.

There is a general custom in Lisbon which is particularly offensive to strangers, and that is, throwing all filth and nuisances of every kind out of their upper windows into the streets, as few or none of the houses have back yards or sewers. This gives the streets in general in warm weather a most offensive smell. A passenger has two choices to make, either to walk in the middle of the street and run the risque [sic] of being rode over, or constantly to have his eyes about him and run off directly if he hears a window open near him.

Another criticism was the extreme levels of noise in Portuguese towns.

In all large towns in Portugal a man's ears are constantly serenaded with the ringing either of convent or chapel bells. Another great nuisance in Portugal is the great creaking that the car wheels make, as the axles are wood, and the people are forbid to grease them to prevent smuggling. These are drawn by two bullocks, who bear the whole weight of the car by a bar of wood which rests on the neck near the horns which is attached to the pole.

The dangers of nocturnal perambulations were not confined to Lisbon, however. William Bragge wrote of similar problems at Castelo Branco.

9 January 1812 Castelo Branco
Of evils choose the least, If you walk close to the wall, you certainly tread in a p[oo], more in the centre are deluged from the house tops and in the middle are in a gutter up to your knees in water.

One huge problem in Lisbon was the great numbers of feral dogs. Ensign Charles Crowe of the 48th Foot spoke of the French attempts to rid the city of this plague.

25 November 1812
In most of the old streets the ruins left by the earthquake of 1755 still stare you in the face, and form dens for the innumerable half wild

dogs which lurk therein by day, and by night act partly scavengers to the city at large by feeding on the refuse thrown from the various houses, to which they rush in swarms by the instinct of experience, and many quarrels occur while the more peaceably disposed members of the community cull the choice morsels! When the French occupied Lisbon, Marshal [sic] Junot[3] gave an order and two thousand of these dogs were killed one night!! By the numbers we saw we should not have imagined that such a slaughter had ever taken place.

Clerk Robert Duffield Cooke wrote at great length to his father of his experiences in Lisbon: he did not like anything! Indeed, once he started what was intended to be a short postscript, he could not stop himself.

Lisbon, 29 June 1811

According to my promise I write you first opportunity acquainting you with my safe arrival at Lisbon on Wednesday last. Would have written before but the mail goes this afternoon. . . . I got my quarters yesterday, I was obliged to have recourse to the police to get admittance. I do not like the Portuguese at all, they are all thieves and the dirtiest set I ever saw. . . . I cannot speak the language which is very unpleasant. Everything is dearer than in London even wine and fruit. I wish with all my heart I may go with the army for I hate Lisbon, 2 of my comrades want to go back to England. . . . There is nothing in Lisbon but fleas, bugs, old women, cats, dogs, mosquitoes and all sorts of vermin; will write a long letter by next mail if possible.

P.S. This letter is merely to you, I am well and safely arrived which I know [will] make you happy. In my next I will give you an account of Lisbon and its inhabitants. But what a disappointment when I got there, instead of finding a delightful place I found it the dirtiest stinking hole I ever saw for it really is without exception the filthiest capital I ever wish to see. We went to the best hotel in the town where I expected to meet with things a little decent! . . . However, we managed to get some *squash* there which looked just like what we *brought up* in the packet. We could not get beds there, so we went to another *hot-hell*[4] where I

---

3. General Jean Andoche Junot, Duc d'Abrantes (1771–1813) commanded the French army which occupied Lisbon from November 1807 until defeated by Wellington at Rolica and Vimiero in August 1808 and was evacuated back to France by the terms of the Convention of Cintra.
4. A play on hotel.

had the pleasure of sleeping with an unknown *gentleman*. To be sure we had 2 beds in the room but that did not alter his kind intentions, for in the morning I found he had walked off with my shirt, stockings and one shoe and left in the place an openwork nightshirt of his *own*, I took it all very quietly till I found the above article and then my pretty temper began to show itself for the dirty scoundrel had thrown his lousy shirt on my pantaloons which was soon covered with a livestock, so I walked them both into the Tagus, kicked up a famous breeze in the house and packed off bag and baggage to another English place where I kept till I got my quarters, and very glad I was when I got them, for it cost us nearly 4 dollars a day without being able to eat their stuff, or sleep in their beds for the mosquitoes; the first night I could only open one eye besides being covered with bites in other places. They have likewise plenty of fleas and bugs but mosquitoes prevent your seeing the places they make by biting all over you. The quarters I have is one room very well furnished with a long staircase leading to it likewise very well furnished in the hotel style, you will not believe me when I tell you there is not a *petit maison* in Lisbon or indeed do they know what it means. I am obliged to do as the Portuguese ladies and most of the English officers do, that is use Polly White[5] and throw it out of the windows, which is another of the customs of the inhabitants and of course makes it dangerous for the passengers at night, and causes that effluvia which is natural to Lisbon and serves for the cows to graze on in the morning as they have no fields, nor have they above a dozen cows so they fare very nobly. The milk they use is goats, which is but middling. Now, for a description of the inhabitants; there is not a gentleman among them, they seem to be a wandering set of brutes, every fellow wears a cocked hat and an amazing large cloak wrapt [sic] all round them. The women are as dirty if not dirtier than the men. They are extremely lazy. The only hard working people are water carriers, foreigners that come from Galicia and cannot be pressed for soldiers, there are some very fine buildings. The aqueduct is an amazing one and conducts the water from the distance of 20 miles over the valleys and mountains, one of the arches I am told is 387 feet high. It is so strong that the earthquake which upset all the houses never hurt it. If that was to be pulled down by the French there would not be a drop of water in Lisbon, of course it is well guarded.

---

5. Colloquial name for a chamber pot.

Lieutenant John Maxwell Tylden of the 43rd Foot even wrote home about Lisbon when far away in Coria in Extramadura on 23 July 1809.

> . . . I did not by any means like the city, it is by far one of the most filthy places in existence, it is an impossibility for an Englishman to conceive the thing without seeing it, they absolutely never appear to clean their streets and the smell that is occasioned by this is enough to knock one down. Was it not so, Lisbon would be a fine city, the houses are certainly uncommonly well-built and there are some good streets, but there is nothing in its appearance to give it the air of a fine city.

It is clear from these numerous sources, that their first arrival at Lisbon was a huge cultural challenge to them on every level, but it is easy to over-emphasize how awful Lisbon was from these accounts and some balance must be applied to this dreadful picture. The general poor cleanliness of the Portuguese, combined with the profusion of fleas and lice, was very evident to all and understandably criticised, along with the nocturnal showers of effluent from the rooftops and the resulting dreadful smells in the streets.

However, much of the remaining criticism, including the general levels of poverty, the strange foods they ate, their incomprehensible language, the profusion of clerics of every kind and the poor quality of accommodation, was more a consequence of the great cultural shock evinced on landing in such an alien world, rather than an outright detestation of anything and everything in Lisbon. Some, as we have seen, saw past this deprivation and admired the remnants of its former grandeur and even enjoyed some aspects of the city.

Indeed, some troops had their first encounter of Spain and Portugal at various other locations and they were similarly described as both poor and filthy beyond their comprehension. Captain Edwin Griffiths, whose comments we have already heard regarding his first arrival in Lisbon in 1813, had however already encountered the Spanish town of Corunna some four years earlier, with similar results. He wrote to his sister-in-law from Corunna on 13 November 1808 that:

> . . . the extreme poverty and wretchedness is past all description; . . .
> I live on shore but sleep on board my ship in preference to a lousy, filthy, buggy, Spanish bed which I must turn into as soon as she quits the harbour . . .

His nephew Cornet Frederick Philips, also in the 15th Hussars, described how he found Corunna to be a miserable place and also full of filth.

Corunna 11 November 1808

I went ashore on Thursday to see the place which is something like a miserable Welsh village, it is certainly much larger, but to describe the filth and dirt that incommode the streets would be impossible. They are the most extraordinary set of *animals* I ever beheld . . .

Indeed, most would soon discover that in many ways, Lisbon was actually better than a lot of the hovels that they were to inhabit in the future whilst on campaign. Lisbon was never viewed on a par with the grandeur of London or Paris, but it was probably not as bad as these shocked and horrified young men describe on their first encounter with the Iberian Peninsula. Their views changed subtly with time and their experience of other regions of Portugal and Spain.

Chapter 3

Long Marches and Cold Nights

Within days of the infantry regiments landing at Lisbon, they usually received orders to march up country to join the army. Cavalry and artillery units needed much longer to get their horses fit after a long period confined in a ship's hold and the equipment in good shape, so they were often moved just outside the city to allow them time to recuperate fully. Quite a typical march is described by Lieutenant Colonel George Bingham commanding the 53rd Foot.

> Convent of Santa Tirja near Oporto, 20 May 1809
> We have made very long marches in excessively wet weather, and on roads scarcely broad enough to admit of more than one man abreast, and literally knee deep in mud; frequently without bread, and seldom less than twelve hours under arms.

Various equipment was issued to the troops from the vast stores established at Lisbon, while officers sought to purchase horses and mules to carry their baggage, hire a local servant and complete their personal supplies before marching inland, where it would be far more difficult, if not impossible, to procure them. Band Master Westcott of the 26th Foot recorded the equipment supplied to his battalion at Lisbon in 1811.

> The equipment of a regiment of infantry, in taking the field in Portugal, is one canteen and haversack for each man, one iron camp kettle for every ten men, one bill hook for every ten men.

The following entrenching tools were also supplied per battalion:

> Five spades, five shovels, five pickaxes, five felling axes.

They also received:

> One tent for each field officer, one tent for the officers of each company, and one tent for the Staff officers in case the officers chuse

[sic] to find the means of carrying them. The regiments will receive an allowance of twenty pounds [sterling] for each company, (paymaster and surgeon [also]) for the purchase of mules to carry the company kettles, paymaster's papers and surgeon's medicine chest, and the commissariat department will furnish a mule to carry the entrenching tools, 13 pack saddles and bridles, 13 nose bags for the public mules.

As regards the heavy baggage of the regiment which could not be carried with the army:

> The whole of the heavy baggage belonging to each regiment is to be removed on board a transport, and an non-commissioned officer, or steady man left in charge of it, the women and children (if any), will be quartered at Belem and receive rations at the government's expense . . .

Each regiment was officially allowed six wives for every 100 men, to travel overseas with the troops, receiving a half food ration, children accompanying them only receiving a quarter ration. It is clear, however, that a number of the women and children chose to follow the regiments on the march, rather than remain at Belem.

> It was recommended by Lord Wellington, that very few woman should accompany a regiment, when it marched to join the army, and [those] having children or with child [pregnant], were not on any account to proceed with a regiment, when marching to join the army. A spare cart were [to] accompany the regiments on the march, for the purpose of carrying forward, any men, that may fall sick on the road, and which is on no account, to be appropriated for any other purpose whatsoever and always if possible to follow the regiment as near as possible. The commanding officers of each regiment will report when their battalions are equipped and ready to take the field, as soon as possible after landing.

Some changes of uniform were received with enthusiasm.

> 17 July [1811] – The mules of the brigade went off to Vila Franca, the white breeches and legons [black knee length gaiters] of the regiment were packed up and sent off with the baggage on board the *Elizabeth* transport under charge of a sergeant, the regiment afterwards wore grey trousers, while they remained in Portugal which was much more serviceable and easier for the soldiers.

Ensign Crowe of the 48th Foot detailed his purchase of a canteen set:

> Lisbon 25 November 1812
> I purchased a canteen consisting of an oval hamper covered with an undressed bullocks hide containing the following appurtenances. A tin boiler capable of holding a gallon or more, another within that into which went a tea kettle and a pot, with shifting handles, pepper box, a salt cellar, and a gridiron occupied a half of the space. The next partition was fitted with two tin canisters filled with two pounds of moist sugar and about a pound and half of tea. In the other compartment were two tin plates, two knives and forks, two iron spoons, two earthen cups and saucers with pewter spoons. For this ordinary fit out I paid twenty dollars, or £6/5s/0d![1] I grudged my money excessively at the time, but every day's experience made me better satisfied with my purchase.

By far the most important purchases made by the officers were their horses for riding and mules to carry their baggage. These cost a small fortune, often requiring funds from home to pay for them. Lieutenant George Barlow of the 52nd Foot wrote briefly from Lisbon on his priorities.

> Lisbon, 14 September 1811
> I purpose reporting myself to the Adjutant Generals [Office]; I shall then seek out for some of our officers, who I know are in this city and shall confer with them on the best means of procuring mules &c &c. Tomorrow, which is Sunday, I shall employ in putting my baggage into the saddlebags and making all the necessary preparations for my march which is nearly 300 miles . . . Barlow

A little while later, however, Ensign John Blackman of the Coldstream Guards was writing home in great detail to explain why he had already been forced to spend all of the allowance that he had been given to last the entire year on horses.

> Sunday 24 May 1812, Castelo de Vide
> . . . I therefore, write candidly to inform you that I have already drawn to the amount you was so good as to allow me for one year viz

---

1. About £300 in today's terms.

£150.[2] This you will say is a very large sum to be gone in so short a time in which, my dear father, I must agree with you; but in the first place mules are excessively scarce and dear and I have been very unfortunate though not particularly so in my animals. I set out from Lisbon with 2 mules, one to ride, the other for my baggage, we went by water to Vila Franca and on marching the next morning I found one mule could not carry all my baggage, in fact it fell down before it had gone many yards. I, therefore, loaded them both and marched that day on foot.

At Azambuja I had the good luck to fall in with a burro, or ass, and was able to ride till I joined the army at Albuera; I had not been in camp with them 2 days, or rather 2 nights, before I lost my baggage mule, a thing that frequently happens in camp, as the inhabitants seize every possible opportunity of stealing them away; and everything being new to me, I could not be supposed to manage so well as those older in the service; I was then left with my riding mule and burro; I must now tell you what these animals cost. Riding mule 120, baggage mule 90, burro 20, [total] 230 dollars.

I found we were to march the next day and was at a loss what to do, however, I had the misfortune to light on a mule, which belonged to a sutler; misfortune I call it for it turned out to be a bad one; for this he demanded a hundred dollars, I got it for 5 dollars and gave him a draft for 95 dollars: the next day we began our march and had continual marching direct north, where the roads are very bad, we then turned to Castelo Branco where the mule either would not, or could not, proceed any further, and I could only get 20 dollars for him. I then walked 3 or 4 days after which I bought a fine mule off Captain Lascelles, (having more animals than he wanted) for which I gave him a draft for one hundred dollars; the price he gave at first.

I then had in possession, this mule, my riding mule and burro; we then marched on to Nisa and before we marched to that place, my burro knocked up. Now, however, as we halted at Nisa for a long time I got him round again and sold him for 20 dollars, the price I gave for him and bought a baggage pony for which I gave a draft for seventy dollars: I, therefore have now the baggage mule I had off Lascelles, the baggage pony, which is well known in the brigade, having been with it for some time, and my riding mule, making 2 very capital baggage beasts and the other a very good one to ride; so that I am at last set up. I hope to

---

2. About £8,000 in today's terms.

have no further trouble and be at no further expense on that head, at least for some time to come.

Cornet George Woodberry of the 18th Hussars recorded paying a small fortune for his mule and was also very pleased that he had not lightened his baggage like others by selling some of it off.

> Barquinha, Tuesday 27 April 1813
> My mule at the lowest price, cost me one hundred guineas.[3] The portable beds and tents have been given away on the march or sold for very inconsiderable sums; those very articles are now found an indispensible necessary. Thank God I have all my baggage safe and though it weighs near 400lb [181kg], yet my mule and pony carries it well . . .

Clerk Robert Duffield Cooke also felt the need to explain to his father that he had not been overly profligate.

> Lisbon 15 August 1811
> You will no doubt think me very extravagant when you read of *my horse and my servant* but I will convince you those thoughts are ill grounded. My horse for instance costs me nothing but for shoes, being allowed 80 dollars to purchase him and rations to keep him on, viz 42 lbs [19kg] oats, 36 lbs [16.3kg] straw which is to last 3 days and is more than sufficient for the purpose. My servant costs me nothing but his wages, being allowed the same rations for him as for myself (viz 6 lbs [2.7kg] meat and 9 lbs [4kg] bread and 18 lbs [18.1kg] of wood which is to last 3 days for both, which is also a good allowance, the wages I pay him is 6 dollars a month which is more than customary but he is an excellent cook, can shave and dress hair, manage a horse, make my bed, cleans boots and shoes etc etc. Indeed father, to speak the truth, it would be very ridiculous not to keep a horse for I should not only lose the allowance and rations but likewise my *consequence* which must be kept up now. When I first came here they all told me I could do nothing without a servant. I could not cook my own dinner and the first week I was here I was obliged to give all my rations away having nobody and no place to cook them in, therefore a servant is an absolute necessary and as you must have one, you may as well have a horse and be at the expense of shoes.

---

3. This equates to around £5,500 today, a huge sum.

32 *Marching, Fighting, Dying*

Lieutenant Colonel George Bingham recorded the number of baggage animals he found it necessary to use.

> Camp near Abrantes 16 June 1809
> I have now completed my allowance of baggage animals, five; three would answer if their backs were made of iron . . .

George Woodberry of the 18th Hussars listed his baggage in great detail.

> Luz, Monday 22 February [1813]
> Had the whole of my baggage on the mule and find he can carry it well. I take the following articles with me. 2 Pelisse's, 1 Dressing Gown, 1 Jacket, 2 Blankets, 1 Dress Waistcoat, 1 Rug, 4 Regimental Pantaloons, 1 Bearskin Bed, 3 [pairs] White Pantaloons, Dressing Case, 1 Leather Pantaloons, Writing Case, 2 Blue Waistcoats, 10 Books, 2 White Waistcoats, 1 pair Hussar Pistols, Cotton Drawers, 1 Pocket Pistol, 2 Flannel Drawers, 1 Powder Flask, 3 Flannel Waistcoats, 1 Pinch Belt Plain, 12 Hose, 1 Pistol Belt and Pouch, 12 Shirts, Dress Sword, 4 Black Handkerchiefs, 6 Pocket ditto, Dress Sabretache, Plain Sword, 2 Foraging Caps, 1 Hussar ditto with oil skin cover, Plain Sabretache, Sword Knots, 1 Cap liner, Racing Jacket, 1 Sash, 2 Feathers, 1 Pelisse Liner, 6 pair Boots, 3 pr. Gloves, 1 pair Shoe, 2 Night Caps, 2 pair Slippers, Canteen, Breakfast & Dining, 1 Hussar Pipe Service complete, 1 Leather Trunk, Hussar Horse Accoutrements Complete, Double Saddle Bags, 2 Horse Cloths Basket with Locks, 2 Horse Blankets, Spy Glass, 1 Plain Saddle, Great Coat, 2 Plain Bridles, Flannel Jacket, Pack, Saddle, Bridle, etc., Complete Leather Bucket, 3 Shoe Brushes and Blacking 15 Cakes of Soap, 2 Clothes Brushes, 24 Boot Jack Oil skins' and straps to go over the baggage . . .

Lieutenant Henry Hough of the Royal Artillery detailed his 'establishment' on the march, which he viewed as both minimal and essential.

> 21 April [1812]
> I left Lisbon to join the Army. The first day I marched to Sacavem, taking with me two domestics; a country horse, and a mule for my baggage, this being all my establishment, and the only way you can travel up the country.

Ensign John Mills of the Coldstream Guard also retained a decent establishment.

> 13 June 1811
> My stud at this time consists of a horse, *Docktail*, who was taken from the French . . . Two mare mules, *Bess* and *Jenny* . . . a small he mule *Turpin* . . . Mare mules carry the baggage and I ride *Docktail*. My servants consist of William, a private servant, Duckworth a soldier servant who looks after the animals, Joseph [and] a Portuguese boy under him.

George Woodberry listed his establishment at Muskitz on Friday 24 September 1813.

> List of my horses, mules [&] servants – September 1813
> No. 1 Grey horse, *Crafty*. No. 2 Bay horse, *Worcester*, (my Battle Horse). No. 3 Black horse, *Andalusian*, (late King Joseph's). No. 4 Bay mare *Morales*, (for baggage). No. 5 Pye bald mare pony, 2 years old, she is in foal, and stands four feet tall. Named *Belisarda*, (for the small breakfast canteens). No. 6 A mule, *Doctor*, (for baggage). *Fly* and *Swift*, two French greyhounds. *Vitoria*, (dog), my French prisoner, a faithful companion. John Porter, valet and cook. John Ipper, groom. Jossa, a Portuguese servant, hired him at Sovillida, very faithful.

For a more senior officer, however, such a 'military establishment' was totally inadequate. Major General Frederick Robinson, commanding a brigade in the 5th Division, complained that his was very small and totally insufficient for his needs.

> Mondragon on the road to Bayonne 3 July 1813
> You may judge of the severe hardships general officers endure by a description of my establishment, which is very low in comparison with any other; 12 men employed in various ways, four horses, ten mules, five sheep, two goats & a large dog. This is besides my aide de camp & Major of Brigade who live with me.

We have already seen that troops marching from Lisbon could regularly expect to march some 220 miles (350km) or more to reach the army stationed along the Spanish border near Almeida and later in the war this increased to as much as 560 miles (900km) to reach Pamplona, until the port of Pasajes became available. To ease this march somewhat, the infantry were regularly transported by boat up the River Tagus as far as Valada near Santarem, reducing the actual march by some 37 miles (60km). Band Master Westcott's diary entry for 18 July 1811 is typical.

The 26th Regiment marched from St Paul's convent at four o'clock, in the morning and embarked cheering and the band playing at the dockyard, in boats to join the army under the command of Lord Wellington, . . . I went on shore for a few moments at Vila Franca celebrated for its vineyards & wine which is situated on the left side of the Tagus, it has been a flourishing pretty town before the war but appeared a distressed looking place when we saw it . . . our sail up the Tagus was remarkable pleasant, particularly as the naval officer commanding the boats described to us the different positions that had been formerly occupied both by the British, and French armies, and also the different houses that had been occupied by the French generals, and their staff. The regiment landed in the evening at the town of Valada, a very miserable distressed looking place, situated in a sandy soil on the left bank of the Tagus, the country about the place consists of very large fields of Indian corn, and a great quantity of vineyards.

From 1812 onwards, it was more usual to transport troops up the coast by ship to Figueira da Foz, which stands at the mouth of the Mondego river. This reduced the march to Almeida to only 134 miles (215km). Lieutenant George Barlow of the 52nd Foot was one of the first to follow the new route and it caused problems with his horses.

Lisbon, 28 September 1811
. . . I am obliged to commit my horse & mule to the care of a soldier to conduct them as far as Coimbra, a distance of 135 miles, while I am compelled to embark on board a transport with these men and go round by sea to Figueira [da Foz] town & port situated at the entrance of the Mondego River from whence it is thirty miles to Coimbra. This system of sending supplies & recruits, convoys &c to the grand army is for the future constantly to be pursued; inasmuch as the whole tract between Lisbon and the above mentioned city has been so devastated, consumed & ruined by the ravages & long continuance of so large an army of French, as also by furnishing the necessary requisitions to the allied troops, which in numbers were also very considerable, that the government are willing to spare the few remaining & wretched inhabitants as much as possible. In consequence of this, their cattle teams &c are freed from military service, from a certain portion of taxes & all troops are transported by sea to Coimbra, so as to avoid marching them through those tracts. From that city to Ciudad Rodrigo, where the army are at present encamped, the distance is about 180 miles, so that upon landing at Figueira [da Foz] we shall have 200 only instead of 300 to march.

Ensign Charles Crowe 48th Foot wrote excitedly of their first real march, but also gives a few hints regarding the trials of marching in the peninsula.

> 5 December [1812]
> We marched to Azambuja and every one of the party felt himself a soldier in right earnest. The men felt the weight of their knapsacks loaded with a blanket in addition to their usual contents, surmounted with their tin canteens containing the remains of three days rations, and of their cartridge boxes charged with sixty rounds of ammunition; and the officers, followed closely by their loaded burro's, marching in the rear, felt their responsibility for any misdemeanour of their men.

Lieutenant George Young of the 38th Foot wrote a typical list of marches and counter marches across the peninsula from a camp near Arronches on 1 July 1811.

> I arrived at the army on the 19th of May after a very long and fatiguing march and joined my regiment at Nave de Haver, near Almeida on the frontiers of Spain; from thence we marched to Espeja with an intention to attack the French of a Sunday morning, but they came on in such force we were obliged to retreat in great hurry. They hung on our rear for three days, during which time we marched without intermission night and day. Their advance guard would be marching into a town at one and our rear guard marching out at the other. You must think we had not much time to spare. We crossed the [River] Coa at Sabugal and took up a very strong position on the heights and formed in line of battle with the pass of the river very strongly defended with the 9th, 1st Royals, 30th, 4th, and 38th and 24 pieces of Artillery. They came and reconnoitred our position and then thought it better to retire. We were then ordered for this place, where we arrived on the 28th of June after a march of 180 miles over a mountainous barren country where we saw nothing but rock and wood. I am surprised how I stayed it out so well, where we march from six to eight leagues per day, which is about thirty English miles a day, and without roads, and the sun so hot that about one we are obliged to get under the trees, otherwise we would faint with the heat.

Indeed, the troops marched huge distances in a campaigning season. Troops joining from Lisbon in 1811 marched at least 600 miles (965km) during that campaign; while in 1812 the troops already on the Spanish/Portuguese frontier marched in excess of 900 miles (1,450km); and in 1813 they marched on average at least 620 miles (1,000km). None of these figures quoted include the routine marches to change position or cantonment, to receive victuals and replacement uniform or to attend hospital. The average soldier could probably add another 50 per cent to his list of marches each year for such routine reasons.

These marches were made early in the day whenever possible, to avoid the unrelenting sun and unbearable heat while wearing a woollen tunic more suited to the British climate. The times of march varied anywhere from 1am until 6am depending on the length of the journey and the commanding officer's whim; but night marches were generally avoided unless it was desperate as they were generally found to be counter-productive, the rate of march being much slower, with great confusion attending their desire to keep on the correct route and they proved extremely exhausting to the men.

Private George Woolger of the 16th Light Dragoons regularly recorded the times at which they marched each morning and as a random, but pretty consistent example, he recorded:

> 3 August [1809]. At 2 am we were ordered to saddle;
> 5 August. We march at 4 am;
> 6 August. Marched at 4 am still over mountains.

This inconsistency in times of marching is very evident in Lieutenant Charles Madden's journal:

> 1 October [1810] Turned out at 5 am
> 6 October [1810] Turned out at quarter past 3 am
> 16 November [1810] Marched at 4 am
> 25 March [1811] Got orders to turn out at 8 am but did not march till 10
> 11 April [1811]. Marched at 11 am
> 16 April [1811] Marched at 2 in the morning
> 16 June [1811] Turned out at 3 am.

The quality of the road and the length of march were of course also major factors in the relative difficulties and duration of any march.

There are a few famous marches associated with the Peninsular War, especially the forced march of the Light Division under General Robert Craufurd of anywhere between 40 and 60 miles (64 and 90km) in 24 to 30 hours depending on which of the various sources are referred to. Others are linked to disasters, including the dreadful retreat to Corunna in 1808 ably described by Captain Charles Pierrepoint of the 20th Foot, who was serving on the Staff as a Deputy Assistant Quarter Master General.

> 25 December Mayorga
>   Sixteen miles march from the last cantonments (near Sahagun) through melting snow, rain & mud, the baggage and artillery could

proceed but slowly. The troops came into their quarters wet through and through, chopped straw, fuel of the country afforded no relief to men crowded by 20 to 30 into small houses. The necessity of quartering ten regiments in a small town not above 300 houses forced upon us new modes of billeting troops. The place being divided into ten parts each corps was shown to what had been allotted to them. Soldiers forced themselves into houses, most of which had been abandoned.

Pierrepoint continued his diary on 1 January 1809, when the discovery of large stores of wine had made the retreat infinitely worse.

Under arms and off again an hour before daybreak to march 24 miles more on the road to Villafranca [del Bierzo] through a country not mountainous but hilly, populous and highly productive of *wine*. This last word accounts for the considerable increase of our stragglers on that day, some lame, some sick, fell into the hands of the French, I am very sorry to add many many drunken. Carts overturned and dead cattle had begun three days before to trace strongly the retreat of the British Army. My horse who at first started and turned back at the sight of a dead carcass, was then brought to pass horses killed on the road scarcely noticing them.

The retreat from Talavera in 1809 and the ill-managed retreat from Salamanca into Portugal in 1812 are further well-known examples. Lieutenant James Gairdner of the 95th Rifles, a seasoned campaigner, summed up the retreat on 19 November 1812.

Thus ended this retreat, one of the most fatiguing and annoying, miserable retreat, for the time it lasted the British army ever made, for though the marches were not long the roads were shockingly bad, the weather for the season of the year very cold and rainy and the want of provisions very great, much more so than from the nature of the case it ought to have been.

It is calculated that the army have lost in prisoners, who were through fatigue & illness unable to keep up, more than 4,000 men, the loss in stores &c &c is immense. I here talk of the retreat from Salamanca to Rodrigo alone . . .

These marches were truly awful, for obvious reasons and they cannot fail to colour our views of the soldier's life in the peninsula, but were they typical of the ordinary demands on the men or are they a grotesque distortion?

Private George Woolger recounted in a letter from Villaviega on 26 October 1809 how hard his march was to join the army.

> The last time I wrote to you was from Tomar, we marched from Tomar the 2 July over a mountainous country, we were 11 days on our march without halting, the sun excessive hot & the roads very dusty. We arrived at Placencia the 13th, we halted here 4 days to rest and shoe the horses.

Little would appear to have changed over the ensuing four years, as General Robinson wrote to his wife from Outeiro on 25 May 1813.

> We have had a most fatiguing march of about a fortnight, over mountains and rocky roads hitherto deemed impassable for artillery. In many instances the horses were taken off and the guns were dragged up by five or six hundred men.

This punishing regime was confirmed by Lieutenant George Barlow of the 52nd Foot, who wrote from a camp near Vitoria on 20 June 1813:

> My dearest uncle,
> I take the opportunity of this, our *first* day's halt during more than *three weeks* of incessantly rapid forced marches to give you some further account of our still successful progress.

Lieutenant Edward Fox Fitzgerald of the 10th Hussars, wrote home from Villa Olite on 4 July 1813 claiming that:

> . . . I have marched now from Galegos to the foot of the Pyrenees and back to this place without a single day's halt, upwards of eight hundred miles.

Marching across Spain and Portugal in the summer heat, on seemingly endless dusty tracks and swarmed by a myriad of flies was certainly exceedingly challenging. Lieutenant John Tylden of the 43rd Foot wrote to his brother William of these exhausting marches.

> Coria in Estramadura 23 July 1809
> It is not for want of inclination that I have not before written to you, but since we commenced marching the weather has been so uncommonly hot, that I have generally been glad to lay down

immediately on arriving at our quarters instead of being able to write, particularly as we marched every morning at one o'clock to avoid the excessive heat & though one might attempt it, it is nearly an impossibility, one is so bothered with flys [*sic*] fleas, and all manner of devilment.

Band Master Westcott of the 26th Foot wrote similarly on 20 July 1811.

> The regiment marched at four o'clock in the morning from Santarem to Golega a very fatiguing day's march through a sandy road. The country covered with a kind of long heather, and olive trees, in general the country had a barren aspect with very little water, the country almost destitute of inhabitants, what few houses or rather huts, we passed were in ruins. The regiment had three days provisions with them, which with their knapsacks and ammunition, made it very fatiguing in such a broiling climate, and at the most sultry time of the summer.

A week later, things had become far worse.

> 27th July – The regiment marched from the village of Pego at a quarter past three o'clock in the morning for Gaviao and for want of a guide, which was a neglect, lost their way, and were marching and counter marching, over a barren uncultivated heath, until five o'clock in the evening, the sun uncommonly hot, and not a tree or shrub to shade the regiment from the most excessive heat we ever experienced in Portugal. We halted repeatedly on the desolate heath, while detachments went voluntar[il]y in different directions in search of water, some of the men went a league before they could find any, others could find none. For my part I could find none, but was favoured with a drink by a soldier who had been more fortunate, nothing but friendships alone could procure a drop, money was of no use here, officers and soldiers alike, all would sooner part with gold than water. This was one of the longest and certainly the most fatiguing days marches that ever was travelled by the Cameronian Regiment in any country and never can be forgot by any man who was present that day and experienced the desert silence of the scene, all occasioned by neglect in not procuring a guide before we commenced our march. About fourteen hours marching in an uninhabited part of the country without roads, in the burning sun of July in Portugal we experienced this day before we entered the town of *Gaviao* which place we occupied, it's a ruinous distressed place, we quartered within the walls of uninhabited houses, where we were happy in being able to rest ourselves from the heat of the sun, without any other accommodation.

Private Woolger of the 16th Light Dragoons also described the tough conditions.

> . . . we marched, the whole of the British army over the mountains, a very bad road, very hot & dusty & scarcely any water to be met with on the road, we were fortunate enough to camp 2 of the days by rivers.

Ensign Robert Garrett of the 2nd Foot was a little cooler on his march despite the sun.

> Mealhada Soida 20 May 1811
> . . . The first ten days of our march was hot in the extreme, but before we reached Celorico we had not that to complain of, a great part of our march being over mountains, on the tops of which snow, in some places , laid very deep . . .

The state of the roads was often a major issue, particularly for the artillery, as Lieutenant William Swabey described in his journal for 1811.

> 24th September – This day's march was by far the worst we had encountered, the mountains we had to cross and the sudden ascents and sharp turnings in coming down the hills required much labour and perseverance on the part of both horses and men.

However, a few days later he had encountered even greater obstacles.

> 28th [September] In descending the steep hill through Pena Macor no.2 ammunition waggon overpowered the shaft horse and he was precipitated clean through a wall three feet thick, neither man or horse being hurt. The march from Vila Velha to Nisa, four leagues, took us from 7 in the morning till 6 in the evening, the brigade of foot artillery that passed yesterday had their howitzer precipitated over a rock and two wheel horses killed; we were obliged to use ten and twelve horses to one carriage. This is the worst march for artillery in Portugal.

George Woolger described similar problems during a retreat in 1810.

> 6th August – Marched at 4 am still over mountains. We now begin to feel the hardships & calamitys [*sic*] of a retreating army; cars break down, bullocks drop down dead with fatigue & hunger, artillery horses also, likewise troop horses and the infantry are obliged to be yoked [*sic*] to the guns to draw them up these steep mountains. It was 3 o'clock on the 7 August before we halted and we were forced to cover the artillery.

We then rested till 6 am [when] we march again over the highest mountains I ever saw, infantry still at the guns. About half way we came to more level ground, we march 5 leagues, water scarce & bad, no wine to be had for money this day a handful of rye flour was served out, no bread, we halt here one day.

Gone were the days when war was restricted to the summer months, indeed winter quarters were now rarely used for long periods. However, the cooler conditions brought their own problems. Lieutenant Charles Crowe, now serving in the 27th Foot recorded a difficult march in the depths of winter.

19 December [1812]
We marched to Espinhal. We had to pass over the summit of the Estrella Mountains, which run diagonally across the western part of the peninsula of Portugal and are very lofty. The road was cut on the side of the summit for the chief party of our route, in a strong clay sodden with wet, which drew the soles off from many of the soldiers' shoes. The baggage animals had the greatest difficulty to get on. On our right hand the precipices were quite appalling to look into, and a large stone thrown down made a noise equal to the report of a very large cannon. The wind raged tremendously and frequently blew the soldiers down before they could draw their feet out of the stiff clay to steady themselves. I was riding in rear of the detachment, to enable the men to pick the best path, on the left of the road, when a furious gust of wind blew my pony and self fairly off our balance and laid us on to the clay bank, or slope of the summit where we both left as perfect an impression of our forms as ever intaglio[4] left on the finest wax.

The following June he described an equally difficult time.

29 June 1813
A halt, to wait for the Light Division moving parallel with us. They encountered so bad a march that they did not reach their campground until ten o'clock this morning, leaving, of course very many stragglers, knocked up by fatigue. This morning was very fine,

---

4. Intaglio engraving, as a method of making prints, was invented in Germany in the 1430s, whereby the image is incised into a surface, known as the matrix or plate, normally made of copper or zinc but can be wax.

and everyone was busily occupied in drying and regulating his baggage when a sudden and most tremendous storm of rain set us all afloat.

Lieutenant Benjamin Ball of the 39th Foot wrote of a wet march from Albuquerque on 15 November 1811.

> The day before the action,[5] we marched at six in the morning & continued on the road till eight at night, halted in a new ploughed field till two, while the rain almost beat us into the ground & being forbidden to make fires, could get nothing to eat. Marched again at two, came up with the enemy at five & continued our pursuit over the mountains till four in the evening, having had nothing to eat or drink from 5 o'clock in the evening of the 26th, till 9 at night of [the] 28th, incessantly on the move & constantly *wet through*.

Lieutenant George Woodberry of the 18th Hussars recorded the miseries of a march in early May 1813.

> Cabacos, Monday 3 May. A wretched day's march this, we left Tomar very early, at the time it was raining excessively hard.
> Espinhal, Tuesday 4 May. At 4 this morning I arose from my bed which was a table I had passed the night on and commenced our march across the Serra da Estrela mountains.
> Cortizes [Sao Martinho da Cortica?], Friday 7 May. Never did troops march in worse weather; a very rainy morning and a most uncomfortable march I had; it never ceased raining until after we arrived at this place, which has suffered most severely.

Private Henry Willis of the 1st Life Guards also endured a difficult march in 1813.

> Vitoria 28 June
> We left Pinheiro [Grande] on the 21st of April last, since that time we have been continually upon the march from one place to another. Some part of the time, the weather have [*sic*] been very wet, which made it unpleasant.

---

5. Arroyo dos Molinos, 28 October 1811.

Private John Morris Jones of the 1/39th records how the constant marching in 1814 also saw large numbers of stragglers.

> Our movements were at times so quick, that many of the poorest marchers were often left struggling in the rear; and this was particularly the case in our advance upon Aire; more than a hundred of our regiment being stragglers that day. Indeed it was not at all surprising, considering the wretched state of the roads, if such abominable tracks were deserving the name of roads, flooded in many parts in consequence of the continued heavy rains that then prevailed; and rendered still worse by being cut up by the cavalry and light artillery in their headlong progress in pursuit of the retiring enemy. Besides which it was very often a sort of steeple chase, across rough tracts of country; over fences and through ditches, where it was not possible any order could be observed. Add to this the necessity of frequently fording turbid[6] and rapid streams, swollen by the rain and those often more than waist deep and occasionally dangerous. We were more than once indebted to the additional weight of our arms and appointments to keep a firm footing on the bed of the stream. It is well known to military men that a slight obstruction to the head of a column of march, will inconceivably confuse and harass the rear; so much so, that in a broken country, the rear of the column is alternately at a dead stop and on the run; which ere long, throws the weakest marchers behind their fellows; and when once well in the rear, they are very seldom able to come up before the column halts for the night.

Most officers would prefer to ride a horse on the march if they could afford it, few seeing it as an extravagance. Indeed, officers usually viewed a horse as invaluable, allowing them to arrive at their destination each day without being so tired. This left them better able to perform their duties regarding the overseeing of the billeting of their men, ensuring that they also received rations and that they were personally capable of carrying out any picket duties they may have had to perform that night. In a letter dated 31 October 1812 from a camp near Tordesillas, Thomas Maynard, Assistant Surgeon to the 1st Battalion the Coldstream Guards, added a footnote to his friend Ensign John Lucie Blackman's letter of 3 May 1813, desperately supporting his friends attempts to convince his father to provide finance for his horse.

---

6. Turbid – thick and muddy.

John Blackman, too has been singularly unfortunate, what with the loss of one beast at Albuera, his Portuguese servant making off with another and the best part of his baggage, and some unlucky choices he has made since we came here, his catalogue of misfortunes is dreadful, and all this without any fault. Every sergeant keeps a beast of some kind, who can, and I would throw away half my baggage before I would part with my riding pony. Our marches sometimes lie through plains almost entirely under water and through fords up to a man's breast and these so frequently occur as to try one's strength and constitution. Besides an officer's duty is not done when the march is over, he has to go on picquet or some more active duty, perhaps on legs that would require other usages than standing or running all night. No! Let him keep his riding horse at all events.

As can be seen, rapid marches in such difficult terrain often led to the troops struggling to get any food at all and falling out on the march in significant numbers, but it seems that the German soldiers were better able to maintain their morale in such terrible conditions. Band Master Westcott of the Cameronians noting that:

24th November [1811] – . . . at two o'clock in the afternoon, the 26th Regiment and the rifle company of the 60th Regiment, marched at seven o'clock at night we went one league out of our road in consequence of our guide taking the regiment to the wrong village through mistake of the name, the night was very cold the regiment marched very fast in order to keep themselves warm, the moon being up it assisted us very much in marching over the rough ground we were amused on our march through the night by the rifle company of the 60th Regiment singing their national German songs, that battalion of the 60th were all Germans, to do them justice they certainly sing better, at least together, they sing more musical in parts than any of the British soldiers, indeed they appear to be more fond of music than any of the British soldiers, singing and smoking is the German soldiers chief amusement. We arrived about twelve o'clock at night to the village of Sobral da Serra, where we remained that night, occupying whatever quarters we could find, which was chiefly but ruinous houses without inhabitants . . .

This is confirmed by Second Lieutenant James Gairdner 95th Rifles in a diary entry at Vera on 6 October 1813.

It is very beautiful to hear a whole troop of German dragoons on a night march, strike up with one accord, and instead of roaring away on one discordant key (as many Englishmen would do were they inclined to be musical) sing a regular first, second, and third to their national martial airs.

On arrival at their destination, their quarters for the night varied immensely from superb to absolutely desolate. Lieutenant William Bragge of the 3rd Dragoons wrote home describing the wide variety he had experienced.

Fundao, 4 February 1812
The variety of lodgings I get into on a march is really amusing; at Sabugal my bed was composed of a pillow, a rug, two dirty petticoats and two large towels and all this in a house where they take Portuguese lodgers. I got some lice of course and the next night had a superb suite of apartments at Caria with a bed in the patron's library. I should not have been so miserably off at Sabugal but my old horse who was honoured with the baggage took an opportunity of lying down in the river, much to the annoyance of my bed and blankets.

For officers, the loss or theft of their baggage mule made their experience infinitely worse. Lieutenant Benjamin Ball of the 39th Foot explained his predicament in a letter dated Albuquerque 15 November 1811.

To add to my comfort, my baggage was carried back to Portalegre during the fight & I was left with only the clothes on my back & these in no very Catholic condition, until a few days ago, when it was restored to me in a most melancholy plight, one half of my things having been stolen & those which remained, utterly destroyed by the wet & my horse almost dead from ill-usage & starvation, so you see I am no great gainer by these wars.

Lieutenant George Barlow explained how devastating the theft of his mule was to him:

Camp near Vera, 20 August 1813
You probably are in ignorance of my mule having been stolen in the night owing to the negligence of the sentinel appointed to take charge of the animals, two days march *from Rodrigo*. No resource was left but to transfer the baggage which it carried to my horse, who was unequal to it & got in consequence a very bad sore back. No mules could be procured but at Salamanca & good strong ones bore a tremendous price. We halted one day & were under orders to march early the next

morning. No alternative remained but to leave the best part of my baggage & comfort behind at the very outset of a most active campaign or purchase one on the spur of the moment coute que coute;[7] I could meet but with *one* animal for sale, which I was obliged to buy & pay the sum of *one hundred & fifty dollars* in those gold pieces I procured in London. This pretty nigh ruined me as I had calculated upon the above sum to last certainly to the conclusion of the present campaign. The beast is [a] very good [one] of the sort & my only consolation is that I may regain my money when I find it convenient to dispose of him, as also that my £120 granted by the medical board will pretty nigh cover the £140 drawn upon you & beyond my allowance for the year, which I received on quitting England and which debt upon my father's purse I desire may be liquidated out of the above £120 as far as it will go. Dollars here cannot be procured under six shillings apiece.

After the hardships he had endured on the march, Private John Bald of the 91st Foot went so far as to write home advising his brother not to join the army.

15 November 1809

Give William my advice not to go with soldiers, for he is better off where he is. No man knows what a soldier comes through, only those that endures the hardships of an expedition. I have been sixteen months without a bed and most of that time in the open fields lying in our clothes. I was eight days without provisions being served out to me, only what I could forage for myself in the country.

It would appear to be the case that many of the marches in the peninsula were difficult and exhausting and that the famous marches, which are notorious for their extreme hardship, were not that much worse than many routine marches endured throughout the war, except for the complete absence of provisions. This clearly shows the terrible conditions which Wellington's soldiers often endured on the march throughout the entire six years of campaigning. The only reason that they were discussed less was probably because they had become somewhat inured to the harsh conditions and because their expectations had been markedly lowered over the years of hard campaigning. It needs to be recognised however, that the intense and constant marching took a far greater toll on the troops than any other element of their lives on campaign.

---

7. Coute que coute – at all costs.

Chapter 4

Sun and Sickness

The constant marching in the excessive heat or the interminable rains rapidly wore out the soldiers' boots, and combined with a poor diet, led unsurprisingly to very high levels of sickness. Many viewed hospital as the very last resort, however, as the rudimentary medical services there meant that far too often they simply turned into their final resting places. Lieutenant William Cowper Coles of the 40th Foot wrote about the unhealthiness in the very first campaign from a camp near Lisbon on 26 September 1808.

> My dear father,
> The army have not as yet entered quarters and owing to the dampness of the weather, fevers and complaints peculiar to the country have become prevalent. For the comfort of the soldiers I most earnestly wish that the general would allow the regiments that have borne the hardships of the campaign, to enter Lisbon. It would be some recompense for their labours and besides would be the means of preventing farther sickness.

However, over four years later, Ensign John Hamilton of the 2nd Line Battalion King's German Legion (KGL) wrote similarly to his wife from Fuenteguinaldo on 31 January 1813, describing the hardships they had endured in their march up from Lisbon, particularly as he could not afford to purchase a horse.

> We had rather a long route from Lisbon to this, 22 days, I walked the whole way and destroyed nearly three pairs of boots, the roads were very rugged in some parts and it was almost continually wet . . .

Even experienced officers, such as Lieutenant Colonel Andrew Barnard of the 95th Rifles, wrote home from La Encina on 2 February 1812, just after the siege of Ciudad Rodrigo, that:

> The rains have commenced. It poured torrents last night and as few houses in the country are water-tight we were drenched in our beds. How lucky we were during our operations before Ciudad Rodrigo;

the weather was in general intensely cold but always dry and the divisions employed have not sent a man to hospital since, excepting wounded.

Captain John Ewart of the 52nd Foot agreed that cold, dry weather was far more healthy than rain.

> 17 January 1812
> Our batteries ceased firing from 4 pm till daylight on the 17th as the night was foggy and some of the platforms and embrasures required repairing. Most of the division were again thirty hours out and all the men suffered from having to ford the Agueda, taking off their shoes and stockings; the sick list, however, is wonderfully small, 1st [battalion] 52nd not 30; cold night, but no rain.

There is little evidence here of General Craufurd forcing them to ford the icy streams fully booted, as a number of accounts claim, something that surely went against all sense in the battle to maintain the health of the troops.

Periods of retreat, when a lack of sleep and the stress and dangers were often heightened, certainly made the situation even worse. Brevet Colonel John Keane of the 60th Foot described how:

> Fuenteguinaldo 21 November 1812
> . . . never was there a more trying day for the troops, it rained dreadfully and the country we passed was knee deep, no rations of any kind were issued previous to starting & towards evening the poor fellows from weakness occasioned by famine & fatigue struck off the march by degrees & fell into the enemy's hands

Such trials often led to fevers, or agues as they commonly called them. These typically came on with little warning, but with a little care these short bouts could be overcome. Captain Henry Mellish with the 87th Foot recorded one such occasion in his diary.

> Badajoz 19 September 1809
> I have had a most severe attack of fever & ague. It attacked me three days ago most violently the next day I felt tolerably well in the morning, but had my attack again in the evening & yesterday it attacked me at eleven o'clock in the morning & lasted till ten at night. I am now free from fever but much reduced & dreadfully weak. I suffered terribly yesterday but I trust I shall be able to shake it off.

The lucky ones recovered in a few days, but some found that the fever had really taken hold and they fought it valiantly for lengthy periods before they either finally recovered, or more often, succumbed. Band Master Westcott of the Cameronians wrote in December 1811 that whole regiments were going down with fevers.

> 26 December
> A fever of a very dangerous nature has spread through the 26th and 79th Regiments, a number of deaths has taken place within this few days in both regiments occasioned by irregular living and lying cold at night, some of them having no covering but their great coats, which the 26th Regiment had on two expeditions before to Spain, under Sir John Moore, and to Walcheren, which wore them out nearly before they arrived in Portugal. It's the general opinion that the both regiments will have to leave the army until recovered, the sick were again sent off in spring waggons to the city of *Pinhel*.

The following summer they were still in poor health and were eventually sent from the theatre as being too unwell to continue the fatigues of campaigning.

> 15 May 1812
> The 77th Regiment marched into this city from the army in front having been sent down to Lisbon by Lord Wellington to recover from the late campaign, this gallant regiment have suffered very much since they landed in Portugal having lost above three hundred brave fellows who landed from the island of Jersey with the Cameronians the fifth of last July. The Cameronians were inspected this day by the General doctor who in consequence of the weakly state of the men, ordered them to bathe in the salt water every second day for which purpose, the regiment were to go by wings every day to bathe at a place near Belem, about four miles distant from Campo de Ourique Barracks – the right wing tomorrow morning at four o'clock, the left wing of the regiment to go the next morning at the same hour, and also in consequence of their weakly state, Major General Peacocke the commander of Lisbon, has ordered the Cameronians to be struck off the duty of Lisbon, which is in future to be done by the detachments of Belem until further orders.

Captain John Duffy of the 43rd Foot wrote in his 1810 daily diary as he tried to fight the ague and struggled to continue to fulfil his duties, until he was forced to admit defeat. Michael Crumplin believes that he had a severe case of parasitic malaria which had inflamed the spleen.

June 22: Relieved at 4 am from piquet.

June 23: Taken extremely ill this morning with a burning heat all over and fever not able to take any liquid but water all day which continued all night.

June 24: Still Feverish unable to taste any food whatever. Cooler in the evening.

June 25: At ½ past 4 am went on piquet though extremely ill at the time. Posted at Bridge of Marialava with 40 rifles besides my company. Subaltern's piquet of hussars in the village. About 9 o'clock the enemy advanced, drove in the cavalry & formed on the heights of Carpio. Their numbers about 4,000 cavalry. Their skirmishers come down to the Azava, fired repeatedly at our piquet but we did not return it. The brigade moved out to support us but the enemy did not attempt to cross the river. About 11 they retired. Owing to being exposed to a burning sun my fever returned with double violence so that I was obliged to return to Gallegos, continued so all afternoon and night.

June 26: Removed at daybreak to Fuentes & in the evening to Castello Bom. [Saw] the doctor of the sick of the division. Miserable old castle. Still unable to take any sustenance.

June 27: Taken with the ague & fever afterward in a dreadful state all day.

June 28: This day much better in the evening, took a little soup and butter which is the first I have tasted (except once before soup) for 5 days. Heat excessive.

June 29: Attacked again with ague and as usual followed with fever & pain in my side.

June 30: Better, very faint.

July 1: Ague again at 9 in the morning followed by fever at 11. Continued till sunset.

July 2: The Field Hospital removed from Castello Bom to Azenal across the Coa . . .

July 3: Attacked again with ague & fever and a severe pain in my left side which the Staff Surgeon thinks is occasioned by a lobe of the fever. Informed that a Medical Board is on orders to assemble at Alverca.

July 4: Left Azenal for Alverca . . . Not being Medical Officers sufficient at Headquarters ordered on to Selorico [*sic*] 4 leagues. Waited on Dr Franks[1] who kindly procured me a good quarter.

July 5: Ill as usual. The ague & fever now regularly attacks me every alternate day about the same hour & continues till evening. The Board assembled on me this day at 11 o'clock. Mr. Irwin[2] S[taff] Surgeon President and after a short examination the president waited on the Inspector with the report and afterwards returned & informed me that I was at liberty to proceed to England, the Board having recommended me for three months leave of absence. Dr Franks called in this evening examined my side again & pronounced the disease spleen, told me that I was in too weak a state to take bark or any medicine for the ague. Advised my leaving off Calomel which I have lately taken for my side, told me of my leave which he would forward immediately.

Band Master Westcott of the 26th Foot described the serious effects of heavy marching in the middle of the day on 6 August 1811.

In consequence of several men of the army having dropped down dead by having their heads uncovered in the heat of the sun, the commanding officer is determined to punish any man who may be found bare headed hereafter.

By the 11th Westcott was suffering himself, but he was temporarily relieved by a halt on the march.

. . . this halt of the army was very fortunate for me, for had they continued their march one week longer, I should have had to fall to the rear, to some hospital for during the whole of this march with the army I was very unwell, nothing but the dread of going to an hospital prevented me leaving my regiment. In the course of my existence, I never was so tired of life, all occasioned by the excessive fatigue of marching through a mountainous country in such a hot climate and sleeping almost every night in the open air with no shelter but the trees (sometimes even no trees) and of course we never in such camps could take any clothes off at night, the dews being very heavy far

---

1. Actually Inspector of Hospitals James Franck who was Principal Medical Officer in the peninsula until 1812.
2. Henry Irwin.

more than in England. But through the assistance of the Almighty, I recovered my health and spirits without ever being absent from the Cameronian Regiment during their marches in Portugal.

Clearly there was no understanding of the dangers of sunburn and many of the men burnt exceedingly, while many of the officers developed a very un-gentlemanlike suntan. Ensign John Mills of the Coldstream Guards recorded at Fuentes de Onoro on 8 May 1811 that:

> I am tanned to the colour of a dark boot top and my hands from not wearing gloves to two degrees darker than mahogany.

Their woollen uniforms made it intolerably hot. Lieutenant Henry Dawson of the 52nd Foot described the heat.

> Castello de Vide 28 May 1812
> If a woodcock was now to take a walk with his clothes off he would find himself agreeably roasted in ten minutes. The sun appears to be perpendicular during the whole day . . . I have some thoughts of turning frog and sitting all day in the water.

Many were too keenly aware of the general misery and illness that pervaded the greater proportion of the army. On 9 November 1813 Ensign Edmund Wheatley of the 5th Line Battalion KGL wrote:

> I could not help observing this morning as we stood round the fires how pallid and deathly every countenance appeared. Perhaps my own state of mind exaggerated every appearance as there is something very awful in reflecting that another hour and we may be summoned to that 'bourne from whence no traveller returns'.

However, Captain George Widdrington of the 34th Foot wrote of a generally accepted 'cure all' which he was convinced had kept him well and was the answer to all their ills.

> Badajoz 8 December 1809
> I am perfectly well and the climate agrees with my constitution, nevertheless I take all possible care of myself and for the time I remain in this country I shall be a great smoker [sic] as a preventative against all disorders . . . Judge of our loss since the Battle of Talavera, by sickness alone, which amounts to upwards of 2,200 men, and at Elvas

(the sick depot) the soldiers are dying at the rate of 10 to 15 nightly so unhealthy are the troops . . . it is singular how much the sickness extends to the ranks, and the officers exempt from it; but it is terrible the miserable state that the men have been in for want of common comforts. Till within these few days not even a blanket was issued out to them, and they absolutely lay on the damp bricks without a covering to keep them from the cold which is very intense . . . The French are even more unhealthy at Salamanca, than we are, as they lose [many?] men.

His concern for the men was admirable, but to claim that the officers were exempt from sickness because of their more comfortable life cannot be supported by the evidence. Lieutenant James Crummer of the 28th Foot recorded his concerns for two of his fellow officers in 1812.

Abrantes 13 September

Poor Power[3] is very ill at Elvas with a fever, he sent for his wife & children to Lisbon, they are now (unfortunate family) on their way to see him, I trust to hear of his speedy recovery but I fear all hopes are over.

Badajoz 24 September

I saw poor Boggie[4] and Power at Elvas, very ill indeed, the former is getting better, but the latter I fear we shall lose, he has got his wife and family up with him from Lisbon where both move to as soon as their situation will admit of travelling. I trust sincerely he has had a change for the better, as his death would be an irrecoverable loss to his wife & three unprovided children.

I assure you I have not met with a single officer who has a dollar, such is the scarcity of money. I have not a farthing even to get a shirt washed, but we hear that our division has got pay up to May last.

Captain Power luckily survived his fever, but it must have been disconcerting for his family and even more so for the troops to see that their surgeon had also gone down with the ague. Having his wife and children at Lisbon was unusual but not unknown, but officer's wives rarely followed the army at the front. The mention of money is also very significant. The shortage of coin in the peninsula was a constant problem and the immediate need to pay the owners

---

3. Captain William Power of the 28th Foot.
4. Surgeon John Boggie of the 28th Foot.

of the mule trains and the merchants for their supplies, to ensure the continued resupply of the army, meant that the troops were often many months in arrears with their pay. The chief problem this caused was that neither officers or men could supplement their rations or provide themselves with better footwear or warm clothing, without stealing. This of course was seriously punished if caught.

Fevers were not, however, the only problem they endured, with others suffering from a myriad of complaints as this letter from Captain George Dansey 88th Foot to his brother Second Captain Charles Dansey explains:

> Tarbes, 26 March 1814
> You will of course be surprised at hearing of my being left here which arose from a total incapability of going further by my seat having become quite raw and full of blisters originating at first in boils, but by the continual irritation of riding I was at last compelled to give up the chase, but not until I was actually bedridden, although perfectly well in health. I now expect to be detained here about a week in order to go through an alternative course of medicine (Fraser can explain the term). Barring my sore rump and a scorbutic irruption in my leg, I never was better, and although I have suffered great pain was always free from the slightest degree of fever.

Robert Duffield Cooke of the Pay Masters Office made his two complaints clear in a letter to his father.

> Oporto 21 November 1811
> I thought a few days back I had got a little touch of the itch, which is a very fashionable complaint here I assure you, but I believe the Portuguese remedy which is very simple (viz scratching) has entirely effected a cure.
> When the 'Ordor Shitembum' is a little abated I shall begin [to move] myself, but at present it rages with such fury that I think myself well off if I get into quarters without being upset as I unluckily must pass the door of headquarters to go to my own. That headquarters, at present, the seat of the whole family where they retire not as a relaxation from business but to renew it with redoubled vigour.

Lieutenant William Bragge of the 3rd Dragoons had a similar complaint and was equally descriptive of the symptoms.

> Belem 14 September 1811
> Except for a few fits of the King Agrippa I have continued in as good health as ever.

Sun and Sickness 55

Something he suffered with again the next year.

> Vaiamonte 6 May 1812
> Continual riding, change of weather or want of vegetables brought on so many unpleasant symptoms, that I had almost made up my mind to a fever or ague fit, but upon applying to our pompous Aesculapius, I was informed the Golden Duct was stopped, liver sluggish, internals out of order etc. However a few calomel pills hurried all the evil genii through the Golden Duct with tremendous explosions, leaving me in as good health as ever.

Band Master Westcott listed a number of the other hazards on the road in his journal entry for 2 January 1812.

> . . . the day was snowy, the road was uncommonly rocky and rough, a soldier of the 79th Regiment fell and broke the cap of his knee. The most of the road was hilly and the snow being on the ground made it very dangerous walking, we passed a great number of mules loaded with ammunition going up to the army in front. We passed a Portuguese lying dead on the road, this is the third person we have seen lying dead on the roads to Portugal, the first was a young woman apparently very handsome which the First Division of the army passed, no appearance of any violence upon any of them, what occasioned their death on the public roads I cannot explain.

The unexplained deaths were almost certainly caused by a combination of malnutrition and hypothermia. Two days later the regiments were ordered indoors because of the severe weather and the sickly state of the men. A novel approach was taken to ensure that the men kept dry and warm, being ordered to remain indoors except on duty.

> 4 January – The two regiments halted this day on account of the severity of the weather, we had heavy rain and a most uncommon hurricane the whole day, we were granted the indulgence of halting in consequence of the sickly state of the two regiments.

> 7 February – Heavy rain almost constantly day and night from the 29th of January to this evening, and far more heavy than what generally falls in Britain. During the rain no soldiers were on any account excepting on duty, to appear in the streets, in consequence of their sickly state.

> 8 February – The sick of the 26th Regiment has increased one hundred and ten men since we entered this city notwithstanding every precaution having been taken to prevent it. The number dead of this regiment one ensign, three sergeants, two drummers and fifty-four rank and file, that is what they know of, but the returns from the different hospitals have not been received by the regiment, consequently a number must of died that we have not yet heard of.

Henry Mellish, now a major and Deputy Assistant Adjutant General on the Staff, wrote of an unfortunate injury he had suffered at Abrantes on Monday 26 June 1811

> When I tell you I am very well, you must be satisfied without my writing a long letter, as I am lying in bed with my ribs broken by the kick of a mule . . . I am doing surprisingly well & expect to march after the army by Thursday.

The army did not rely completely on foot power, with sickness amongst the horses being just as devastating. Lieutenant William Cowper Coles now of the 4th Dragoons wrote from San Roman on 4 May 1810 of losing a baggage horse the first day of the march, but luckily procured a mule to replace it.

> . . . Was extremely unfortunate in losing a valuable baggage horse on our first day's march. He was taken ill in the night & died the following morning. I had the fortune to meet with a tolerable good mule which I replaced him with; they are extremely useful in this country and very hardy, consequently better for baggage than horses; I am afraid Government will not allow me anything for my loss as he neither was killed in action or died of the glanders which are the only grounds upon which you can make a claim. My mare turns out admirably, I was offered a very fine horse for her and thirty guineas, but knowing her worth refused it . . .

Lieutenant Charles Madden, also of the 4th Dragoons, had similar bad luck.

> 7 August 1810
> Lost a very fine mare which I had bought as a second charger from the remount sent from England for the 4th, having got the commander of the force's leave. She was first seized with a fever in her legs, and her hoofs began to separate from the hair, and would have fallen off her in a short time. I had bought her three weeks before for £46.[5]

---

5. Nearly £2,000 in today's terms.

Indeed, serious sickness amongst the horses could force the whole army to halt, as Lieutenant James Crummer of the 28th Foot wrote from Coria on 2 March 1813, regarding the delay in opening the campaign.

> Still does the army remain inactive owing to the bad state of the cavalry (who with the exception of the late reinforcements) have not a horse fit for active service nor can they move until the green forage (that is the young corn) brings them about, which will be fit for use in a fortnight.

Ensign John Mills of the Coldstream Guards summed up the awful picture at Quintana del Puente on 14 September 1812 and was not afraid to blame the commander-in-chief.

> The weather is now so bad that campaigning is more than a joke. We are never under cover even of a shrub for this country is not favoured with anything bigger than a vine. The rain comes down in torrents. Headquarters and the staff are always snug in houses and do not care about the weather and you must know that our noble marquis is not gifted with much feeling, ambition hardens the heart. He only regards the comforts of his men as far as it is actually necessary to his purposes; all have their faults and this is his.

However, despite the very difficult conditions, Lieutenant Colonel George Bingham of the 53rd Foot was impressed to see his men maintaining their morale and discipline.

> Coimbra 6 January 1810
> The coolness of the weather enables us to get on famously, and some little help is necessary to our poor fellows, who have now a blanket as well as a great coat; three days bread, sixty rounds of ammunition; and when besides all this you know they have not slept on a bed these nine months, you will be inclined to believe a soldier's life is no luxury on service. They however laugh and joke and don't appear to feel it. They are in high favour with me at present, they have conducted themselves so well during the whole march; no pilfering or petty larceny, of course no necessity for punishment.

It is clear that life in the army in the peninsula was very unhealthy, but it is also evident that the men slowly became used to the hardships and the regular bouts of fever that swept through the army. It was for this reason that Wellington was so reticent to send home his experienced troops, who were better inured to the challenges of campaigning on the peninsula, and sought to retain them in Provisional Battalions.

Chapter 5

Bad Food and Little of It

Keeping the army supplied with its rations was a logistical nightmare on the Iberian Peninsula, food frequently having to be transported by thousands of mules for hundreds of miles over rugged terrain on often terrible roads. Initially the Commissariat Department struggled badly and the troops often went without their rations, but the system clearly improved as the Commissary staff gained experience and generally succeeded in feeding the troops. First Lieutenant William Swabey of the Royal Artillery passed through the great supply base at Abrantes on 19 September 1811 and wrote of the mule system.

> Here is the grand depot of the army . . . all the stores are forwarded to the army by mules, which are pressed and become regularly the property of government. The pay for a mule which carries about 320 lbs of corn or 28 gallons of wine or spirits in casks or 280 lb of biscuits is one dollar per diem. To keep up the communication with the army many thousands of mules are employed. The owners take them in charge and receive besides the pay per mule, 18 dollars per month for themselves.

However, there were a number of infamous occasions when the supply train broke down badly, particularly on both the advance from and retreat to Corunna in 1808–9, as described in a series of letters by Captain Henry Packe of the 1st Foot Guards.

> Santiago, 1 November 1808
> The commissariat department have made no sort of arrangements for the provisioning the troops on the road hither, consequently we arrived at Caral (a village consisting of not more than eight miserable hovels) with neither bread, meat or wine to be found for our men, luckily a convoy with these necessaries passed through the place at the time, destined to form a depot at Santiago, upon which we laid violent hands of course. The country we passed through the first and part of the second day, was extremely beautiful, very luxuriant and well cultivated, but as we advanced, the country became bleak and not so productive.

We expect to remain there until the necessary depots of provisions, are found for the army on its march

Los Villardes de la Reyna, 10 November 1808
  The army was put in motion from our cantonments in the neighbourhood of Salamanca on the 14th, since when until the 20th we have been retreating rapidly with all the attendant miseries of such a movement, increased by the badness of the roads, heavy rains, and (worst of all) want of bread, the which the army went without for four days, this last distress has been by far the greatest we have had to contend with, but I trust it is now at an end yet the consequences must and will be felt very severely, the strength of our men is worn out, sickness increasing hourly, and it is said we must yet retire still further, not from the enemy *man*, but from *famine*; this unfortunate country is so drained of every kind of provision, that it is impossible for us to remain above a day or two more where we are. In our retreat I have fortunately been perfectly well & am so now thank God and my losses have been a pony a tent with some other small things which are comparatively nothing. Our baggage animals are in a wretched state from want of forage. We are obliged to send them into the woods & fields to pick up the dead grass, or what they can get; mine are now in the act of eating acorns from the evergreen oaks, of which there are abundance.

This also occurred in the retreat after Talavera in 1809, as described by Private George Woolger of the 16th Light Dragoons.

  3 August . . . at 11 we were ordered to make for Ponte Ozos de Bispo, we had had no bread for the two last days, here we had 1 biscuit & ½ served to each mess, which was 10 men
  5 August We march at 4 am over a mountainous country, water scarce & bad, no bread.
  6 August Water scarce & bad, no wine to be had for money this day a handful of rye flour was served out, no bread, we halt here one day.
  9 August This day we had 5 small biscuits served out, which was previous our famisht harts [*sic*].

Another instance was the retreat from Salamanca to Ciudad Rodrigo in 1812, which caused the troops to suffer dreadfully. The comments of Lieutenant James Crummer written at Saugo near Ciudad Rodrigo on 25 November 1812 are typical.

> . . . our retreat, which thank the Almighty is at an end, and which I have got through in good health, has been severe to an extreme, attended with all the misfortunes that can render the same miserable and distressing accounts you must receive of it by the papers . . . I have not time to repeat the many sufferings, privations & starvations we have endured since our commencing the retreat, no doubt John Bull will make much noise about it . . .

Pay Master Clerk Robert Duffield Cooke also wrote of the retreat on New Year's Day, 1813:

> I wonder how the devil I managed to come off so well as it hardly ever ceased raining and I without a great coat of any description and for 3 days only half a biscuit, which was for dinner, breakfast and supper.

However, this cannot be deemed as being in any way typical, so let us explore comments in their writings home regarding their supplies in more normal times. Captain Henry Mellish of the 87th Foot, then a Deputy Acting Assistant Adjutant General, wrote home from Oporto on 22 May 1809.

> We are just returned from seeing Marshal Soult safe out of the Portuguese territories. Our march has been most harassing for four days & nights it never ceased raining, all the villages through which the enemy had passed were burnt, so that after marching all day in the rain, we had nothing to do but to lie down to sleep in it & that frequently without anything to eat from the badness of the roads being such as nearly to prevent the possibility of forwarding supplies. Added to this we have had no means of getting our horses shod & frequently none of getting them any forage, so that we have been riding in misery both to ourselves & them.

Only a few months later, following the retreat from Talavera, he looked for an improved situation regarding rations.

> Merida 27 August 1809
> Thank God, we have now got a supply of bread & I trust the men will have their full rations henceforth. What with fatigue & the scarcity of bread, the army has fallen very sickly, but I trust rest will in a good measure bring it round.

Gunner Andrew Phillips of the Royal Artillery described a recent shortage of provisions which was then thankfully over.

Cadiz 12 March 1810
. . . I have lived on an ounce of bread a day and sometimes nothing for 2 or 3 days and 4 days but thank God we have now we have plenty at the present.

Lieutenant Colonel George Bingham of the 53rd Foot was very concerned regarding the health of the men following a difficult campaign and gave his views as to the cause:

Camp near Lobon 27 August 1809
Sickness made great ravages in our army during our stay on the banks of the Trio Almonte, a scarcity of everything, and a total want of vegetables and salt, introduced dysentery amongst both officers and men to rather an alarming degree.

A few weeks later the situation had not improved.

Camp near Badajoz 13 September 1809
. . . the army is still sickly, nor is it to be wondered at considering our men have been six months without having had their clothes off at night and have not had a blanket to cover them. The days have been excessively hot and the nights again as cold and disease naturally follows bad living and violent fatigue.

By November 1809, it would appear that the supply situation had improved but was not yet perfect, as Captain Widdrington of the 34th wrote from Esperagalego near Merida in Extremadura on the 20th.

The army still remains inactive in the plains of Extremadura, where they are quartered in different small villages and are more healthy than they were a short time ago. The weather is so extremely cold we are half starved; and this morning the ice is an inch thick. I never felt myself in better health notwithstanding our bad fare.

In comparison, Lieutenant William Freer of the 43rd Foot had only the local bread, which was made of rye, to complain of.

Arzinhal 25 February 1810
The inhabitants scarcely know what wheat bread is, nothing but black rye bread is to be bought except you send to Almeida (a league from this) for it.

This comment is quite typical, particularly amongst officers, but not exclusively so, and it is clear that they often supplemented their rations by purchasing extras, but this was only possible when they had ready money to purchase them. When the pay of the troops was seriously in arrears because of a lack of coinage, this became a major concern. Even Brevet Major Alexander Gordon, a captain in the 3rd Foot Guards, serving as an aide de camp to Wellington, wrote on 30 September 1810:

> I really have not a farthing in the world, I have no pay here whatever.

Lieutenant Freer later wrote of the greater complications of resourcing wine for the entire Light Division:

> 4 April 1810
> I have within these few days returned from Pesquiera near the Douro where Booth & myself with a small party were sent to escort wine up for the division & a troublesome job I assure you it was; firstly the procuring the wine which the inhabitants would not give for this reason, some time before, Crawford [*sic*] had sent down for wine from a merchant there, who agreed to procure the quantity at a price to be fixed by the Oporto Wine Company, but after receiving the wine (by the people's account) he deducted 20 dollars from each pipe & more over had not paid him when I left. The consequence was we were obliged to break doors to come at the wine, after that another difficulty was started, the procuring carts & oxen to convey [*sic*] it & when we had got them, the drivers were continually concerting among themselves means to escape with their oxen . . . but management succeeded & I lost but two pair out of forty, notwithstanding we had only ten men to guard them for seven days and nights, in general requiring three & four sentries continually over them. We had altogether a very pleasant time of it, making a rule to go to the best house in the town & of course [were] treated with civility.

Lieutenant George Barlow of the 52nd wrote home describing his rations while at Lisbon on 29 March 1811, but he had to bolster it as he was unwell.

> The king allows me a lb of meat (*bone included*), a lb and a half of bread (the latter hard & four or five days old) per diem. I stew the former into poor soup & poor enough it is. Things to be sure are not so dear as in London otherwise I could not stand it, but such as they are, it falls heavy upon my purse. My signora furnishes me with lodging and candle only, eatables I provide myself with & as I cannot eat solid meat like beef

I must furnish every day a dinner at my own expense, if I follow the surgeon's directions.

Band Master Westcott of the Cameronians wrote of supply problems in late 1811.

> 11 December – The biscuit served this day amounted to no more than an ounce per man, in consequence of the commissary not sending sufficient quantity to the brigade, nor neither could bread be bought, for money. Indeed, the brigade has been very badly off for provisions since they came on the plains of Almeida, owing to the difficulty of bringing it up so far, beef we had a plenty as the cattle travelled with us and was killed after the march, but it was the most miserable meat ever eat, after a fatiguing days march. The cattle was killed in a feverish state from walking and cut up, and divided immediately, and cooked instantly, and often eat without salt, as each individual must provide themselves with salt or go without. No man wants ever [to] eat such beef unless like them for mere hunger, when bread was scarce having nothing else fit to be eat. We were miserably bad[ly] off, so with bad feeding and bad quarters and hard marching, the brigade lost a number of men, who deserved a better fate. The 26th Regiment lost two sergeants, one drummer, twenty-seven rank & file and two women, the sick of the regiment amounted to six officers, five sergeants, seven drummers, and two hundred and three rank & file.

It appears that the men were only then being issued with blankets for sleeping at night in the open air.

> 18 December – The regiment received sixty blankets more, which was still far too little, as they were falling sick every hour through want of cloaths [sic] at night, the working party returned from Almeida, the regiment had Indian corn bread served out to them this day.

Only a few weeks later Ensign John Carter of the 30th Foot was complaining of being unable to afford a piece of mutton from the regimental butcher.

> 30 Dec 1811
> Paddy Wire the butcher desired the doctor & me for the payment of a little mutton which we had bought of him in order to make the times appear a little more like Christmas. Neither of us had a farthing to pay him.

Lieutenant George Barlow also witnessed difficulties with the supply of rations that winter.

> Martiago, 18 December 1811
> Provisions have of late become very scarce; the troops have not received any bread for four days together; and the officers have been obliged to purchase it at the rate of 3s the loaf, much about the same size as the English bakers quarter;[1] and what appears still more incredible the 1st Battalion were unable to procure it at a less price than 5s in a neighbouring village; but purses are not very long at present and a little longer continuance in these parts, as such an expenditure would soon reduce us to beggary.
>
> It has been actually some weeks on the route & in the meanwhile some of our company cannot come to parade on account of nakedness. The country is also pretty nigh exhausted; for four days together, the men have been without bread or potatoes, this however is in some measure the fault of the commissary against whom complaints have been forwarded to the general.

Captain John Ewart, also of the 52nd, found it impossible to procure anything beyond his rations with which to celebrate his birthday.

> 28 July 1812
> *We* dined on rations, *no* wine and *no* money – how differently should I have passed this birthday in England among my friends!!!

George Bingham, commanding the 53rd Foot, saw that the junior officers particularly suffered when they had no pay:

> Almofala 10 May 1813
> . . . we have not received any pay since December . . . it is most severely felt by the junior officers, who are absolutely starving on their pound of meat and pound and a half of bread which goes but little way with young gentlemen who have been used to gorge themselves at a regimental mess.

---

1. A quartern loaf was a very large loaf, often cut and sold in quarters. The London Bread Act of 1822 stipulated that the loaf before baking had to weigh 4lbs 15oz (2.2kg).

Another regimental colleague, Lieutenant Charles Dawson, wrote from Martiago on 2 December 1811 confirming the food shortages, but also highlighted the severe shortages of clothing in some battalions.

> I am sorry to say that our commissariat is not as well conducted as it ought to be. I can [only] answer for the Light Division. Our poor fellows have not had any bread for some time, not until the last 3 days & then only half rations and at a time when they have no money, 3 month's pay due to them & have been obliged to feed themselves upon chestnuts & acorns. The inhabitants refuse to bring bread to market as the commissary presses it and pays only by paper, [giving] a receipt for it. The men have 1½ or 2 lb of meat when they have no bread, but without salt or potatoes, they would prefer ½ lb of bread. Our 2nd battalion [is] almost naked and have been excused outlying picquet. We cannot muster 30 shirts amongst them, no stockings, coats & pantaloons patched like harlequins . . .

The desperate situation that winter is particularly highlighted by a diary entry of First Lieutenant William Swabey of the Royal Artillery.

> 15 January 1812
> I superintended the shooting of a horse as I went to dinner . . . passing by the camp an hour afterwards there was not a remnant of him except his bones to be seen.

Ensign John Blackman of the Coldstream Guards wrote of the added expense occurred when in encampment, to keep up standards.

> 24 May 1812
> Now with regards to living, of course in marching, I get nothing but my rations, but in halting it becomes expensive as then we are very glad to get mutton & bread and butter &c, &c. all which things advance in price every day and that most enormously, but I shall be very happy to appeal to my brother officers whether I do not live as cheap and much cheaper than many of them.

Second Lieutenant Henry Hough of the Royal Artillery wrote of another problem. Rations were issued but were so poor that they were inedible. It is quite possible, however, that his standards were a little too high, given his comments over the replacement he bought.

25 April 1812
   The rations we drew at Santarem were not eatable. Met with a fish, something like salmon, which we bought and dressed part of it for dinner. Could not get any vegetables in the place, and had no sauce, so that we made but an indifferent dinner.

He also found problems in acquiring adequate provisions for the battery's rations while covering the siege of Burgos on 5 November 1812.

   I . . . dispatched orderlies in several directions for intelligence, and also to endeavour to obtain some rations; the former was very unwelcome, and I could only procure 2 days meat without bread, biscuits or anything else, for my detachment to subsist on.

Lieutenant Colonel George Bingham of the 53rd Foot found the scarcity of wood so bad that he was forced to extremes.

Camp in the position of San Cristobal near Salamanca 10 November 1812
   Wood is so scarce, I was obliged to burn my tent mallet yesterday, to boil my kettle. All wood that is to be procured comes from the houses . . .

Not everyone was finding it so difficult to procure food, however. Major the Honourable Edward Cocks of the 79th Foot and his colleagues clearly had other priorities.

22 June 1812
   The mess I belong to finished its last two bottles of champagne, we have nothing left but Bucellas[2] and Claret.

On 19 July 1812, only three days before the Battle of Salamanca, he wrote again with some better news.

   We get plenty of lemon ice cream and I received yesterday a strong reinforcement of claret but am still badly off for champagne. Very little game or poultry is stirring.

---

2. The white wine Bucelas, or historically Bucellas, comes from a region near Lisbon, which has the highest wine classification in Portugal.

Lieutenant William Bragge of the 3rd Dragoons also indicates that the shortages were not universal.

> Villayerna, 3 miles from Burgos 18 October 1812
> This climate certainly has agreed with my constitution wonderfully well hitherto, and will I hope continue to do so. I am become immensely heavy and fat and shall have a very respectable bay window by the time I return to England . . .

Certainly Wellington and his staff were saved from running out of fine wines by a major capture, as mentioned in the letter of Henry Johnson, aide de camp to the Prince of Orange.

> 11 May 1812
> Great news the valiant guerrilla Longa yesterday presented to our Lord one thousand bottles of prime Claret taken on their march from France to Madrid for the private tippling of his Majesty Napoleon El Chico, alias Joey,[3] who must now put himself on short allowance. These were only a brigade of a strong division, the remainder having been distributed amongst Generals Castanos, Walker, Alava &c not to mention that Longa may have detained a few for himself. This prime stuff was escorted by 300,000 dollars and certain conscripts. We shall drink his health in high style, in addition to 'the passage of the Douro', this day three years. This month is nearly blocked up with gala days. We must see if we cannot decorate June with a few red-letter days this summer.

Indeed, an invite to the duke's table was a sure way of sating a ravenous appetite. Lieutenant Edward Fox Fitzgerald of the 10th Hussars was very glad of the invitation.

> Subijana 26 June 1813
> I dine with Lord Wellington this day at 3 o'clock, which is a very good windfall, as we are all at short commons and have had no bread for these three days . . . I am in good health and very happy, but very hungry!

That winter the troops were well fed and there are no complaints at all of lack of rations. Individual officers did find it hard to feed their horses, however.

---

3. King Joseph Napoleon of Spain was the Emperor Napoleon's older brother.

Ensign the Honourable Orlando Bridgeman of the 1st Foot Guards wrote of his problems on 20 March 1813, but recognized that other officers not so well off financially were really struggling.

> You have no idea what difficulty there is in getting forage for ones horses here, the commissaries seize it all, & it is scarcely to be bought, except what the poor people can hide in their houses & they are very loath to part with it. Nothing but offering a high price will get it from them at all, you know they only allow a subaltern forage for half a horse, this I own is shabby, it is impossible for any to go on at all without two & with no comfort under three, there are more officers with four than three. Those of the line who have not money are *actually* obliged to steal & Lord W[ellington] *obliged* to wink at it. Think how officers with nothing but their pay go on at all; the army have been paid up to November, this is March, so they are four months in arrears, now officers who have nothing but their pay, must be hard put to it, as you will plainly see.

Newly-arrived cavalry resting after their voyage near Lisbon enjoyed plentiful and regular rations from the city, as Lieutenant George Woodberry of the 18th Hussars described.

> Luz, Thursday 18 February. 1813
> Our daily rations arrive every morning from Lisbon and are delivered out to the regiment about midday; my rations are as follows, one pound of bread, rather brown but very good, ¾ lb of beef, generally killed a few hours before, a pint of sour wine, 6 pounds of hay, 8 pounds of corn, and 9 pounds of wood for which I am charged three pence. An officer may live very well indeed in Portugal on his pay, particularly after he gets up country. An ill constructed cart is employed, drawn by two bullocks, driven or rather led by a stout fellow who walks in front of the animals; he has a stick with a small spike at the extremity to goad them occasionally. This vehicle being extremely long, narrow and clumsy will carry from six to eight hundredweight, and as the Portuguese have no idea of greasing the axletree, when loaded they send forth a horrible noise. Twenty or thirty of these carts bring our rations daily.

Brevet Colonel Frederick Robinson (he was to become a major general two months later) describes arriving to take command of his brigade. He enforced changes of supply with the Commissary and was soon reaping the benefits.

Lamego 27 April 1813

The first thing I did on joining my brigade was to examine the state of the men's messes and the hospitals; and obliged the reluctant commissary to issue good wine instead of bad rum, bread instead of biscuit and two ounces of rice per man per day to put in their soup . . . I tasted one kettleful so often the other day that the men began to look devilish sulky, but my putting down a twelve sous piece to buy some salt restored their smiles. I have been reaping the benefit of these regulations for ten days at least, 150 men have been restored to the ranks and no more new cases have occurred than would have happened in any other country.

The rapid advance of 1813 again put the Commissary under great strain but they started well prepared. Lieutenant James Crummer of the 28th Foot rejoiced to get on the march again, the troops being fully prepared for the campaign.

Camp near Gallisteo 16 May 1813

At last I address you from the field, once more have we assembled to advance against the enemy, whose advance posts are within a few leagues of us. Tomorrow we advance five leagues, which does not prevent our celebrating (by a division) the anniversary of the Battle of Albuera. Great preparations are making, whole trees on fire, roasting, boiling & stewing, so that . . . we take the field under the happy auspices of *plenty*. I cannot describe the satisfaction and pleasure everyone [feels?] at moving again . . . in the hope of deciding the fate of the Peninsula this ensuing campaign . . .

Lieutenant James Gairdner of the 95th Rifles described how they marched through a seemingly barren landscape but found themselves in a land of plenty.

15 June 1813

Marched at the usual hour, left in front, through the same miserable barren country & crossed the Ebro at Puente Arenas near which we bivouacked. The bed of the river is very far below the level of the country through which we have been marching, consequently the pass down to the river is very steep, it is the most formidable (with the exception of Barba del Puerco) I ever saw. The valley through which the river runs, which opens to the view in descending the pass now was the most beautiful I ever saw. It is abundantly plentiful in fruit, corn, vegetables & everything & is such a contrast to the barren mountains & precipice which surround it, for there are most terrible heights on both banks of the river, that it is the most heavenly spot I ever saw. There is a great quantity of fresh butter selling hereabouts, every species of provision is very cheap here, our mess bough[t] 7 loaves of bread for 4 vintems & 3 quartos each. An officer of the 2nd Battalion told me he bought 3 sheep & a 4-pound loaf of bread for 2 dollars.

Charles Crowe, a lieutenant in the 27th Foot, recorded that the rapid advance inevitably led to shortages as they outmarched the Commissariat. The greatest problem however was a lack of salt, on which they blamed their dysentery.

13 June 1813

We marched with dawn of day, leaving behind us our sick men, according to order. There were 53 from the whole division, of which only three were of the 27th Regiment. Here was a strong proof of the indomitable spirit of the British soldier under bodily sufferings, for many men in the division looked more like moving mummies than able soldiers. We have been three days without bread or biscuit, our advance has been so rapid that the commissariat stores from the rear cannot overtake us. Consequently, an extra half pound of meat per man has been supplied. This was highly expedient, but, salt, wherewith to flavour this pound and half of beef, reeking from the fresh slain bullock was not to be procured. For nine days we have been destitute of this, lightly esteemed, blessing of providence. No one at home duly appreciates the value of this inestimable, but apparently insignificant ingredient because all food is savoured with it by the cook, but the nausea with which we swallowed our soup meagre, and the sodden flesh, lacking salt, made many of us painfully sensible of its great value. The effect of the want of this important article, was that all of us suffered dreadfully from diarrhoea, our eyes, and our noses, told us how woefully some of our men were afflicted, and their pale hollow cheeks and their nether garments confirmed the fact, for the flux ran from them as they marched. Late in the evening, when we encamped in a rich vale, near two small villages, we received for our rations, rum of the very worst quality, it must have been more than half turpentine. My chum and I did not drink our quota. How fervently did we wish that the rascally contractor who sent such vile stuff could be made to suffer like our poor soldiers. It would have cost him more for physician's fees, than he had gained by his villainy.

George Barlow of the 52nd Foot spoke of new stores arriving to clothe the army.

Abrantes, 4 May 1813

Everything indeed announces the immediate opening of the campaign. The men of our regiment were ordered from [Fuente]guinaldo to escort a convoy of new great coats; but a general order has been given to the army, for everyone to leave behind his great coat & to take only a blanket, a pretty sure sign that his lordship intends to try the hardihood of our feet.

However, during the march, he also wrote of temporary shortages.

> Camp near Vitoria, 20 June 1813
> Today we halt as I imagine on account of the supplies, which such rapid marching have left considerably in the rear; for two days no bread has been served out to the troops and for *the three* preceding them, but half a pound per man which is little indeed for those who are constantly eight or ten hour's under arms, make rapid marches in these mountainous tracts and have no substitute whatever, excepting a quarter of a pound of flower [*sic*] & sometimes not even that allowance.

Major Edwin Griffiths of the 15th Hussars wrote down the secret of the most valuable food that they sought to procure.

> 11 June 1813
> Eggs were the greatest luxury that *could* be procured in this country; they not only formed a pleasing variety in various shapes at dinner, but also made an excellent substitute for cream with our tea . . .

Luxuries were still very difficult to procure, as clearly shown by George Woodberry's account of the sale of a dead officer's effects which went for quite exorbitant prices.

> Olite, Thursday 1 July. We had a parade this morning, for the inspection of horses, they are in a very bad state, and only rest will bring them about . . . Poor Captain Carew's baggage was sold yesterday, it was truly ridiculous to see the prices given for the eatables, two bottles of sauce were sold for 35s/-, cheese of about 7lbs weight sold for 73s/6d, two tongues for 27s/-. The principle purchasers were Lord Worcester, General Hill, and Mr Fitzclarence, and Somerset. Lord W[orcester] gave 34s/- for a pair of brass spurs. I bought a bridle, which cost me £4, a monstrous price, and cloth for a pair of overalls at £2/14s/0d, which all thought was not sufficient for that purpose, but the tailor of the regiment says it's full enough.

While encamped in the Pyrenees during the winter of 1813, there was again very little complaint regarding the supply of rations. With the advance into

Southern France there was indeed usually great plenty and complaints become very rare, although Charles Crowe had a minor one during the autumn.

> 6 October 1813
> We could obtain nothing but salt meat, or regular junk for our rations at Renteria and moved off little satisfied with our cargo.

This comment would indicate that in normal circumstances they were then receiving better than ration of salt beef. Indeed, William Swabey of the Royal Artillery felt able to give away beef to his landlord, something apparently rarely eaten in the area.

> 23 November 1813
> Gave my poor landlord a couple of pounds of fresh meat, which he has not tasted for many years, he says. The poor peasants live upon chestnuts and sour wine.

Major John Tylden of the 43rd Foot was also highly complimentary of the abundance of fine food.

> 11 March 1814
> We have hitherto found an abundance in the country, in spite of the exactions of the French and I have no doubt shall continue to do so, some parts that we have passed through equals England in point of cultivation and beats it in point of the general appearance of farmhouses.

Edwin Griffiths of the 15th Hussars was very impressed with the levels of agriculture in France, but still found some items he regarded as basics which remained almost impossible to procure.

> Gargas near Toulouse 25 April 1814
> This part of France very much resembles England and notwithstanding all Bonaparte's taxes & conscriptions, it is extremely populous & well cultivated and there is more general comfort & less appearance of poverty than any country I have ever been to yet . . . The market towns are well supplied & attended, meat, bread, vegetables, fowls & eggs much cheaper than in England, but there is one article they are almost entirely deficient of and which we miss more than any other, there is neither milk or butter to be got for love or money.

There were clearly times when the Commissariat was under intense pressure, even at times other than the infamous retreats already highlighted. Rapid advances could soon outrun the supply chain and halts had to be ordered simply to allow them to catch up. The winter of 1811/12 also proved to be a very significant challenge for the commissaries. However, outside of these periods of great difficulty, the issues with obtaining sufficient rations for the troops are significant for their general absence in any of the communications with home, a clear indication that the troops were being adequately supplied and that there was no reason to complain. This would indicate that the machinery of this enormous supply chain actually worked exceptionally well for most of the time, perhaps not the picture that is often conjured by later memorialists, and this has perhaps tainted the judgements of some historians too much.

Chapter 6

The Allied Nations

Early encounters with Portuguese and Spanish troops often led to many soldiers harshly judging their proficiency, but not always. As the war progressed and their understanding of the very difficult conditions they were operating in grew, this did change, although national stereotypes did persist.

As regards the Portuguese army, it is undoubtedly true that initially British soldiers looked on them scornfully, but is it any wonder that they were in a very poor state? The Portuguese army had suffered badly from decades of inertia, lack of investment and corruption and many of its officers were elderly and habitually absent. This meant that the weak French force that virtually crawled into Lisbon in November 1807, following a disastrous march through barren countryside, found the Portuguese forces completely unable to mount a defence against them. General Junot, commanding the French troops, then systematically disbanded much of the army. There is little wonder, therefore, that these hastily reformed units garnered such scorn from their British allies. Typical of this attitude are the comments of Captain Henry Mellish of the 87th Foot.

> Oporto 22 May 1809
>
> . . . It is right that people should be informed correctly of what assistance we may derive from any Portuguese army, as I see statements in the English papers that Silveira has 15,000 well disciplined troops . . . .The truth is that Silveira's army (if such it ought to be called) does not much exceed 2,000 men, at all events does amount to 2,500 & these the most miserable irregular banditti that were ever seen. I am certain one good regiment of dragoons would cut them all to pieces.

Lieutenant Colonel George Bingham of the 53rd Foot echoes these concerns.

> Fonte del Pipo 9 April 1809
>
> Much is expected from the Portuguese, but I am afraid little reliance can be placed on them; certainly some of the new levies commanded by British officers appear tolerably well, but I am afraid want the necessary spirit. There certainly exists a hatred towards the French . . .

At the same time, much was also hoped for from the large Spanish armies fighting the French, although experience was to show that little reliance could be placed on their official numbers. Views of the Spanish troops varied quite a lot during the early days of the war, but the more positive comments may have been engendered more from hope than with any confidence. Captain Henry Packe, 1st Foot Guards, wrote disparagingly of them during the Corunna campaign from the camp at Comvases (Carneros?) near Astorga, 28 November 1808

> I am afraid Spain cannot, or will not resist the French much; the total defeat of [General] Blake's Division seems to have cast a damp over the ardour and patriotism of every Spaniard, and there is great reason to believe they have not above seventy thousand men in arms, and all the accounts you have heard in England have been greatly exaggerated.

Captain Mellish, however, was impressed by his first encounter with Spanish troops, rating them far more highly than the Portuguese, but his opinion seems to have changed quite rapidly.

> Abrantes 17 June 1809
> I am just returned from a pleasant little ride of about 150 miles to see [General] Cuesta's Army. I like the Spaniards very much, there is ten times more military spirit in them than in the Portuguese.

> Talavera de la Reyna 25 July 1809
> Cuesta cannot meddle with them [the French] without us, as his troops, although tolerably good in appearance are very deficient in confidence & in organisation. The army may one day be 35,000 & the next 5,000 as every man goes home as best suits his pleasure or convenience.

> Badajoz 9 October 1809
> As to the *Army* of the country, if a regiment of French cavalry shows itself to ten thousand of them, off they go, leaving their artillery, arms &c as we saw pretty plain proof of at the Puente d'Arzobispo, where they lost 21 pieces of cannon merely on the crossing of a small force of cavalry over the river.

Captain George Widdrington of the 34th Foot was damning of both the Spanish and Portuguese troops after the Battle of Talavera when writing to his father.

> Badajoz 8 December 1809

> You will have heard of the battle between the Spanish and French; and how poltroon-like the former behaved on that occasion, in my humble opinion the Spaniards see their fate as irrecoverable and to spare the expense they heartily wish us out of the country. No sign of cordiality appear on their side towards us; and we are forced often to insult by threats before we can obtain a billet or any trifle we may want. Every article that is sold is an enormous price and these are our friendly allies!
>
> You ask me to let you know what sort of soldiers the Portuguese are. You may thank your stars that you never embarked as brigadier; you have no conception, my dear father, of the badness of the troops; although you allow them to be the worst in the world; they in reality do not deserve the name of soldiers either in conduct, skill, or appearance; and sorry should I be to see you and myself in action with such inability on the side of the men and officers as we must have met with had we been employed with them.

However, with a British officer – William Carr Beresford – placed at the head of the Portuguese army in the rank of field marshal, with a brief to reform it from top to bottom, it was not long before very different views were becoming evident. As early as 14 January 1810, Captain John Tylden of the 43rd Foot, despite having little hope for a successful outcome for the campaign, wrote from Pinhel that:

> To tell the truth I am sick of carrying on so hopeless a cause as this is. Not that the Portuguese themselves want energy in the business, on the contrary they are actually exerting themselves much more than I had conceived the natural idleness of their character would have allowed. The regular army consist of about 40,000 men, infantry & cavalry, tolerably well drilled by English officers. They have besides a militia, but worth very little. Several English officers now in the Portuguese service have assure me that they can place great reliance on the men, that they are practicable, willing soldiers and fond of being taught, but that the Portuguese officers are not worth a sous . . . The people certainly do detest the French, which is something. It really makes me pity them when I think that probably in spite of all their endeavours, a French force will overwhelm them, as it threatens to do and shortly will do Spain . . .

Captain William Gomm could also see a growing confidence in the Portuguese troops, even before their excellent performance at the Battle of Bussaco.

Portalegre 21 August 1810
    The Portuguese troops on every occasion have been behaving admirably and they talk of puzzling the Frenchmen and are as saucy as you please.

Lieutenant Charles Madden of the 4th Dragoons had clearly not expected much from either the Portuguese or Spanish troops – particularly from the latter – at the very bloody battle and near defeat of Albuera. In his diary entry of 16 May 1811, he had to admit however that they had both fought hard and had performed much better than he had expected, although he attributed this solely to the brave example shown by the British troops. Even after such a stubborn performance by them, he still could not refrain from denigrating the Spanish troops.

> What made our situation more critical, [was that] three-fourths of our army were composed of Spaniards and Portuguese, the former of whom were greatly deficient of discipline, and from frequent defeats by the French had an utter dread of them. However, Providence inspired all our united force with steadiness and courage; and both the Portuguese and Spaniards endeavoured to follow the glorious example of the British troops. Our loss was dreadful. In one division, which consisted of 4,000 men, we had killed, wounded, and prisoners 2,990, the two first in command killed, and an equal proportion of officers; our whole loss out of about 8,000 or 9,000. British [losses] amounted to 4,000, with 2,000 Spanish and Portuguese . . . [but night did not relieve our anxieties] with a prospect of the engagement being renewed at daylight, or an attack under cover of the night. Much was to be dreaded, as we had a most experienced general (Soult) to guard against, who had an utter contempt of the Spaniards. who formed one-third of our army.

He was joined in these views by Lieutenant James Crummer of the 28th:

Elvas 22 May 1811
    I am happy to say that the Spanish cavalry performed very well indeed & should think the infantry would have behaved equally as well had they been engaged.

However, the Spanish were still capable of terrible massacres in their quest for vengeance, as Private John Insley of the Royal Dragoons recorded in his diary:

12 May 1811 Barquilla
    On enemy's retreat a Spanish general fell in with their sick and wounded about 30 carriages and 200 men and put every man to death

and took away a deal of ammunition, in revenge of the enemy's killing of his wife and child.

Brevet Major the Honourable Alexander Gordon of the 3rd Foot Guards made a short note regarding his concerns over the Portuguese troops captured at the fall of Almeida, but then admitted that it had been a ploy to escape.

> Gouveia 13 September 1810
> In my last letter I mentioned to you that the 24th Portuguese Regiment of the line taken at Almeida had entered into the French service. Since which however, every man and officer has deserted and returned to us.

Within a week he was crowing over the delight shown at Wellington's headquarters at the performance of the Portuguese at Bussaco.

> Convent of Bussaco 27 September 1810
> We are in high spirits at the Portuguese behaving so well.

Band Master Westcott of the Cameronians had very positive thoughts while watching a Portuguese militia battalion at church parade on 12 January 1812.

> We saw the Viseu Militia parade and march to church, they were something better than six hundred men on parade, their clothing was new, and the uniform blue with yellow facing which had a handsome appearance. In general they were a fine looking set of young men, and made a very military appearance. The people of Britain, has not the least idea that the Portuguese troops are so fine and so well equipped and disciplined. The Portuguese army before the war were a despisable [*sic*] looking set of undisciplined men, badly equipped in every particular, and in such a state altogether as not to be able to defend their own country against any regular army who might invade them. But since the war with the assistance of a number of British officers who got promoted in the Portuguese service, and with long experience fighting with the British against the French, they now are an honour to their country, both in military appearance and in bravery. In many hard fought actions through the peninsula, assisted by the British they proved themselves sturdy determined soldiers against experienced French armies, commanded by the best generals of France.

A week later he saw the Portuguese Ordenanza, or local militia, muster. They were clearly not of the same calibre, but had previously proven useful using guerrilla tactics.

> 19 January – The whole of the city was very much crowded with the armed peasants, some armed with fowling pieces and others with old rusty pikes, who were obliged to come in and show themselves and arms on particular days, to some magistrate. Those people were found to be very useful through the war, in the mountains, in destroying small parties of the enemy and in cutting off supplies of provisions. They were a very unmilitary looking set, more like rebels than anything else, yet they answer the purpose of mountain warfare, but very often in the most cruel manner they would treat those unfortunate stragglers who fell in their power, having no discipline or humanity among them. Many a brave French soldier, has been butchered by those set of beings when straggling, from the rest of their countrymen, and often their bodies left unburied on some mountain as a savage trophy of the cowardly achievement committed upon a human being, who was over powered by numbers and where his body lay as a brutish spectacle to the view of those mountain canibals, his friends and comrades, not knowing where, or how he breathed his last. At Macal do Chao several men who were left behind the French army through sickness in their last retreat from the lines at Torres Vedras under the command of Marshal Massena was cruelly butchered by some of those miscreants at the house I quartered at in the village, they had the arms and clothing (as a trophy) of one of those unfortunate soldiers, who belonged to the Eighth French Regiment ...
>
> It may be said that the Portuguese had every reason to be exasperated against the French, to behold their country laid waste, their altars destroyed, and their towns and villages a heap of ruins, no true patriot certainly could stand and tamely view this melancholy scene, without a spirit of retaliation. Yet no brave man would ever take the life of a defenceless prisoner for the tyranny of his commanders, yet it's a misfortune that mostly always attends oppression, which at all times cannot be avoided, that when a nation is oppressed by a despotic army who has invaded their country, who's numbers of experienced veterans fighting under discipline[d] officers often forbids an open resistance. The oppressed exasperated to the highest pitch of desperation often retaliates upon those who may unfortunately fall into their hands, without any consideration of mercy, happy is the country that never experienced such sanguinary scenes of war, and destruction.

Another month later he watched a regular Portuguese regiment march through and was quite impressed.

> 21 February – The 12th Portuguese Regiment of the line, marched into this city, on their road for Badajoz, they consist of about fifteen hundred men, a very fine looking well-disciplined regiment, they have five English officers.

Lieutenant Colonel Charles Macleod of the 43rd Foot was impressed with the Portuguese troops. Indeed, he believed they were better than the British troops in some circumstances.

> Elvas 17 June 1811
> The Portuguese troops are really beyond what I expected; for many services they might be preferred to British. Their officers are not good, but the soldier is sober, obedient & patient, they work capitally, so will the British if they are in the humour, but if not, it is difficult to rouse them . . . I also became very intimate [with] Lieutenant Colonel McCreagh commanded a corps of riflemen cacadores, all Portuguese and as good light troops as you can conceive; I don't mean they will rival the 43rd but still they are not to be sneezed at.

Band Master John Westcott later recorded watching a number of Portuguese regiments passing through Coimbra in 1812 and was very impressed.

> 28th February . . . several passed through Coimbra, the 4th, 10th and 11th Regiments of Portuguese Cacadores (rifle regiments) and the 1st and 16th Portuguese Regiments of the line and the 1st Battalion of the 11th British Regiment entered the city on their march to Badajoz. The uniform of the Portuguese Cacadores is something of a snuff colour, like the bark of trees, with black horn buttons and black accoutrements, a very fine uniform for woods as riflemen, they were faced like other regiments with a different colour from their jackets. The whole of those regiments were very fine looking young men with a number of English officers in each regiment. The 16th Regiment are said to be the finest of the Portuguese Army, the whole of those regiments marched into Coimbra in grand style with their bands playing at the head of each regiment, and to do them justice they made an elegant martial appearance. The cacadores appear to be the Portuguese chief pride.

Things continued to improve and Lieutenant James Crummer of the 28th Foot praised the Portuguese troops for their performance during the Battle of Salamanca in 1812.

> Lisbon 8 August
> The Portuguese troops have not been backward in assisting towards the glory of the day and of course every praise is due to these young but promising soldiers.

However, being disturbed by the band of a Portuguese brigade a few months later was not so much to his liking.

> Badajoz 24 September 1812
> I have again been disturbed by a brigade of Portuguese, who have now marched in with bands, drums, and all other noisy instruments of war which foreign troops are excessively particular to. If this constituted a good regiment, the Portuguese ought indeed [to] be very fine.

Ensign John Mills of the Coldstream Guards was less complimentary about the Portuguese troops during the siege of Burgos.

> Burgos 21 September 1812
> The rascally Portuguese work very ill, consequently are more exposed and get more frequently hit than our men. I hope that their conduct will be fully exposed and that no more will be said of their distinguished conduct which few have had discrimination enough to find out.

Ensign the Honourable Orlando Bridgeman of the 1st Foot Guards, writing from the siege of Cadiz on 12 June 1812, was very disparaging of the Spanish troops. He could not understand why they could not continue the war in a more gentlemanly way.

> I cannot say I like the Spaniards in general, . . . there are some fine regiments in the service, but few of them have any clothes & they all want officers, but I really think if well clothed & with good officers they might be made a good deal of. The Portuguese are very superior people, they are grateful to us for all we do for them which the Spaniards are not & their soldiers are much better & in finer order.

Lieutenant William Bragge of the 3rd Dragoons, writing from Villayerno (-Morquillas) one league in front of Burgos on 25 September 1812, was not impressed by the Spanish troops of the Army of Galicia.

> The noted Galician Army have at length joined us under Castanos and look much like an army of mendicants with brown cloaks on.

Lieutenant Colonel George Bingham of the 53rd had a similar view.

> Camp before Burgos 21 September 1812
> The Spanish army under the command of Castanos, 11,000 strong, joined us on the sixteenth; such a set of scarecrows I never set eyes on!! Complete jail birds! The officers being in appearance little better than the men, no discipline amongst them. . . .

By the following year, the Portuguese were gaining universal credit, many soldiers equating them with British troops, a high honour in their eyes. Captain Duncan Robertson of the 88th Foot wrote to his father following the Battle of Vitoria.

> 23 June 1813
> I rejoice to say that both the Spanish and Portuguese troops who were engaged, fought like lyons [sic] nay some of the Portuguese battalions showed both discipline and gallantry equal to any of the British even, I speak not from reports but from what I saw with my own eyes for two Portuguese regiments fought alongside us the whole day.

Orlando Bridgeman wrote again on Sunday, 25 July 1813 from Palencia revising his views of the Spanish troops a little.

> What George had said to me about the Spaniards came to my mind, I thought I had been to blame in forming a bad opinion of all by what I had seen in Cadiz, which he himself allows to be very inferior to the north & I determined to alter my opinion, but I have done so only in a very small degree. In the poorest villages all is well, great civility, with great pride, but the higher one looks, the less the civility, & the greater the pride. The Spanish soldier I abhor & he only is bad, because his officers make him so, they really are not commonly civil to an English officer, they appear to look down upon us & heaven only knows why, except it is from jealousy. However I do own that the Spanish peasant, is a very fine being, generous to a degree, & that *he* only can be liked by an English *soldier*.

Brevet Colonel Andrew Barnard 95th also rejoiced in the improvement in these troops.

> Lesaca 4 August 1813
> In this part of the world the Portuguese behaved admirably on every occasion and were very much engaged. The Spaniards are beginning to show symptoms of [im]provement and [with] the force of example in a very short time I expect to see them show confidence. The soldiers are naturally as brave a set of fellows as exist but they have so often fallen a sacrifice to the ignorance and rascality of their generals that it had ruined their morale, which the direction of an able chief will improve gradually.

However, following a number of incidents where French people were murdered in retaliation by vengeful Spanish troops after the army marched into France, much of the Spanish force was sent back into Spain by Wellington. Colonel Andrew Barnard wrote home from Vera on 27 November 1813.

> The Spanish army are returned to Spain to be near their supplies which is rather a pleasant circumstance as they were not quite on such good terms with Monsieur, as we his old enemy are.

Although formally part of the British Army, the British troops also held their own views on the German troops serving alongside them and their views do not always abide to the accepted view of the King's German Legion. The Honourable Edward Cocks of the 16th Light Dragoons thought highly of the German cavalry, but not of the infantry and he gave reasons why he thought it was so.

> 9 July 1810
> Though I have not a very high opinion of the infantry belonging to the German Legion, yet I must bear the most unqualified testimony to the courage, skill, zeal and marked good conduct of the cavalry. The fact is, the first are foreigners of all descriptions and exactly the same species of troops except being finer men, as the French armies. The cavalry are old hussars, almost all Hanoverians and many of them men of great respectability. These men are perfectly to be depended on and understand outpost duty better and take more care of their horses than British dragoons.

Ensign John Mills of the Coldstream Guards made a comment on German troops in both armies:

Nave de Haver, 3 September 1811
Very few of the French desert, the Germans on both sides make a practise of it and continually get shot for it.

Ensign Edmund Wheatley, a British officer in the 5th Line Battalion KGL, was able to describe his perceived differences, from personal experience.

29 October 1813
The Germans bear excessive fatigues wonderfully well and a German will march over six leagues while an Englishman pants and perspires beneath the labour of twelve miles; but before the enemy a German moves on silent but mechanically, whilst an Englishman is all sarcasm, laughter and indifference.

Captain George Miller of the 95th Rifles also thought very highly of the German cavalry but was very disparaging of the British cavalry.

Camp La Bagmilla 7 November 1813
I cannot tell you in what utter contempt the cavalry of this army (Germans excepted) are held by the infantry at present. They are said to be the most arrant cowards imaginable and have actually run away upon many occasions. They have no chance at all with the French dragoons on equal terms. To say so in England, I suppose, [w]ould be reckoned little less than sedition. It is really lamentable that they have not some officers at their head who know how to manage them.

Lieutenant Colonel Henry Murray of the 18th Hussars made a significant comment on the German cavalry when a KGL regiment replaced the 10th Hussars in his brigade:

Plasencia 6 July 1813
Perhaps we shall learn more by being with the Germans & that regiment in particular for they are first rate & always keep their horses in the highest condition when others are starving. They are also perfect masters of outpost duty & much may be learnt from them if the 18th could believe they did not know everything better than anybody else when in fact they are more deficient than anybody.

It would appear to very clear that the Portuguese infantry and artillery had become so good that the British regarded them as fully their equals. What is also clear is that the Spanish troops had also improved markedly, although they still had some way to go. The rank-and-file Portuguese and Spanish soldiers had clearly earned the respect of the British troops. The difference was in the poor quality of the officer class. In Portugal this had been improved with the help of seconding British officers, whereas the Spanish army was not so far advanced in their improvement because of their refusal to allow British officers in. Whether this is a biased view by British soldiers or entirely accurate is however far beyond the scope of the present work.

Chapter 7

Thoughts on Portugal, Spain and France

As the troops marched further into Portugal and then Spain, they took time to describe the various landscapes they passed through and the people they met. Their letters are often full of comments on the different cultures and their character, the crops and farming techniques, their religion and the sport. Indeed, they wrote on every conceivable aspect of these – in their view – alien lands.

Cornet George Woodberry of the 18th Hussars was initially captivated by Portugal, although there were new dangers to avoid, but he soon began to roundly criticise the Portuguese character and particularly their lack of cleanliness.

Luz, Saturday 27 February [1813]
I begin to like this country more and more daily, for I think it a paradise to England with regard to the climate. Lizards and snakes are here in abundance about this village, [you] cannot walk out without meeting them on every path, particularly if near an old wall and ruins, in which they live. At this time, every tree except orange are in blossom, the hedges and gardens look quite enchanting; perhaps in England all my friends are enjoying themselves round a roaring fire, while I am here sitting in the shade writing this, sweltering to death with the heat of the sun. The climate agrees very well with me at present, though so very hot.

Luz, Tuesday 30 March
What monkeys the Portuguese make [of] their children, fancy a boy of eight years old dressed as follows: – round hat, frilled shirt, and neck cloth, a long shirted coat and waistcoat, pantaloons and hessian boots, generally with a walking stick. The women wear a kind of boot made very like our hussar boots, these are usually worn by those who have thick legs.

Barquinha, Tuesday 27 April
It is with infinite regret I am compelled to write matters in this my idle companion, against the Portuguese so often. But last night two of our men were robbed and cruelly treated on their way to Atalaia, by a party of Portuguese militia men, whom a generous nation has transported to your shores to combat with an enemy ready and resolved to overwhelm.

Lieutenant William Cowper Coles of the 4th Dragoons was not very sanguine as to the outcome of the war, but he actually believed that a period of French control might actually civilize and improve the country.

> Setubal 28 February 1810
> . . . A change in this part of the world will be of the greatest benefit. Even now the greatest superstition prevails, the country being absolutely crowded with convents, that are inhabited by the miserable victims of priestcraft and religious fanaticism. They will soon feel the effects of a civilised government and the face of the country will be much improved by alterations in the system of agriculture. The presence of the French will in some respects prove of the greatest advantage and the greater part of the population will rejoice at the effects of a revolution of government.

Captain John Tylden of the 43rd Foot also believed that the French would conquer Portugal despite their best efforts.

> Pinhel 14 January 1810
> The people certainly do detest the French, which is something. It really makes me pity them when I think that probably in spite of all their endeavours, a French force will overwhelm them, as it threatens to do and shortly will do Spain . . .

In fact, Captain George Widdrington of the 34th Foot was not at all sure that the Portuguese were worth saving.

> Allegrette 26 April 1810
> My dearest father,
> . . . These are the people for which England drains her treasury, and votes her millions for their use, and sacrifices her brave sons to an early grave, for a race unworthy to be free; and too pusillanimous to feel grateful for our exertions in their favour. The only advantage that can occur to England from Portugal not being in possession of the French, is *trade*.

Major General Sir Charles Colville commented on the empty villages as they retired towards the Lines of Torres Vedras, the inhabitants being forced to leave their homes in a 'scorched earth policy', leaving nothing for the French.

20 October 1810

I cannot pass unnoticed the pitiable state of these poor people. Being recommended by us to quit their habitations, they have mostly complied and Lisbon and the roads leading to it are filled with them. Those on the latter are carrying what they can with them, but that of course is very little and as everything left behind becomes a prey to either friend or foe, it is impossible to look forward to their future condition without apprehension and regret; but they themselves seem to bear their present state with wonderful fortitude and great show of attachment to the general cause and antipathy of the French. I asked in Lisbon what had been done for their assistance and was told that for the poorer classes eating houses had been established, perhaps as efficient a charity as could have been thought of.

Lieutenant Charles Madden of the 4th Dragoons pitied the Portuguese civilians during the retreat.

1 October 1810

The roads were lined on all sides with wretched people flying from Coimbra, who were unwilling to leave their homes and properties till the last minute. Numbers seeing us come on so fast threw down on the middle of the road what valuables they had reserved for future wants and ran across the country hiding themselves in woods for fear of the enemy, not having with them what nourishment would support them for one day. You might see some of what were once the most wealthy people in Portugal with their families, each labouring under a load of bread, corn, or something to supply present wants. Some who made a better provision for future wants, put theirs on carts, many of which either broke down or upset, and were left with their contents on the road. To add to their misfortunes the weather was immensely hot. Such destruction, misery and deplorable wretchedness!

Captain Edward Cocks of the 16th Light Dragoons detected that the Portuguese were deeply unhappy with the British who they believed were abandoning them and he recorded some unfortunate incidents with his foraging parties.

1 August 1810

For some time I have observed increasing symptoms of neglect and dislike in the Portuguese peasantry towards us; they think we are retreating and deserting them and conceive this a proper moment to show all the rancour which has long been brooding in their breasts. I do not blame them for disliking us, the contempt with which Englishmen treat them is a sufficient excuse for it, but I despise them for the manner with which they have hitherto fawned on us and not dared to show their dislike thill they think they are getting rid of us. Today, two of my patrols were attacked in two separate villages, a man of each is badly wounded.

This was not an isolated case, as shown by First Lieutenant Hugh Mallett of the Royal Horse Artillery who had similar problems.

Lisbon 12 August 1810
... I must confess as we are not to be employed, I care not how soon I leave the country. I dislike the people, they are a nasty race, very treacherous & cowardly, three of our men were stabbed at Coimbra in the short time that I was there. In a word the more I see of this country, the more superior appears our own in every point of view; An Englishman should go abroad to learn to value his own country, and he ought to be thankful he was not born amongst such a people as this.

That winter was a harsh one for these refugees fleeing from the fighting and Charles Colville recorded that their pathetic state had compelled many regiments into performing acts of humanity.

Alcoentre 15 February 1811
A good many of the British brigades have established kitchens and other modes for feeding such of the Portuguese poor as for want of other refuge have preferred remaining among the hedges or other cover in our cantonments. The fund of my own brigade proceeds from the heads, feet and insides of our fresh beef, with the exception of tongues and heart. Purchases of Indian wheat, corn and rice by subscription among the officers already gives ample relief to 120 people of all ages and would do more had we better convenience for cooking.

With the coming spring and the retreat of the French army, he now perceived an improvement in the situation of these poor Portuguese, but from the comments of others, he may have been guilty of painting too rosy a picture.

April 1811
The variety from the Portuguese hovels to which we had been lately used, their customary filth rendered much worse by the recent

wretchedness of the proprietors, the change to good weather, a pretty enough country and the cheerful, civil manners of the poor people upon whom we were quartered; all this made me quite pleased with the change . . .

Captain John Ewart of the 52nd Foot witnessed the Portuguese peasantry callously dragging French corpses out of a river to search them for valuables. He does not condone it, but he clearly could not criticise them in their desperation.

20 March 1811
. . . above 100 of the French were drowned in attempting to ford the river, and their corpses now lying in a dreadfully swelled and naked state, presented a most distressing sight. The Portuguese peasants were pulling them out in hopes of getting money, watches etc and looking for the eagle of the 39th French Regiment, which was afterwards found here and sent to England.

22 March
Marched to Pinhancos, . . . found the whole country through which we marched in a most distressing state. Several, both male and female corpses in every village and only a few miserable people to be seen, apparently in a state of starvation and terror beyond imagination.

His fellow officer, Lieutenant George Barlow of the 52nd Foot, wrote a great deal on his impressions of Portugal.

Coimbra, 16 October 1811
Perhaps it may be needless to inform you that a Portuguese is a character upon which civility & kindness produces no other effect, than a return of insolence & ill usage. You must cure them into good behaviour, this is well known to John Bull after a short trial of residence. He has at first plenty of money and very little head and deports himself with the usual good breeding & generosity of his country. He is soon compelled to adopt a contrary system.

However, he soon became aware of the dangers of Portuguese daggers.

On the Saturday night, a soldier of the 95th was stabbed by one of the natives; He was walking in company with a brother officer and proceeding to the spot on the first alarm found a man much in liquor on the hill. Upon asking who had wounded him, he replied that he had been struck with a *stick*. I concluded that he had conducted himself improperly & had received a good drubbing for his pains & ordered him to the barracks, whither he marched off as quick as could be expected from a drunken man. It turned out however, the next morning that he had received two severe wounds in the belly but being so drunk at the time did not feel what might otherwise have been expected. All search after the miscreant was in vain and without any redress we marched off for Montemor-o-Velho on the following Monday.

He then described the countryside and farming practices, recognizing fertile soil and excellent growing conditions, saving his criticisms for the atrocious roads.

... woods of olives and hedges full of aloes larger than any to be seen in England and which grow wild in their country, are everywhere to be beheld; as also fields of Indian corn, which thrives here with scarce any labour or cultivation. The ploughs are wooden; the furrows only a few inches deep and the harvest is sure to equal any which the most laborious & careful farmer amongst you would produce. The roads however are most execrable up to our knees in sand, so as hardly to be passable for carts or vehicles of any description. They almost exceed belief and can only be ascribed to the wretched policy of the country which keeps only two or three intended for the travelling of couriers, to repair & regulate the remainder.

His attitude mellowed somewhat when he witnessed the complete destruction of the towns and villages where the French had been.

Celorico, 26 October 1811
... here I found the tales of my brother officers at Lisbon, as well as the accounts of the newspapers verified to a degree of accuracy which I could have scarcely believed. A fine town, the noble palace of the bishop and other fine buildings totally consumed. All was a dreary silence & desolation; that [not] a house, except a few base walls left standing. The scene was equally new to me never having been before in a burnt city; the change equally sudden on a two hours transportation from the bustle & noise of Coimbra. Men, women & children merely because they were Portuguese were butchered without exception to an extent & degree scarcely credible, was not the testimony the most respectable. A few poor solitary inhabitants had just commenced to return & remove away the ashes of their ruined dwellings. Leaving this sad picture of misery, I bent my course across the mountains...

His solitary journey over the barren wastes eventually exhausted him and there he readily admitted he experienced great Portuguese kindness, from those who certainly could not spare much.

> I bent my course across the mountains; the roads stony & execrable. The ascent continued for some miles; the sun most intense, not a single tree and what was worse, pathways, for they could not be called roads, branching off in every direction. I took that which appeared the most frequented, after having gone upon this for a considerable length of time, I accosted two muleteers who informed me that I had strayed considerably from the proper route; they conducted me to the proper road & then went [on] their way. I continued my course to Miranda do Corvo; about five o'clock I reached a small village called St Jago, four miles on this side of it. Having come twenty-one miles and tasted nothing except a small roll & cup of coffee at Coimbra the whole day (for by the proper road the march was but twelve [miles]), I sat down near the market house literally faint, for want of sustenance. The villagers came flocking about, and one good young girl brought me some cold fish, bread & water, for which she refused to take any money, although the expense to people in her poor state must have been very considerable. I shall always remember with gratitude the poor hovel of St Jago and must here remark, that in the whole of my progress unattended & alone as I then was during a march of fifty miles, I ever experienced from the *peasantry*, the greatest kindness & hospitality, nay respect, inasmuch as everyone took off his hat that passed, to my British uniform. This however is solely confined to the country people.

His eyes were now fully open to the dreadful desolation inflicted by the French.

> In a space of one hundred miles thickly studded with numerous villages, I hardly beheld twice as many inhabitants [as I saw at St Jago] in who chiefly drag a miserable existence on roots & herbs. In one hovel I found a numerous family supping on roasted acorns & water with a little goat's milk. Thus, have the French themselves erected the most insufferable barrier to the subjugation of the kingdom. All the owners of these ruined habitations are become guerrillas, whose hatred & activity is equally great. Not a solitary bullock or house have I seen along the great tract of country but what belongs to the commissariat and would of course be removed on the approach of the enemy. The country is indeed swept to a degree of nakedness & poverty, such as has never had a precedent.

Ensign John Mills of the Coldstream Guards also wrote of the devastation.

> Puebla 21 April 1811
> You can form no idea of what a ruined country this is; the houses in the towns and villages are most of them unroofed and not a vestige of anything that can be called furniture in them. They have burned all the houses that will burn and the others that have no wood in them the French have entirely gutted. When we were upon our journey the inhabitants of the different towns were beginning to return to them from the mountains. They appeared nearly famished, such a scene of distress you cannot imagine.

Lieutenant Colonel John Keane of the 60th Foot rode through the same country two years later and saw little improvement. Indeed, he perceived a war weariness and even perhaps a desire for the return of the French.

> 28 September 1813 Salamanca
> ... Thus far I am safe and sound on my way to the army, such a journey is no trifle, and the difficulties encountered are seldom calculated on. The whole country is laid waste wherever the French have been, they have left evident marks of their brutality, not a town or village from Lisbon to the banks of the Tormes has escaped their vengeance. The inhabitants are ruined and disgusted.it strikes me very forcibly that our welcome, as their deliverers is nearly at an end and that the majority of them would prefer to have the French back again, than be obliged to make an exertion for their independence ...

Ensign John Blackman of the Coldstream Guards spoke of the destruction by the French, but he showed little empathy for the poor Portuguese, viewing the delightful country as too good for them.

> Saturday 28 March 1812, Abrantes.
> All the places we have passed through have a very miserable appearance, the French having ransacked and destroyed everything: they have never entered Abrantes, it being very strongly fortified and very advantageously situated; indeed, I think it would do this place good if the French would pay them a visit, for the people are extremely dirty and indolent, and so insensible to any kind of comfort whatsoever, that I cannot help expressing a wish that this happy climate and beautiful country was peopled by another race of being, having a better idea of cleanliness, activity and other various things which conduce to

the comfort and welfare of the people at large and without which we are nearer allied to the brute inanition which is at present my opinion of the Portuguese.

Others were pleasantly surprised how quickly some parts of Portugal recovered. Lieutenant Colonel George Bingham of the 53rd Foot recorded at Leiria on 1 January 1810 that:

> The town is much altered since we were here last year . . . Now the market-place is crowded with people; every article of life is to be sold, exceedingly cheap, and everything looks like peace and happiness . . .

Other issues constantly occurred, First Lieutenant William Swabey of the Royal Artillery, was particularly upset by a refusal to allow the body of one of his drivers to be buried in consecrated ground as he was not a Catholic:

> 14 October 1811
> . . . read the funeral service over a Driver William Weeks who died of dysentery after a lingering illness. We are obliged to bury in the fields, for the Roman Catholics do not permit heretics to mingle their dust with their own more sacred remains.

Meanwhile Ensign the Honourable Orlando Bridgeman of the 1st Foot Guards commented on the Portuguese addiction to gambling.

> Oporto Monday 7 June 1813
> Such is the love the Portuguese have for gaming, that you might as well give a ball in England without music, as a ball here, without a gambling room.

A number of years later, George Bingham was still perplexed however, by Portuguese politeness on leaving:

> Ranhados 22 February 1813
> . . . they are tiresomely polite and to please a Portuguese, you should have studied the fourteen books of Chinese ceremony, there are so many bows to be made at the top of the steps and again at the bottom of the steps that there is no end to it.

The unfortunate campaign of 1808, which culminated in the dreadful retreat to Corunna, gave many their first glimpse of Spain. This mountainous and extremely beautiful region of Spain did give a very positive first impression of the country and Henry Packe of the 1st Foot Guards seems to have been enamoured with the people.

> Corunna 21 October 1808
> I am much pleased with the bolero and fandango dances with castanets which is extremely graceful and pretty. The country is very beautiful, the verdure very fine and in general the land well cultivated, the meat is very good and fat, particularly the beef, and the markets exceedingly well provided with every sort of vegetables and fruit.

> Santiago, 1 November 1808
> The Spaniards certainly look upon us with a jealous eye, they wish to finish themselves, what they have so gloriously begun, I must at this same time say they pay us every attention, I admire them extremely, I believe the lowest class of the people to be scrupulously honest, I have been a witness to one or two instances of honesty, that would rather stagger some of our own countrymen.

Operating along the Portuguese border for much of 1809 until 1812, there were ample opportunities for comparisons between the Portuguese and the Spanish. They were surprised to find that the countries were quite markedly different. Lieutenant Colonel George Bingham of the 53rd Foot wrote of the bitter hatred evinced by both the Portuguese and the Spanish towards each other:

> Estremoz, 21 December 1809
> . . . allowances must always be made in Portugal for the hatred that exists between the natives of the two countries.

Cornet Charles Madden of the 4th Dragoons spoke at length of the noticeable and immediate changes.

> 11 September 1809
> Marched to Badajoz, a frontier town of Spain, two leagues and a half from Elvas. In going into the town you cross the Guadiana, over a large well-built bridge, consisting of 25 arches. Badajoz is the headquarters of the British Army in Spain. The transition from Portugal into Spain can be perceived immediately by the difference in the appearance of the people, and the cleanliness of the streets and houses. The Portuguese language is very little understood even in Badajoz, and not in the least blended with the Spanish, as each nation has had for centuries a noted antipathy for each other, being in constant war, and though now fighting

in the same cause are jealous of each other. Though the Spaniards are more unfriendly to the English than the Portuguese, and show it in their manner and conduct, yet I think they are a much finer race of people. The dress of the men of the upper class is grander to an extreme, being embroidered from head to foot, and the colours of their cloaths [sic] partake of all the shades in the rainbow. They are particularly civil and courteous to each other. The women dress mostly in dark silk and satins (I mean the higher class) with a great deal of silk lace; being constantly braced up from their infancy they have generally very fine figures. They have generally a shawl or lace over their heads. They have much advantage of the Portuguese women. The ruling characteristic of the Spaniards seems to be great pride, with an inferior opinion of all other nations, but particularly so of their neighbours the Portuguese. The market in Badajoz is well supplied with vegetables, fruits, and game.

Following the terrible retreat following the Battle of Talavera, Captain Henry Mellish of the 87th Foot wrote from Merida on 27 August 1809. He was clearly angry with the Spanish people and saw no hope of success. His comments regarding the French treatment of the Spanish may well be surprising.

... as the people themselves are not in a state to make any resistance, our remaining is only putting off the evil day & subjecting them to pillage & every horror for the resistance they make. The French pay very regularly for everything & keep excellent discipline, wherever the people remain in their towns, but where they resist & conceal everything in the mountains (viz this means rendering the subsistence of the armies difficult) their houses & everything are given up to indiscriminate plunder.

He continued at Badajoz on 9 October 1809:

It may be very fine to talk about deserting our allies & leaving these poor people to their fate, but believe me their fate is of their own chusing [sic] & whatever they may suffer they most richly deserve it.

Lieutenant Bragge of the 3rd Dragoons was struck by the sudden change between countries.

Borba 14 March 1812
The country was entirely new to us and indeed so different from what we had hitherto seen of Portugal that I could scarcely believe

so great a contrast could possibly exist in the same kingdom. The country itself is quite open, tolerably level, and the greater part of it in the highest state of cultivation. The roads equal to any in the New Forest and the towns and villages more delightfully clean and neat than anything we see in England, every house and cottage nicely whitewashed within and without, all the churches and public buildings standing detached, the streets very wide and not a bit of filth to be seen, whilst the pots and pans lightly polished and arranged in order over a good fireplace, render every cottage in the Alentejo a more desirable residence than the most sumptuous houses north of the Tagus.

George Barlow of the 52nd Foot also noted a marked difference as they crossed the border.

Celorico, 26 October 1811

I passed the Spanish frontier at the village of Albergaria [La Albergueria de Arganan]. It was like magic, the country instantly changes from mountains to a fine level, flat plain full of trees, putting me in mind of old England. I was amongst a new people, new languages & everything changed for the better; the natives a fine, tall, stout limbed race of people; carrying themselves particularly upright and in their garb & look, wearing all that Castilian demeanour & pride for which the Spaniards are so celebrated. The villages are clean & the cottages resembling the neatness of those in England. It is impossible to find so great a contrast, as forcibly strikes the mind on passing the very frontier. The Spanish mantle & hat turned up in front of the natives pleased me much; the antipathy existing between the two peoples is most inveterate.

Eighteen months later he crossed the border again (this time for the last time) and was once again struck by the differences, but he noted that the Spanish people were now a little more cautious.

3 June 1813, Camp near Morales [de Toro] two leagues beyond Toro

Having just emerged from the filthy towns of Portugal, Salamanca has the appearance of a most clean & well-built city. The people greeted us with vivas and their joy was no doubt sincere enough, but prudence restrained a too great expression of it, as the French promised to return in the course of two or three weeks and would pillage them again after the manner of last year, on our retreating from thence, for their former patriotic conduct.

Captain John Ewart of the 52nd Foot wrote of the beauty and bountiful nature of the country they passed through. His breakfast was traditional in both Portugal and Spain, but he calls it a Portuguese breakfast from habit.

> 28 December 1811
> After a Portuguese breakfast (mainly meat) . . . We reached about 2 pm Cadalso (two short leagues from Robledillo), a very good, clean town, with many inhabitants. Here we drew billets, left the servant to get ready some dinner for us and proceeded by a mule track along some very bad road and by the side of the mountains to Torre de Don Miguel (half a league), a very good village very like Robledillo, in the midst of olive groves, with its inhabitants looking cheerful and healthy; we reached Cadalso just at dark, after having had an uncommon pleasant ride, particularly made so by the mildness of the weather. In the gardens of this town there were several orange and lemon trees loaded with fruit; upon my begging my landlord to sell me some of the latter he *gave* me as many as I wanted and was altogether very civil . . . All the inhabitants seemed well inclined to the British and received us with *Vivez los Anglesos.*

Lieutenant Bragge was also enamoured by the welcome given by the Spanish people as they advanced.

> Camp near Subijana[-Morillas], four leagues from Vitoria, 20 June 1813
> . . . the fine city of Palencia, which we entered about eleven o'clock on a beautiful summer's morning, four hours only after the departure of the French & the public joy was manifested here according to the usual custom, by hanging out variegated pieces of drapery upon every window and their patriotism was sincere enough, could explicit reliance be placed on the bawling spirits *which the multitude* gave, or the bouquets which were dropped so fragrant from the balconies by the enthusiastic fair to the British soldiery.

Orlando Bridgeman of the 1st Foot Guards was not so fond of the people, however.

> 12 June 1812
> The men are perfect brutes, they stink of garlic & smoking & they hate the English more than their bitterest enemies, there are some fine regiments in the service, but few of them have any clothes, & they all want officers, but I really think if well clothed & with good officers they might be made a good deal of. The Portuguese are very superior

people, they are grateful to us for all we do for them which the Spaniards are not, & their soldiers are much better, & in finer order.

Certainly, the entire country of Spain was far from being universally superior to Portugal. James Gairdner of the 95th recording more negative thoughts in 1813.

10 June
The inhabitants of this part of Spain are uglier, dirtier and worse dressed than on the frontiers or indeed any part of the country I have been in. They are [sic] exactly resemble the Portuguese, both in dress & appearance. The villages are also of the worst description I have seen in Spain.

Lieutenant Colonel George Bingham agreed that Leon was not as nice as further south.

Camp near Villasandino 12 June 1813
The villages throughout Leon are poor, the houses dirty and wretchedly constructed . . . they . . . scarcely cultivate vegetables, so that with a soil and climate the most productive in the world, they are the most wretched. Here the peasants are dirty and ugly in their persons and features; in the south they are clean and handsome . . .

William Swabey of the Royal Horse Artillery was not easily pleased, but even he recorded that:

17 March 1812
The difference in courtesy and cleanliness between the Portuguese and Spaniards is striking.

Wanting to experience all that Spain had to offer, Captain John Ewart of the 52nd Foot even tried a bull fight, but like most of his colleagues, he was horrified by the barbarity of it.

31 August 1812
. . . Went to Madrid to see a bull fight at the Prada de Toro, a large building open in the centre like a circus, very neatly fitted up and capable of accommodating 11,000 spectators. Most of the boxes were filled with British officers who got tickets of admission from the Junta (Earl Wellington was in a large one in the centre with his Staff). There was a guard of about 100 men well appointed, and everything was carried

on in the old style. Eight bulls were fought during the evening from five to eight o'clock and certainly it was most barbarous sport. The bulls were turned into the square one at a time; they were tormented some time by about ten men on foot with large silk cloaks, which they threw in the face of the bull when attacked by them, in doing which and vaulting over the paling when pursued, they showed much agility. There were two fighters on horseback with long spears, who indeed displayed much courage in spearing the bulls and defending themselves against their attacks, but this was carried to a great extent of cruelty, as the poor horses got terribly gored. Two of them were remounted and kept in the square some time after their entrails were literally hanging out. The men on foot next tormented the bulls by sticking short spears into their necks and sides; this they did very actively while the bulls were in the act of charging them. Upon some of these short spears, crackers and squibs were fastened and lighted so as to go off as soon as the spears entered their bodies. This added much to the furiosity of the bulls, two of whom made extraordinary leaps over the paling, near six feet high, and created much confusion among the spectators, but no one was badly hurt. Lastly the matador came forward with a sword and small cloak. With the latter he defended himself with great dexterity and with the former waiting an opportunity of taking a good aim at the spine when the bulls were running at him, he killed them. Once the first blow he made was sufficient, but some bulls he struck often. The bulls after they had fallen were dragged off by three mules gaily harnessed with ribbons &c and bands of music playing. Two horsemen attacked the first four bulls, and two others the last four, but the same men on foot attacked all the eight and the same matador killed the whole; also one bull was baited by three dogs, who got him down in about ten minutes, when the men with spears dispatched him. On the whole it was an extraordinary sight, but very barbarous. Though the Spaniards seemed much gratified by the sport, this day they called it bad, because no men were killed and only two horses!

However, Lieutenant George Woodberry of the 18th Hussars clearly admired the Spanish character.

Subijana [de Alva], Lord Wellington's headquarters 19 June 1813

I am persuaded that the Spanish never will be conquered; they very strongly resemble the English, the frame of their bodies, and even in their undaunted minds. They may be defeated a thousand times, but they will never be subdued. The English newspapers and people are wrong when they explain that they have nothing to fight for, and say give them a constitution, give them liberty. In the first place, they have their country to fight for, their soil, their homes, and against foreigners and invaders, surely this is something And as to liberty, they have as much as they want, as much as they are really capable of [enjoying]. With respect to constitution, you might as well say, give them English roast beef, they have no idea of it, they know nothing about it, and, therefore, neither knows the want of it, nor desires it. If you were to offer it to them, if you were to tell them of balanced powers, they would decline it. Their cause is their country, and if they chose to put Ferdinand at the head of it, why in the name of wonder should you object. I believe there is a great deal of nonsense in the party refinements at home; they know nothing about these people. They are brave to excess, but of course cannot stand yet veteran and disciplined armies. We will at length remedy this defect. The Spanish armies want organisation.

Colonel Andrew Barnard of the 95th Rifles wrote of French excesses and was impressed by the indomitable Spanish spirit.

La Encina 26 May 1812
  The French army are a good deal dispirited by our late success and show their spite by being more oppressive than ever to the poor Spaniards whose dislike of them appears to increase, but the country is so exhausted that the resistance of the latter cannot keep pace with their dislike of the yoke. . . . They are fine fellows but have been miserably conducted.

Lieutenant Charles Crowe of the 27th Foot tried the theatre, but found it very different to England in so many ways, although he did ultimately enjoy the performance:

20 September 1813
  I am disposed to write as slightingly of the theatre itself: for in the first place it is very indifferently or, insufficiently lighted, and an Englishman must ever feel disgusted by the prompter's box, in the middle of the front of the stage; from whence he rehearses and leads the whole part of every character in so audible a manner, that the audience must hear him and at the same time makes no point of secreting himself from observation; although his awning is full three feet broad and two feet above the stage: but with the head, as well as arms and even book, extended, beckons forward the next character. The performers do not consider it requisite to be perfect in even their own part; for the prompter tells them every word: consequently, their eyes

and attention are fixed on him; and never directed to the audience and having repeated their part, remain motionless and inattentive to the reply, until beckoned, or called, by the prompter, to rehearse a rejoinder. Thus there is no acting, or treading the boards; which gives animation to every character; and is requisite in all. The leading characters are assigned of course to the best performers; who are generally perfect and fully sustain their parts; but are obliged to act behind a semicircle of subordinates in front of the prompter's box. I have seen the real heroine standing behind in the utmost unconcern and indifference, while her rich rival endeavoured to inveigle the affections of her plighted lover!!

There are but few ladies to be seen in the theatre; the house being so badly lighted, there is no opportunity of displaying charms, or dress. A box or balco for as many of a party as might come, can be exclusively engaged for about three shillings and such select parties were often to be seen. Watching them to catch the characteristics of the natives, I was much amused frequently, at seeing an elegant young woman light a paper cigar i.e. tobacco scattered on paper, and rolled up, the size and length of a large quill, and after 3 or 4 puffs, presenting it to her brother or favoured swain. In the front of the pit, behind the orchestra are three rows of seats armed off and numbered; called lunettas, admittance to which is two shillings. They are engaged by those who go purposely to enjoy the play. There are two rows of benches immediately under the balcos: the admittance to which is about nine pence; corresponding with our two shilling gallery; and are occupied only by men; in the other part of the pit all stand; a similar accommodation for women being in front of the upper balcos. On a fair calculation I should imagine that the utmost of a full house would be thirty pounds.

After the above comments, it will only be justice to mention that I saw, with surprise and delight the performance of the *Tragedy of the Wife with Two Husbands*! The characters were well cast and as well supported! The plot good; and the moral plain. It was a performance altogether worthy the attention of an enlightened audience.

He also had to admit to their general sobriety.

Olite, Tuesday 17 August.
The whole time I have been in Spain, I never yet saw [a] Spaniard in liqueur; they are fonder of water than wine. The Portuguese are as fond of wine as the English. I am very partial to their country's wine, and I seldom get up from dinner, without three pints in me.

A few days later he made a number of comments regarding social etiquette and living in Spain.

> Olite, Saturday 21 August.
> The mode of living in Spain is certainly not congenial to that in England, the first order taken in the morning, either in bed, or soon after they rise, chocolate with cakes, or toasted bread, having first drunk some cold water, which is always brought with the chocolate. They dine from 12 until 2 o'clock, seldom later, the tables are about eight feet long and six feet wide, covered with one large table cloth, and a plateau is generally placed in the centre with figures in wax and bottles of wine corked, placed round the brim of it. Bread covered by a napkin, denotes the place of each of the party, the dinners consist of soups and a variety of dishes which encircle the plateau. Each person sitting opposite to a dish, whether of meat, fish, or vegetables, fills his own plate, carves the content, and hands it round, so that during the whole time of dinner, if a large party, they are continually passing and re-passing plates, with something of every sort which passes, the Spaniards always fill their plates, they are moreover very great eaters, some of the dishes are palatable to an Englishman, but their meats are covered with oil and garlic. Their soups are good, the meat is generally boiled in large unshaped chunks, or in pieces and mixed with potatoes, mashed with oil. The Spaniards rarely eat salt or pepper; they seldom use a knife, except in cutting up the contents of the dish next to them, and occasionally stabbing each other. A piece of bread and a fork answer their purpose, as to what is on their own plates. The pastry is particularly good, the fish is a side dish, generally after the soup are two dishes, one of boiled meat, and boiled fowls together, and the other a sort of stew with sausages, of which garlic is a material ingredient.
> Strangers drink and eat as they please, no health drank, and there is not that reserve or respect observed by the servants, who attend the table as in England. They laugh at a joke, set you right where they think you are wrong; both men and women maid servants, are dirty, slovenly and awkward.

Lieutenant James Crummer of the 28th Foot described the callous barbarism shown by the Spanish peasantry towards the French sick and wounded.

> Camp near La Oivada 28 May 1813
> . . . the Spanish peasantry were not wanting in their exertions against this unfortunate devoted corps, as they murdered many of the

wounded & to add the more to their misfortunes they [the French] did not fail in their wanted custom of drinking to an excess when under the apprehension of being engaged, they had each man taken previous to quitting Salamanca two bottles of wine & upwards, which so intoxicated them that many threw themselves into ditches & corn fields to sleep, in a state of insensibility and consequently all that were found by the Spaniards were put to immediate death & their loss altogether is said to amount to 400. Colonel Abercromby relates his having saved a man twice (who was in liquor) from a Spaniard who attempted to throw him into the river, but in the third attempt the exasperated patriot succeeded in drowning him.

Captain Ewart of the 52nd Foot also spoke of the deep Spanish hatred of the French and described how their thirst for vengeance led them to commit atrocities.

28 July 1812
The body of the French General Ferey who had been killed on the 22nd and been buried here, we found near the roadside, his grave having been disturbed.

Lieutenant George Barlow, also of the 52nd Foot, described to his friend Andrew Amos Esq in an undated letter written some time in August 1813, the depredations made by the Spanish guerrilla bands, which were not always perpetrated against the French alone.

. . . the Spanish troops whose licentiousness, more particularly Longa's guerrillas are truly flagrant. These last mentioned chiefs of banditry (for such they are both in appearance & behaviour) amount to several thousands, and no doubt have proved very formidable by the French armies, possessing no commissariat their means of subsistence are truly precarious & they are pretty active in levying contributions and plundering their own countrymen to make up for their deficiency, whom in their indignation I have heard to say that the guerrillas were worse than the French. These roaming bands rob & pillage the whole face of the country, British officers even are not secure from their attacks, one of whom the other day going to St Sebastian, was surprised by a volley from some bushes on looking around saw his servant sprawling in the dust, while a party of these gentry rushing forth seized the baggage & forced him to run with all possible speed.

This is confirmed by his regimental comrade Lieutenant Henry Dawson, writing from Los Agallas on 18 December 1811:

> I was sent last week to Guadepero with a party of dragoons and the inhabitants complained bitterly that Don Carlos d'Espana pressed everything for his troops & that they were actually starving. I offered money for bread, wine or spirits for the dragoons who were with me, but could not succeed and we travelled the whole day without anything to eat. Yet the men do not grumble.

Now lying close to the French border, they noticed major changes once again. The Welshman Major Edwin Griffiths of the 15th Hussars mentioned the language difference, suddenly discovering that the Spanish he had spent so much time learning was completely useless.

> Ascoz, 5 November 1813
> It was at this village [Buenza] that I first found the little Spanish I had learned of no use to me; the native of these mountains talk Basqueyada [Basque] only; a language as different to the Spanish, as Welsh is to English.

He also commented on the very steep conditions they found in the Pyrenees.

> The miserable villages are stuck on the sides of the hills & the communications between them are roads that when you travel you are continually either in a bog, or on a staircase!

On 31 December 1813, looking back over the year, he made a final note on his time in Spain and Portugal with mixed emotions, his sentiments were almost certainly shared by almost everyone in the army.

> It had been a year of great variety. Joy, sorrow, pleasure, ennui, comfort, misery, I had by turns experienced. Memory will often revert to & dwell perhaps with pleasure upon many of the hours I spent in Spain & Portugal, but I don't think I shall feel regret that they are past or wish to experience them again.

Finally entering into enemy country, Assistant Surgeon Thomas Maynard of the Coldstream Guards wrote eagerly:

> 11 November 1813, Banks of the Bidassoa.
> We are invading the country like perfect gentlemen, we touch nothing, take nothing, do no mischief. Guards for the protection of

property are mounted everywhere and members of the Provost Staff enter St Jean de Luz with fresh troops to protect the inhabitants from insult or depredation. What must the French think of this? Is not Lord Wellington a hero?

Lieutenant James Gairdner of the 95th Rifles wrote his thoughts on France.

> 17 January 1814
> Marched at about 9 o'clock to Labastide on the Joyeuse near which we encamped . . . Labastide is a nice village, the people all completely French which language they all talk, even to each other. The peasants about here also all talk French, their mother tongue is the Gascon an infinitely more comprehensible lingo than the Basque, it has a good deal of French in it. The inhabitants of this country are not only civil but remarkably good natured and affable, they are very clean and the younger part of them both male & female very handsome. They live apparently to a great age. The inhabitants are very civil indeed and seem very glad that the English are advancing. How ridiculous now appear to us those doubts and fears we had held out to us of the peasantry rising in arms and the impolicy of entering France. We never have been better treated in Spain or Portugal & the further we advance we find them more glad to see us. The weather is very cold, three of our companies are in houses, I am not one of the lucky ones.

Colonel Andrew Barnard, also of the 95th Rifles, wrote that the initial French fear had subsided and that they now preferred the British to their own forces. Masses of young Frenchmen were also swarming into the British lines to avoid the conscription.

> Mont Marsin 2 March 1814
> The Beaunois and Gascons however showed a little fight at our first appearance but on return of confidence almost immediate, they then overwhelm us with kindness and swear their emperor is a scamp and their army is more abused by them than it was by the Spaniards, all this may be to flatter us but it is evident that they do not consider our entering France as an insult to the country and look forward to the restoration of commerce from it, all the conscripts fly to the rear of the British army as we advance and you never saw such joy as is painted in all their countenances at their escape.

Edwin Griffiths of the 15th Hussars also spoke well of the French reaction to their invasion.

> Urcuray 21 January 1814
> The people are if anything too civil; they quite overwhelm one with kindness; the lower order speak in general the Pyrenean lingo & you seldom meet a person who speaks good French . . .

On their continued march into France he found similar sentiments.

> Nogaro 10 March
> The natives continue very civil & on our entering a new place frequently greet us with 'Vive le Roi George'.

> Gargas near Toulouse 25 April 1814
> This part of France very much resembles England and notwithstanding all Bonaparte's taxes & conscriptions, it is extremely populous & well cultivated and there is more general comfort & less appearance of poverty than any country I have ever been to yet.

Lieutenant James Gairdner 95th of the Rifles found that food was plentiful and cheap in the markets, but did also record some resistance by the local French peasantry.

> 8 February 1814
> To Orthez four leagues . . . an excellent [town] larger considerably than Sauveterre, the market was amazingly crowded, and very well & cheaply supplied. Fowls were selling for 3 francs a pair, turkeys 3 francs each & everything in proportion. It is full of wounded and we got bad quarters. The people are not very civil, I met here with the first instance of incivility I have met with in France.
> The peasants turned out & fired on our foraging party today, they wounded several horses, mine among the rest.

As can be seen, the poor state of Portugal, the dirt and the fleas, did not enamour the country to the British soldiers, although they could admire the beautiful scenery and they would also show great empathy towards a people who never had much, but had been heartlessly stripped of that little and seen great numbers murdered by the French. The general view of Spain was that the towns and indeed the people were infinitely cleaner and more prosperous and that they were a proud people. At times they were detested for failing to support the army with supplies, but generally the Spanish were highly regarded and indeed were seen as more like Britons themselves. It is also clear that there was a great deal of trepidation regarding invading France and the reaction of the French peasantry. They had seen the barbarity of the guerrilla war fought by the Spaniards and they had no wish to endure such a terrible war themselves in France. This generally positive reception which they received in France was therefore a very pleasant surprise and a huge relief to all.

Chapter 8

Billets and Cantonments

Throughout the Peninsular War soldiers on the march were billeted in large towns or villages where this was practicable, but in the vast expanses of both Portugal and Spain, which were far more sparsely populated, this was simply not possible. Therefore, it was normal for the officers to be allocated the few available buildings in the vicinity as their billets, no matter how run down and dilapidated they were, on a strict seniority basis. More junior officers were often turned out of their billet by the arrival of a more senior officer and often had to share a room or use the tents allocated for officers. Any remaining buildings would be taken by the NCOs, rarely leaving any room for the ordinary soldiers. The situation for the officers, no matter how poor the buildings were, was infinitely more preferable to the situation of the rank and file, who were expected to sleep beneath the stars with only a blanket or a greatcoat to keep out the chills and the rain, causing many to become sick. During the long dry, hot summer, this was undoubtedly not seen as much of a difficulty, and they were generally put into farm buildings for the harshest winter months, but the wet spring and autumn was often a huge problem for the men. However, George Bingham, commanding the 53rd Foot, makes it clear that just like the French, the British troops were soon making huts made from branches of the trees and that he found it preferable to his tent.

> Camp near Abrantes, 21 June 1809
> We have now very comfortable huts, which keep out some rain, and are certainly cooler than tents.

Major Gregory Way of the 29th Foot also wrote of a hut encampment, but complained of the insects and the noise.

> 24 June 1809
> Hut camp near Abrantes constructed with young pine trees covered with fern. No scarcity of ant[s], beetles & centipedes; braying of asses & baggage mules all day & night.

In his diary Lieutenant Henry Oglander of the 43rd Foot mentioned the fact that the troops hutted on a number of occasions.

29 July 1810

The division left Celorico at 5pm and marched about two miles to the rear, where we halted & went into huts close to the road.

21 August 1810

Returned to our quarters at sunrise and at midday the regiment marched to a position below the town, where it hutted. The rest of the brigade went into huts near us.

3 September 1810

At 7 am we left this camp and continued our retreat to the immediate vicinity of Sampayo, where we hutted for the evening.

28 October 1810

In the morning we returned to camp and began to build our hut.

Most of the time, however, officers were billeted on the local population. Cornet Charles Madden of the 4th Dragoons got a billet at a large house on arrival at Lisbon, but found himself unwelcome and unable to communicate with the owners.

26 April 1809

Got a billet in a large house in Belem; could not even procure a fire to boil water for my breakfast as all the doors were locked which led to any part of the house where the family lived, and not being able to make myself understood when I met any of the family.

Ensign Charles Paget of the 52nd Foot was not enraptured with his billet, but at least it had no infestation.

30 September 1808

I was shown into a room, which though not good, I thought a blessing, it consisted of a good table, bed on the floor, 8 chairs, two pot de chambres, 2 dish[es] & leaden mug, one window &c. My landlady seemed a tolerable good old dame, she had two pretty daughters & some little brats, the old man devilish sulky, however I went to bed after buying 2 fowls for 3 shillings & slept most soundly, luckily no fleas!

Lieutenant Hugh Mallett of the Royal Horse Artillery was turfed out of his original accommodation at Lisbon to make way for a hospital, but certainly landed on his feet with the replacement.

Lisbon 26 August 1810

    It has been my lot to obtain a very good one, which I have occupied now near a week: the people of the house are very respectable and appear to be in very good circumstances; they are extremely civil to me & try to make everything agreeable as possible. I have two rooms on the 2nd floor: the family (as is generally the case in Portugal) live on the 3rd and as they seldom quit their rooms except to go out in their carriage I have my part of the house as much to myself as if I was living in a barrack . . . the family consist[s] of the owner of the house & his wife, and their two children, a boy & a girl, the one about 8 the other six years old.

Ensign Charles Crowe of the 48th Foot found the garden of his billet at Lisbon very pleasant, writing on 25 November 1812 that:

At our billet we enjoyed the comfort of a regular retreat at the corner of the garden. The walk to it was planted on one side with orange trees, on the other with lemons each bearing half ripe fruit, and an abundance of blossoms.

    Except in the modern streets, the ground floor of the houses is used as a stable, or store for wood and lumber. The large arched doorway is open during the day, facing which is a broad staircase leading to the top of the house; each storey of which is generally occupied by a separate family, who burn frequently during the day lavender and various herbs to drown obnoxious scents. And as every family makes its own selection for such purposes, multifarious are the fumes which assail the olfactory nerves when ascending a flight of these stone steps . . .

Lieutenant William Bragge of the 3rd Dragoons found the life of the family who owned his billet of some interest.

Belem 14 September 1811

    . . . The gentleman amuses himself with a few hours sleep in the daytime, whilst his wife and daughters sit in the parlour windows and amuse themselves with searching each other's heads, a chase which seldom fails affording considerable sport . . .

However, as soon as they left Lisbon, they all had to follow the official procedures to get a billet allocated to them. Second Lieutenant Henry Hough of the Royal Artillery described his first encounter with the system.

> 21 April 1812
> I left Lisbon to join the Army. The first day I marched to Sacavem, . . . Upon my arrival at this village I waited upon *Juiz de Fora* (or chief magistrate) for a billet, according to the custom of the country: found him shoeing a mule, but he gave me a billet upon a house, some distance from the village which was occupied by some Portuguese officers. Had to return for another and after some trouble was well accommodated. Dined off rations, fat salt pork, and went to bed about 9 o'clock.

Lieutenant George Barlow of the 52nd Foot complained that local magistrates were apt to adopt airs and graces above their station.

> Coimbra, 16 October 1811
> In the distribution of billets, the judge of the town is apt to give himself great airs. One of our detachment in begging the use of a few knives & forks for his dinner was peremptorily refused, the next morning the padrone walked into the room and began to converse & behave in the most pleasing way. This so much incensed the officer, that he sent him *neck & crop* out of the apartment. In the course of the day the Portuguese [man] sent up the above articles without any request whatever on the part of his host.

The troops that landed at Corunna in north-west Spain found their billets to be a little different to what they had imagined. Captain Edwin Griffith of the 15th Hussars initially found a more preferable place to sleep than his billet.

> Corunna 13 November 1808
> . . . the extreme poverty and wretchedness is past all description;
> . . . I live on shore but sleep on board my ship in preference to a lousy, filthy, buggy, Spanish bed which I must turn into as soon as she quits the harbour . . .

A few days later, Griffith was forced to sleep ashore and found the accommodation novel to say the least.

> Corunna 17 November
> I am billeted upon a merchant . . . you never saw anything so ridiculous as the figure I cut among them, not understanding a word of Spanish; he has two or three daughters besides a wife. And we all

sleep as it were in the same room, for the recesses where the beds stand are open to it & we dress and undress in each other's presence in the utmost sangfroid . . . in the morning as soon as I am awake one of the handmaids herself with a large cup of chocolate and dry toast which I am forced to eat in bed . . . There are very few tolerably pretty women to be seen & as they have all got teeth of any colour but white, I don't think that there is much chance of my losing my heart to a Donna.

Lieutenant William Cowper Coles, an ex-infantryman now with the 4th Dragoons, believed that the cavalry got better billets generally:

Setubal 28 February 1810
   In this country the cavalry always march in detachments, the infantry in large troops, which render the quarters of subaltern officers very bad in this respect therefore our lot is superior and in many things which might be ascertained on examining the nature of the two services . . .

Billets obviously came in all shapes and sizes depending on where they were, the best and the worst obviously gaining the greatest comment. Lieutenant Henry Hough was far from impressed with his quarters at Abrantes on 27 April 1812.

Abrantes is reckoned the key of the Tagus. It is a garrison town and the regiments always come down to receive their clothing here, which makes the billets very indifferent for officers passing through. I was billeted in a priest's house, but it proved the worst lodging I had had since leaving Lisbon. It was strictly according to Lord Wellington's orders, viz., 'That no British officers was to expect more than bare walls, a chair and table.' The ceiling was burnt in several places, the walls quite black and hung round with cobwebs, and the floor broken-in every two yards, which admitted a refreshing smell from the dirt of my two horses that were in a kind of stable below.

However, Ensign John Blackman of the Coldstream Guards was much happier with his own billet in the same city.

Saturday 28 March, 1812, Abrantes.
   I have as yet been extremely fortunate in my quarters and my present one is a very good one, the bed of course laid on the floor, indeed we are lucky if we get a bed at all, if not, we use our own, which I shall avoid doing as much as possible, till I join the army.

Captain John Ewart of the 52nd Foot came off even better, but at a price.

> 28 December 1811
> I got an excellent bed with fine sheets, and we dined on boiled fowls, pork and potatoes, with the best bread and wine that I had tasted in the country. The walnuts and chestnuts were much larger than I had seen before, but we could get no corn for our horses, only chopped straw and chestnuts, for which, like everything else, the inhabitants made us pay very dear (eggs 2 vintems each) and we were obliged to apply to the alcalde for everything, as there was no market established.

Band Master John Westcott of the 26th Foot mentioned arriving at their quarters for the night but found that it was impossible to get under cover from the rain and they did not even have a blanket to cover themselves.

> 30 July 1811
> The most tremendous rain with thunder and lightning came on which lasted all night. This was the night for reflection, wet, dejected and miserable, we set officers and men, under the cover of trees, without as much as a blanket to throw over us. Our regiment by some mistake received no blankets on marching to join the army nor neither did they through the whole campaign, which was a shameful neglect. I strolled away from the regiment's lines in the middle of the night by myself to a neighbouring village thinking to get under cover from the most tremendous rain I had ever seen, which with the thunder and lightning made it yet more awful, but here again I found myself mistaken, for the whole village was taken up by a brigade of Portuguese infantry and a number of cavalry, even the very passages were completely crowded with men and horses. I offered a dollar to get in a house but was refused, here again I found money of no use so I had to return dejected back again to my regiment's melancholy camp ground, . . . lying out with no covering but the canopy of heaven . . .

In the following September they at least got a covering in old abandoned buildings.

> 30th September
> The division marched at six o'clock in the morning to their different cantonments, . . . headquarters for the brigade, the 26th and 79th Regiments at Macal de Chao, although the quarters of the soldiers in general were but merely a covering from the weather, being mostly in old ruinous houses without inhabitants and our beds nothing but the

floor and that without straw. Still we considered ourselves comfortable in those miserable quarters, having time to rest our wearied limbs and not being in dread of a night's dreary march from an active enemy, we changed our linen not having an opportunity for the days before being in a constant alarm of the enemy.

Private Richard Smith of the 3rd Foot wrote home to his parents around January 1811 (it is undated), describing their situation. His spelling is retained for authenticity.

We shall have a very sharp battall sum wehre about Abrantes in the course of 3 or 4 months, when the wether gets so that men can lye out of doors. The wether now to[o] cold. but the wether is as warm hear now as it is in England in April. The wet season is not come in yet, but we expect it very soon.

Paymaster Clerk Robert Duffield Cooke found an interesting billet.

> Casillas de Flores 26 May 1812
> When I reached headquarters (about 8 o'clock evening) I was informed by the commissariat, the military chest was kept about 4 miles off at a village called Casillas de Flores where I immediately went, saw Mr Gordon and put myself under his orders where I have been ever since (about a fortnight). But the village and accommodations must not go unnoticed; in the first place it is nearly the worst village in Spain. The quarters I have are rather superior to a pigsty, but not equal to a stable. There are 3 women (2 old) and 5 children in arms, 1 pig, my three horses, dogs etc, and myself all in one room and all sleep together. They have not a single utensil of any description whatever excepting a broken earthen pan besides making a trough for the pig. My bed is my own, being made of two blankets bought in Lisbon with some good straw underneath and three sackcloth money bags by way of sheets, with my uncle Mo's leather case for a pillow (all on the cold earth). However, bad as it is, I jump into it at night with as much pleasure as if I was in reality going to a bed and leave it in the morning the last of the family. Indeed it is famous fun to see them all get up; the most disagreeable part of the family is the pig as he runs loose, not having a cord to tie him up.

The daily variation of the billets soon became a source of endless complaint. Indeed, getting a good billet was soon seen as a complete lottery. Edwin Griffiths recording on 10 May 1813 that:

> The country for miles around Celorico indeed as far as we could see, is nothing but a continuation of rough & barren rocks ... As we were now living near the border, the misery & poverty of the villages became more apparent. They presented nothing but an accumulation of the most abject wretchedness. Our accommodation was proportionately comfortless; at Nabais I slept in an old lumber loft over my stable with a very scanty allowance of roof remaining; at Maca de Chao I was happy to take possession of an old poultry house, on the floor of which you might have set potatoes, but we were now familiarised with filth.

A fortnight later he had become a little more philosophical about things.

> 24 May 1813
> The vanity of a soldier's life on service is not the least common part of it. Last night I had two splendid apartments to myself, with matted floors, silken hung walls, glazed windows and a carved ceiling beautifully painted ... Today two of us were squeezed into a loft ... with our servants & baggage, the roof barely kept out the sunbeams, the floor was an inch thick in dirt, the ragged walls hung with cobwebs & filthy garments; the light came in & the smoke went out at the door, no there was neither window or chimney, the bed in which the family slept was separated from ours by a low partition & we all turned in with our clothes on by the dim & cheerless ray of a stinking oil lamp, which had no sooner burned out than a whole host of rats, attracted by the savoury smell of our canteens, invaded the apartment & continued squeaking & racing round & over us the night through.

He still found it good practice to check out the billet thoroughly.

> 9 June 1813
> I was invited by the lady of the house to partake of their family dinner! I had however peeped into the kitchen beforehand & not relishing appearances I declined the feast in favour of my clean bit of tough ox.

Captain Henry Packe of the 1st Foot Guards made it clear that the Guards did not get it any easier, although the officers did have their own personal tents and servants.

> 31 October 1812
> We have never seen the inside of a house since our junction with Lord Wellington, always bivouacking, most of us have small tents which occasionally are sent out of the way, and we of course have

then, no more to trust to, than our men, who sleep under the heavens only, but we have been hitherto fortunate in our weather, having had it continually dry until yesterday.

Encampments in the mountains brought some serious dangers with them. Lieutenant Colonel John Hunt of the 52nd Foot recorded one serious incident.

> Near Huerta 21 July 1812
> About 9 this night whilst we were on the march, came on one of the heaviest storms of thunder, lightning & rain ever remembered; the thunder burst directly over our heads and stunned several persons in our division, but providentially without injuring any one materially although the bolt must have fallen close to us. The report was so loud that it frightened the horses & men rushed forward and was very near through but the most singular circumstance attending it, took place in Major General Le Marchant's brigade of cavalry (3rd Dragoon Guards, 5th & 4th Dragoons) which had just taken their ground for the night, most of the men being fatigued, had lay down in a line in front of their horses which were tied together by troops. The horses alarmed by the tremendous explosion rushed forward over the men and wounded badly near fifty of them, several of the horses afterwards separated having broken their halters and the next morning about 40 were missing, supposed to have galloped off towards the enemy.

However, even officers sometimes did not get a billet. Major the Honourable Edward Cocks of the 16th Light Dragoons, was one of them.

> 13 October 1811 Mafra
> We are enjoying a day or two in quiet here, behind our line of defences which are strong and numerous, which the cavalry very much needed as we have covered the retreat all the way. Neither the captain or myself have had our clothes off now for more than four months and very seldom under any cover but the sky.

The cavalryman William Bragge could spot when the army was about to go into winter quarters, however.

> 1 November 1811 Castelo Branco
> I don't know a better sign of the army going into winter quarters than 4 cars going to headquarters with wine, ham and stoves – this I saw yesterday

Many more of the comments regarding billets are written during the autumn and winter when the troops were all generally quartered in whatever buildings were available. This brought its own problems, as it often caused the troops to be spread over a number of neighbouring villages. Lieutenant William Freer of the 43rd Foot wrote from Arzinhal on 25 February 1810:

> I believe I wrote to you last at Pinhel since which we have been changing our quarters four or five times into villages between that and Almeida, we at present occupy six, so that you may judge the extent and comfort of them & of all barren countries I have seen, this beats them hollow, covered with rocks & here & there amongst them is to be seen a little cultivation.

Captain George Widdrington of the 34th Foot also confirmed how they were spread across a number of villages, where although cold and hungry they remained healthy.

> Esperagalego near Merida in Estramadura 20 November 1809
> The army still remains inactive in the plains of Estramadura, where they are quartered in different small villages and are more health than they were a short time ago. The weather is so extremely cold we are half starved; and this morning the ice is an inch thick. I never felt myself in better health notwithstanding our bad fare.

Charles Madden found a similar situation.

> 24 March 1811
> I did not get to the quarters of my regiment till between eight and nine, as they had marched about two leagues from Campo Major, and were cantoned in some small villages and quintas, the principle of which was Aldea de St. Vincente, the quarters of my troop and two others.

However, the average Portuguese or Spanish house lacked some basic necessities as far as the soldiers were concerned and contained others they could well have gone without! George Barlow described a quite typical winter quarters.

> Zamarra, 26 November 1811
> Last night, there was a great deal of ice, with as intense a frost as I have ever felt in England . . . for the present to a miserable hovel; open to all the winds, rains and elements; full of smoak [*sic*], there is but one apartment, in which ourselves, our servants, batmen & the miserable

inhabitants are crowded all together in addition to a large quantity of logs & timber for fire wood.

He wrote similarly of another billet a month later.

26 December 1811

Martiago from whence I write the present, is a miserable little village and not the best of quarters. Two of us are huddled in this little hovel, for it deserves no better name. There is no light but which proceeds from the door, above a clumsy roof of tiles from whence the azure itself of heaven may be perceived through the fractures and which admits rain and snow a plenty, indeed we were deluged by it yesterday, and filtering through our walls which as well as the floor are made of earth. My bed a couple of wooden benches with a pair of blankets is considered as [the] most comfortable one amongst us. A tin cup, with a cast [iron] knife, fork & spoon composes the whole of my dinner set, and two pair of saddlebags my wardrobe.

Ensign Charles Crowe of the 48th Foot mentioned one common issue.

5 December 1812

We marched to Azambuja, . . . This place showed the devastation of war, few houses were habitable, and scarcely one had escaped injury. The inhabitants we found remaining were emblems of poverty and dirt. My bed, nay the walls and the floor of the room, swarmed with fleas. Truly 'their name was legion!' and they were as avaricious of English blood as their masters [were] of English money. I was regularly fleabotomised! I had no fear of plethora,[1] on the morrow, for my body corporate was far more dense, studded with punctures than this paper is with letters! And the muschetos [mosquitoes] maintained a full share in the concert.

Captain William Bragge suffered similarly.

13 October Abrantes 1811

The Portuguese beds are most abundantly stocked with a race of fleas more venomous and hungry than any to be met with in England.

---

1. His meaning of plethora on this occasion, is an excess of blood in an area.

These devils attack me instantly and in about 10 minutes dislodge me for the night.

Lieutenant George Woodberry mentioned another pest and the ever-present threat of thieves.

Luz, Sunday 7 February 1813
I slept in an empty house, on the ground, rats and mice running over me all night. There were no locks or handles on the doors, and with the horrific information I have been given on these scoundrels of inhabitants, I slept very little. This morning I began to examine the village which is a poor miserable little place. I obtained another billet to a second empty house nearer the barracks where I removed to, a palace with a garden, but not a single piece of furniture, without fireplaces, except in the kitchen. A very fortunate fellow I am, last night in the bustle some of the rascally Portuguese stole my cloak; the very thing I shall most want up the country, to wear on a night picquet.

Two days later thieves made an attempt to rob a group of fellow officers and the incident became potentially very serious.

Luz, Sunday 14 February
. . . Last night the house wherein Kennedy, Smith and Dolbel sleeps at in Benfica was attempted to be broken open by a banditti of 9 fellows, those Portuguese scoundrels. Dolbel fired a pistol at one and Smith discharged the content of a pistol at another, they then made off.

This was not an isolated incident, as Charles Crowe wrote.

6 October 1813
. . . We passed through Oiartzun; and between one and two [in the] afternoon took possession, for the night, of a forsaken house, by the roadside. The valley was very picturesque, the day fine and the clear river most inviting; that we took a cold bath before dinner. I must admit our quarters were capacious; but by no means accommodating, or comfortable; for as the night advanced the wind and rain drove in most bitterly; and the shutters to the windows in front having been destroyed we were compelled to force the doors off the back apartments to fence out the weather. Moreover, our situation was so lonesome, that we considered it requisite to keep watch throughout the night. Fortunately the ground floor, was a wine store, and had no opening but the main entrance to the

house. Over which was a wooden balcony; under whose partial shelter, our servants kept a good fire with the abundance of fuel, which we had providentially secured; and we ordered them to stand sentry by turns and give the alarm, should any person approach. Pollock and I did not undress but with drawn swords in hand, crept under our blankets. This precaution was soon tested, for about 11 o'clock my servant being on duty, fired a shot, and called out, 'Stand to your arms!!' My friend and I had not long made our appearance below, when a very suspicious and desperate looking fellow, a pisan, came towards us, pretending to be looking for his lost mule. We told him very plainly that we knew this was flam;[2] for the sentry heard him conversing with his comrades, before the shot was fired; and that if he, or any man, or any number of men dared to come near the house, during the night we would show them no mercy. During this parlance we frequently stirred up the fire with our drawn swords. Our vigilance and alertness had a good effect: for although we kept a dog watch,[3] we rested ourselves unmolested for the remainder of the night.

Ensign John Hamilton of the 2nd Battalion KGL wrote of the main design flaws with the buildings in the peninsula in general.

[Fuente] Guinaldo 31 January 1813

At present with us it is extremely cold, as much so as with you in England, the ice is thick and the houses are not by any means calculated to keep out the cold. They have no glass in the windows, nothing but window shutters, which you must open for light, of course it lets in the cold as well. This is the plan of all the middling houses, we have neither fire or chimneys, except a little fire of wood in the kitchen, and to a man not accustomed, it is unbearable the smoke, we console ourselves the warm weather is not far distant.

Lieutenant Edward Fox Fitzgerald of the 10th Hussars was determined to move into the room with the fire at his billet but was fearful of the consequences.

Selma de Pampeluna 21 October 1813

I am in a most wretched house with neither glass for the windows or even shutters, and I am so dreadfully cold I can scarcely hold a pen. When I am not out I sit wrapt up in my cloak all day long; and of

---

2. Flam – a lie or hoax; a deception.
3. Dog watch – a late night watch.

course you know that there are no such things as fireplaces in Spain . . . tomorrow I intend to take up my abode in the kitchen and no doubt shall make my appearance with a few day's residence there like a dried tongue.

Many officers could not stand the open fire in the middle of the room and installed chimneys themselves, much to the horror of the inhabitants. William Bragge was one.

Aldeia da Ponte 20 January 1812
The village itself is truly wretched, but some heretic soldiers having built a chimney and fire place in the corner of almost every room, it is during the present severe frost by far the most agreeable place after sunset that we have seen in Portugal.

Ensign John Mills of the Coldstream Guards also commented on the Spanish distrust of fireplaces.

Pinhel 25 December 1811
Frost has usurped the place of rain and it is as fully as cold as in England. The native brutes sit wrapped up in snuff coloured cloaks over a pan of charcoal, roasting chestnuts and think us savages for building fireplaces.

Major General Sir Charles Colville also improved his quarters – although he certainly didn't make the changes himself.

December 1811
I find great comfort in the chimney and other improvements I have made to my house, not forgetting my oiled-paper windows . . .

It is not true, however, that no Spanish properties had fireplaces. George Bingham of the 53rd Foot found one.

Estremoz, 21 December 1809
Our billet was an excellent one, having a room with a fireplace in it, a luxury confined to the middle-class people residing in small towns . . .

Lieutenant Henry Hough discovered that senior officers of all armies stayed wherever they could, noting that they were therefore protected from pillaging or even destruction.

25 April 1812

I went to Gollega, 5 leagues. Was billeted in the same house one of the French generals occupied, when retreating. It was very little destroyed.

Lieutenant George Woodberry of the 18th Hussars went one better.

Cortizes [Sao Martinho da Cortica?], Friday 7 May 1813.

I am billeted in an empty house, no windows or any comfort belonging to it. We made a good fire and suspended our canvasses over the front windows and the door. My servants were lying downstairs. It was once a very fine house and well furnished, it was honoured so the padrone informed me with Marshal Massena [for] six nights and Lord Wellington for three. The whole village presents a complete skeleton.

Officers could also have major problems with their servants, although new servants could sometimes be obtained from an unusual source, as Lieutenant Edward Fox Fitzgerald of the 10th Hussars explained to his grandmother.

Villa Olite 4 July 1813

I suppose you will be much surprised that Robins, my servant, turned out quite different from what I expected. As long as we were in snug quarters and had no hardships to undergo he did very well, but when we came to march seven and eight leagues a day and sleep on the ground, he began to grumble and to be very careless and disagreeable, taking care of nothing but himself. But at the fight at Morales he seemed so frightened that I began to suspect [him] and at the Battle of Vitoria I missed him till eleven o'clock at night. So that I thought it best that we should part, but the immediate cause of my parting with him was being in a state of British drunkenness for two days. I paid his wages by a bill on you for £57 and got clear of him I now have a most capital French servant that we took with some baggage in a skirmish near Burgos; he is by far the most useful fellow that ever was. I gave him thirty guineas a year and he finds himself in everything, which you must allow is not dear for the following qualifications which he possesses; a valet, a cook, a shoemaker, a capital taylor [sic] and a sad bit out of my ration beef he makes as good a dish as I wish to eat even in England . . . keeps all my cloathes [sic] in good repair. He talks German and Spanish and prefers staying with me to going back to France as was offered him. . . . I certainly intend bringing him home to England, if he turns out well. Robins has got a place with an officer of the 18th. so he is not thrown upon the wide world.

Rain was by far the worst for encampments, Lieutenant Charles Dawson of the 52nd Foot wrote of their trials at the siege of Badajoz.

> Badajoz 21-22 March 1812
> Since we have been on this ground we have not had a single day or night, not hardly by 3 hours together without heavy showers of rain; the first night we arrived here it was bitter and a dreadful night, raining and blowing the whole time, the men no cover but their blankets and but few officers with tents . . . . All the tents were blown down that night by the violence of the wind and rain. Now all the army are encamped regularly in tents, which adds so much to our comfort.

Lieutenant George Barlow of the 52nd also wrote of this period.

> Camp before Badajoz, 19 March 1812
> The season at this time of the year is not very pleasant for those who live under canvas; a great deal of rain has lately fallen accompanied with high & tempestuous winds, the camp is moreover very inconvenient in two most important respects. Water must be fetched from a considerable distance & that not of the best; and which in summer must be particularly unwholesome, from being stagnant. It is a considerable distance to the Guadiana and the whole country around a sandy, barren flat, almost as naked as the palm of my hand and almost destitute of wood for fires & cooking; these are indeed two great inconveniences much felt.

However, as the war progressed and the 'fighting season' was extended well into the autumn, with operations even extended at times into the wet and freezing winters, a radical rethink was required. For the campaign of 1813, large bell tents were issued, to be carried on mules and the troops were able to encamp each night under the protection of canvas. Lieutenant Colonel George Bingham of the 53rd Foot reported the change in a letter home.

> Almofala 12 March 1813
> The mule that formerly carried the camp kettles is to be more efficient and to have three bell tents as a load instead and tin kettles are to be served out instead of the iron and to be carried by the men as you may recollect the Portuguese troops did.

However, it was exactly a month later before he could finally record:

> 12 April – our tents have arrived . . .

Lieutenant James Gairdner of the 95th Rifles explained how the tents were carried in this campaign. The men had now also been issued small camp kettles, which were light and easy to carry, rather than the old cast iron pots which were very heavy.

> 10 June 1813
> The public mules which used to carry camp kettles for the men, now carry three tents each per company.

However, any ardent camper will know that living under canvas does have its own challenges. Indeed a number of correspondents make it clear that the merest hovel was still preferable to a tent. Ensign Orlando Bridgeman of the 1st Foot Guards certainly thought so.

> St Jean de Luz Sunday 5 December 1813
> ... it is now raining, the weather is also very cold, I have nothing like a fire place in this house & am at this moment so very cold that I can scarcely hold my pen, however compared with a camp, it is paradise; the quantities of rain that has fallen here has rendered all immediate movements out of the question, the Pyrenees are entirely covered with snow ...

Lieutenant George Woodberry still continued to take quarters when he could, a surprising decision when he describes what it actually consisted of.

> Bivouacked on the left of the road to Toro at Fresno de la Ribera, Tuesday 1 June 1813.
> The house I am quartered at is a poor wretched hut, my horses are in the parlour, our mules in a kind of sleeping room and myself in the kitchen, which is a receptacle of all kinds of animals, and amongst them the old grandfather of the family, who though not seventy years of age, exhibits 'Shakespeare's' last stage, sans teeth. I am exposed to the hungry appetites of myriads of fleas, and entertained all night with the grunting of pigs, squalling of cats, coughing of the old people, braying of mules, squalling of children; in short it beggars all description.

He was also guilty when in France of treating the locals harshly, just like a French officer would.

> Chapel of Hasparren, Monday, 10 January 1814
> My apartment is so miserable I thought already of changing it; but having discovered a good room occupied by the people of the house,

I quickly took possession, to the dismay of the poor wretches, but 'need has no laws'.

Lieutenant Charles Crowe wrote of the camp just after the Battle of Vitoria:

22 June 1813

On returning to our bivouac I scrutinized the scene around. Had a skilful artist been present he might have taken an interesting sketch of 'The morning bivouac after a great battle' but words cannot describe it. Behind our large tree, not a dozen yards from where our weary heads had rested, I saw one of my bullocks, its throat had been cut ad libitum.[4] This spot soon resembled an ant heap on a large scale, for numerous soldiers came to cut for breakfast. My musing was broken by the cheerful shout of my chum, 'Barry Carr! Take the fore quarters of that mutton to [Robert] Pollock,' then turning to me 'Come old boy, we are to breakfast with our friend Carlile, his servant pounced yesterday on some coffee and sugar, and sure now won't we have a hearty meal once more!' The canopy of heaven was our saloon, the green sward our table cloth, and some five or six of us were well pleased with our repast.

A few days later the rains came down and all hell broke loose.

29 June

This morning was very fine, and everyone was busily occupied in drying and regulating his baggage when a sudden and most tremendous storm of rain set us all afloat.

I made four channels through my tent, and fortunately, thereby succeeded in keeping my chattels dry. For two hours not a man could leave his tent. A scorching sun then burst upon us, and soon dried everything. I took a hint from what had occurred, and shifted my tent to the reverse flank of the regiment, on a shelving bank, I made one trench above and through my tent like a Y to effect which, I had to cut away furze bush with my sword, which made me a most luxuriantly soft and dry bed.

Many of the tents were actually flooded and the streets in camp were ankle deep with mud. The poor soldiers were in a most deplorable condition.

---

4. Ad libitum – Latin for 'At the discretion of the performer', i.e. to act as they wish.

However, Lieutenant George Barlow has the last word in explaining the hardships of being under canvas.

> Camp in front of St Jean de Luz, 8 November 1813
> Let happen what will, any change for us in our present situation must be for the better. The severity of a Pyrenean climate in winter is very well known & we already begin to feel the effects. Torrents of the heaviest rain constantly fall by night & day attended with violent westerly winds. Our camp though on the top of a hill is a perfect swamp and many of the tents little better than sieves (to use a joke current amongst ourselves), we need not look far for a draught of water. Make a small hole in the ground & a spring rises in the middle of the tent. But speaking seriously, nothing can exceed the misery of being constantly wet both by day & night, with a thermometer almost as low as freezing point; the weather is extremely pinching, the animals half-starved and despite of the double allowances of grog given to the troops, they will soon suffer most terribly if a change into the low country does not very soon take place, this however we know will very soon happen.

The use of tents came later in the war, as we have seen, but being under canvas was not always preferable to the shelter of a solid building with a roof and the opportunity of maintaining a warming fire. However, the idea of the poor infantryman having previously to lay out in all weathers throughout the year without any covering beyond their blanket has been shown to be a myth. During the autumn and winter rains the troops were placed within buildings to protect them from the worst of the weather if at all possible. Indeed, the need to provide dry accommodation for the soldiers was fully appreciated by the senior officers to avoid wholesale deaths.

Chapter 9

Camp Life

During the worst of the winter weather and sometimes during a lull in the fighting, cantonments often became long-term quarters, forcing both officers and men to seek alternative pursuits to while away the many monotonous hours and a number of activities came to the fore. Edward Fox Fitzgerald of the 10th Hussars wrote of his boredom and what he did to pass the time.

> Villa Olite 4 July 1813
> . . . I wish some of you would write oftener as we have nothing to do here but learn Spanish and flirt and talk of England . . . Every day here passes exactly as the preceding one, except now and then there is a ball, where there are always plenty of partners to be had. There is also a tennis court here so that in general I go to bed very tired and sleepy . . . [I am] a man now just as much at my ease as if I was in England. I dine at five, go to bed at nine, and get up at six to play tennis; and then have my chocolate which my French servant makes admirably.

Some, unfortunately, lost their means of amusement while on the march. Lieutenant James Crummer of the 28th Foot was one who was more concerned about his dogs than his colleagues.

> Saugo near Rodrigo 25 November 1812
> I have lost the greyhounds [during the?] retreat, they I fear fell into the enemy's hands, as did poor Mrs Blair & husband with the colonel's baggage & many men.

It seems that having hunting dogs was quite common. Lieutenant James Gairdner of the 95th Rifles mentioned that his friend Captain Jonathan Leach owned one.

> 6 June 1812
> Leach has one of the Spanish Bulldogs who killed a leveret today.

Hunting and shooting were popular pastimes to while away the hours – from the most senior officers to the most junior. Major Edward Cocks of the 16th Light Dragoons recorded the duke's passion for hunting.

> 24 Nov 1811
> Lord Wellington keeps foxhounds which hunt twice a week and have already killed three foxes.

Ensign John Mills of the Coldstream Guards, however, thought that the hounds at headquarters were owned by others.

> Val de Ayres 13 November 1811
> Lord Tweedale has got a pack of hounds at headquarters . . . Lord Wellington goes out regularly and I hear they have good sport.

Lieutenant Colonel Andrew Barnard of the 95th Rifles wrote of a wolf hunt that Wellington attended.

> La Encina 26 May 1812
> We manage to kill time as usual by hunting for which we go out at a very early hour. A grand wolf hunt took place the day before yesterday, 800 persons to beat the woods and three or four hundred posted in different parts of the wood to shoot the wolves, Lord Wellington posted on a hill to look on with a double barrelled gun. [They saw little of the wolves] that gentleman liking the society of sheep, donkeys and mule better than that of Christians with guns in their paws – so ended the great chase.

Lieutenant Crummer soon got over his loss and still got out riding with other dogs.

> I have had Scott here for this week back, during which time we had very good fox hunting with General Hill's hounds.

James Gairdner also went out shooting when he could.

> 13 May 1813
> Went out quail shooting today, killed a brace & missed a good many more.

> 9 April 1814
> I went out partridge shooting today, the number of partridges here is very great.

Lieutenant George Barlow of the 52nd Foot was more of a bookworm himself, but he agreed when writing from Martiago on 3 December 1811 that for most officers:

130 *Marching, Fighting, Dying*

... the earlier part of the day is generally employed by them in coursing or shooting, both of which diversions are to be had hereabouts in the highest perfection.

Lieutenant William Swabey of the Royal Artillery also took part.

15 November 1811
Amused myself greater part of the day in coursing, killing one hare.

Captain James Gubbins of the 13th Light Dragoons made short work of his fox.

23 December 1813
Went out with the foxhounds found and killed him in a quarter of an hour ...

Ensign Robert Garrett of the 2nd Foot also talks of the passion for hunting in the army.

Mealhada Soida 20 May 1811
... There are a great many greyhounds, guns and pointers in the division, which will be an inducement to me to go out coursing & shooting, there being great quantities of hares, rabbits & partridges near here.

There was also horse racing, although more often performed on mules, as their best chargers were far too valuable to risk being injured. Ensign John Mills states that they were held very regularly.

Castello de Vide 28 May 1812
We were extremely gay during our stay at Niza. We had races almost every day at which [General] Graham presided. Mules and ponies were the principal operators and showed admirable sport.

In fact, Lieutenant Swabey wrote on 18 November 1811 that the officers of the Light Division.

... appears to have the start of the army, they have all sorts of amusements in their cantonments, coursing, cricket, rackets, fives &c.

But they weren't the only ones, Lieutenant Colonel George Bingham of the 53rd Foot describing his life in winter quarters as:

Olivenza, 9 December 1809
. . . nothing but racing, coursing, dinners and suppers since I wrote last.

Lieutenant James Gairdner of the 95th confirms that racquet sports were another option.

27 February 1813
We have made a racket court here against the church.

Exploring their surroundings was another way to enjoy their time, although as Lieutenant William Freer of the 43rd Foot records, it was often fraught with difficulties.

Sierra d'Estrella, 21 November 1810
I made an excursion up the mountain (the highest in Portugal) with another officer, we started at 2 o'clock in the morning and after walking for 12 hours we found ourselves on the top. I must now explain the reason of making this extraordinary excursion. On the top of this immense ridge of hills are three lakes not very wonderful for size, but one is so from being unfathomable. This was the object of our search but guess my disappointment and rage when the fool whom we had taken for a guide after showing us two, shrugged up his shoulders and told he did not know where the lake we were so desirous of seeing was. I certainly would have used a stick about 3 yards long upon his bones had not the recollection of our being in the confines of numerous goat herds prevented me, who might have retaliated on my bones for ill using a countryman. So I contented myself with eating some prog [food] and admiring the very extensive prospect of the country around.

Others took to books and study, but it must be admitted that they were a rarity. Lieutenant George Barlow was a serious young man who preferred to read, ride and gamble very moderately.

Martiago, 3 December 1811
Every day after breakfast & parade till one o'clock I study Spanish and military drawing. Should the weather prove fine I ride until between four & five. In as much as I like to visit every village and be well acquainted with all the country in our neighbourhood. Our mess consists of but four & is as moderate as possible, we drink little or no wine, take a cup of hot chocolate or tea and generally go to bed by ten or eleven at latest.

I seldom or ever play at cards & when that happens we play but shilling points. Such is the turn of our life at present, I possess however this difference, that I am the only officer who possesses any books & indeed who use them much . . .

However, Lieutenant William Swabey and his fellow officers found a novel alternative use for books.

During the winter of 1811 we inhabited part of a house belonging to a Portuguese Marquess in the village of Salgueiro. A large room was occupied by some of us which served as a library, and there was a long book case with heavy volumes on ecclesiastical subjects, those we did not indeed read, but we turned them to good account by pushing them suddenly back and crushing the rats which congregated behind them.

Eating, drinking and socialising were also popular pastimes, and William Swabey wrote triumphantly:

18 December 1812
We hired a cook who is wife to an artillery soldier, whom we likewise retained. Dinner very elaborate, sauces, ragouts, hashes, roast, boiled, and baked, not to be sneezed at.

Lieutenant James Gairdner also wrote of his love of music but was unable to practice.

Camp near Vera, 6 October 1813
How does the music come on? You ought to be a capital performer and the other young ladies ought to be making good progress. My fluting has died away for want of practise. I lost my flute last campaign with the rest of my baggage, and have not played since, not having been able to get another. We have an excellent band in our battalion, I do not think there is a better in the service, they have a very good collection of Spanish music. When we come to England I will get you copies of the best of what they have. English music, especially what is new, is a rarity here, it is only from the bands of regiments lately come out that we hear it. I think after all I have heard no music equal in real harmony, no music which appeals so directly, so forcibly to heart, as the original simple Scottish airs. The Spanish music is however very pretty though there is no great variety in it, the patriotic and national songs are very good and very pleasing when sung by two females, for the Spaniards, as

well as Portuguese and Germans have a natural taste for music which is not in the English, if two, four or any number of persons to beguile whatever work they may be about strike up a song, they divide themselves into first, second and even third and sing a treble, tenor and bass, as correctly as if it were composed for them.

Lieutenant James Crummer also wrote of music and dancing.

Coria Spain 1 February 1813
. . . our time at present is tolerably pleasant in imitating common civility at home, in the shape of dancing and theatrical amusements.

Band Master John Wescott of the 26th Foot clearly had a passion for music too.

3 March 1812
A large fair was held in the town, the officers of the Cameronians gave an entertainment in the evening, to most of the principal ladies and gentlemen of the place. The ball was held at Don Frederic's house, the colours of the Cameronians decorated the assembly room, several boleros and fandangos were danced in good style, and also some good waltzes, but the English country dances, they knew very little about but appeared to like them very well one of the ladies sung several beautiful Portuguese airs and accompanied it with the guitar.

Ensign Carter of the 30th Foot was determined to enjoy Christmas with his fellow officers – he was not to know it would be his last.

26 December 1811
The doctor & I were so merry the night before that we asked a whole lot of fellows to dine with us, neither had much money, but the doctor raised 2 dollars, which enabled us to buy a ceg [sic] of wine, this together with the ration rum we got the day before wined us pretty well, the adjutant also was so good as to send up three pints of whisky. We were very much puzzled as to how to get a table & table cloth however I proposed to the doctor that we should bring up some planks which were in the yard & rest them on a chest & a made a table, now we did not know how it was possible to procure a cloth. Coming up from the kitching [sic] to my great astonishment I saw the doctor very busy spreading a cloth & bestowing great pains to brush some dirty yellow spots off it. When I asked him where he had raised that, he told me that it was one of the sheets which he had taken from the bed & that it would

do very well after he had brushed the lice & fleas off. Dinner was served up everyone seemed to enjoy himself very much

But six weeks later he was being severely irritated by other people's revelries and took matters into his own hands.

> 11 February 1812
> . . . About 12 o'clock at night the doctor returned from a dance, & also the people of the house, but when the doctor got into bed, we were disturbed by the people singing below stairs, we asked them to be silent & go to bed for we wished to sleep. They made reply that it was their intention to dance & sing all night. This enraged us so that when they were in the midst of their glory we employed the contents of the chamber pot in the midst of them, They with the greatest fury laid siege to our room. The girl of the house whom I had told that I was the son of a parson, called me the son of a father & a bastard. After soaking them pretty well with water & turning them out of doors they were quiet.

The dancing often took a lot out of them, however. Lieutenant George Woodberry of the 18th Hussars complaining on Monday, 17 January 1814 that:

> Last night's ball has slammed us all; the floor of the room had no elasticity!

Sometimes the organized dances failed because of a small hitch, but the incident with the band, recorded by Woodberry was presumably a little unusual!

> Olite, Friday 9 July
> A very laughable affair on the evening of Lord Worcester's Ball, he had engaged our band to play, but at the appointed time, they never came; a non-commissioned officer was sent in search of them and found the whole in a room dancing, completely naked, except having their pelisse's slung across their shoulders. I understand there were some women present but have not heard whether they were stripped or not.

However, one of the most talked-about recreations was the theatre, with military personnel performing for their comrades. Famously the Light Division converted a ruined chapel at Fuenteguinaldo into a theatre, Lieutenant Colonel Andrew Barnard of the 95th Rifles recording that:

> El Bodon 5 November 1811
> We are therefore returned to our old quarters and in the absence of Mars we cultivate the acquaintance of the Muses *Thalia* and

Melpomene.[1] We have made an excellent theatre out of a ruined chapel at Fuentes de Guinaldo where the 43rd are, and, our scenery and drapes are superb considering the small means we have to work on, Lord Wellington comes over to our next.

This, however, was not the only theatre that was set up that year, as Major Cocks says that:

24 Nov 1811
   Several theatres have been established. At the Guinaldo theatre, set on foot by the Light Division, I saw *Henry IV* the other night, got up very respectably.

Lieutenant William Swabey went to the Light Division theatre as well to see *Henry IV*.

18 November 1811
   Captain [John] Kent of the 95th in Hotspur was excellent, the rest of the performers exceedingly good. And Falstaff received great effect from an officer of the 95th.

The following winter the theatres were set up again and seem to have been much more ambitious.
   Lieutenant James Crummer of the 28th Foot confirms that General Hill's troops had a theatre, in which Crummer acted.

Coria Spain 1 February 1813
   General Hill has his quarters in this town, some of his staff being admirers & connoisseurs of the stage, we have knocked up a theatre and I assure you have an excellent company of military comedians, your humble servant at times assumes & imitates the great man, the hero, the beggar and in fact all characters but *one*, which I shall not here mention, but leave to your fanciful mind to discover.

A month later he reported the plays they had performed.

---

1. Two of the Greek Muses, *Thalia* represents Comedy and *Melpomene* Tragedy.

Coria 2 March 1813

    Our theatre gets on most famously, we have acted, *The Rivals*,[2] *The Poor Gentleman*[3] and *The School for Scandal*,[4] with suitable entertainments, the scenery is most beautiful, being painted by officers, altogether it is the neatest thing I have ever seen & of course affords very irreverent amusements.

Lieutenant James Gairdner of the 95th Rifles listed the performances of the Light Division Theatre in 1813. They performed at Gallegos this year and it seems that it was not only officers who performed.

18 January 1813

    The Light Division have got up a theatre by subscription; the chapel at Gallegos is the theatre, the first performance is to be this evening and is to be the comedy of *She Stoops to Conquer*.[5] The hussars are invited to dine with us today.

4 February

    The theatrical geniuses of the division perform *The Rivals* this evening. The hussars are invited to dine with us.

12 February

    Rainy. *The Rivals* is to be performed over again tonight & Lord Wellington will be there. The hussars & 2nd Battalion are invited.

7 March

    The *Raising of the Wind*[6] & *Fortunes Frolic*[7] were performed last night & very well done.

10 March

    The soldiers perform *The Brothers*[8] & *The Poor Soldier*[9] tonight.

---

2. A comedy by Richard Sheridan, first performed in 1775.
3. A comedy by George Colman the Younger of 1802.
4. Written by Richard Sheridan in 1777.
5. A comedy by Oliver Goldsmith, first performed in 1773.
6. A farce produced in 1803 by James Kenney.
7. A farce produced in 1800 by John Allingham.
8. A comedy written in 1653 by James Shirley.
9. A farce written in 1783 by John O'Keefe.

11 March
I was not at the soldier's play last night but understand it was very well done.

15 April
The theatricals of the division performed at Gallegos this evening, *She Stoops to Conquer* and *The Apprentice*,[10] Lord Wellington was there.

Henry Johnson also went to the Light Division theatre regularly in 1813

Freineda 16 February 1813
Our theatricals! In a chapel which previously had been metamorphosed into a hospital, thence into a stable, by the bye Covent Garden stands on ci devant holy ground. '*She stoops to Conquer*' overcome only by '*The Rivals*'. Sir Anthony Absolute, famously fiery as he well might have been having been blown up and considerably singed at the storm of Ciudad Rodrigo, while Lydia Languish and Julia were quite sister graces; and after supper, what songs; solos, duets, trios, not to mention the retrospective glances of Mrs Malaprop to the future fame of the theatre ducal of Gallegos.

As to these actors: Sir Anthony Absolute was played by Lieutenant Cooke Tylden Patterson (43rd), Mrs Malaprop by Captain Samuel Hobkirk (43rd), Lydia Languish by Lieutenant the Honourable Charles Gore (43rd) and Julia by Lieutenant Lord Charles Spencer (95th Rifles).

Camp life was clearly noisy, smelly and often tedious, with little to keep the ordinary soldier occupied, leading to increased levels of petty crime and drunkenness. However, many of all ranks sought other preoccupations to pass the time a little more enjoyably and healthily. It does however confirm the old adage first published during the First World War, that war is and always has consisted of 'Months of boredom punctuated by moments of extreme terror.'

---

10. A play written in 1756 by Arthur Murphy.

Chapter 10

Corresponding with Home

Anyone who served abroad in the armed forces in the era of 'blue letters', before the advent of email, will fully understand how important they were, often being the only means of corresponding with loved ones at home. The Napoleonic Wars were really the first conflict where there was an organised mail system to and from the forces abroad, allowing family to maintain a regular correspondence with the soldiers fighting across Portugal and Spain. Many of the themes brought out in these letters will resonate fully with anyone serving prior to the twenty-first century, including complaints that no one was writing to them, descriptions of the difficulties of writing in camp, family issues and requests to post both luxuries and the necessaries of life which they could not get themselves, are all very reminiscent of the author's own experience in the Royal Navy in the 1980s.

The delight at the receipt of mail from home is a pleasure not to be described, although many tried in an effort to impart to their families how important it was to them. Ensign the Honourable Orlando Bridgeman of the 1st Foot Guards had only just sailed from home, but his delight at finding mail for him in Portugal is clear.

> 29 June 1812
> The pleasure I derived this morning from the arrival of letters I cannot express, the packet came in last night, & we got our letters at ten o'clock today, I received one from you dated the 13th of May which has reached Portsmouth after I sailed, they sent it from the Post Office to the Orderly Room in London from whence it was forwarded to me, also I received a letter from George & Henry, but none from Lucy which rather disappointed me, pray thank H[enry] for his . . .

Captain George Widdrington of the 34th Foot explained how important mail from home was to him.

> Allegrette 26 April 1810
> I am looking anxiously for the arrival of a packet from England, in hopes of hearing from you all, that it fills my mind with melancholy and uneasy thoughts of the worst, if I do not hear at the usual times of

receiving letters from home. Therefore my dearest beloved father, do not neglect writing often when you commence your journey and till you return, and I must also entreat that because you are absent that my beloved mother does not continue silent, but writes as often as she has leisure, as you do not know, we have few things to make us happy and comfortable in our minds in this country; and that hearing from our friends is our chief enjoyment and what we look to *all*, with the utmost impatience; and when a post arrives that only brings letters for a few, the mortification is dreadful to those who are not so fortunate as [to] receive any.

The vagaries of the wind meant that letters occasionally arrived very rapidly indeed, although most of the moans were of long delays because of contrary winds. Captain Henry Dawson of the 52nd Foot was delighted that a letter which sailed to Lisbon and was then transported by mule overland had reached the army in only 15 days.

9 July 1812
A mail arrived here from London in fifteen days, up to the 23rd.

More often the weather delayed the mails significantly, as Lieutenant George Barlow of the 52nd Foot noted.

Martiago, 12 November 1811
We have had no news from England for some time past, no less *than four* packets are at this moment due at headquarters and I only fear less some accident at sea should deprive me of some of your letters.

Indeed, Ensign John Mills of the Coldstream Guards thought that more were missing.

Val de Ayres 13 November 1811
The wind for some time past has been so unfavourable that we have now five mails due. The latest papers we have are of the 24th September.

It was also not unknown for packet ships to be captured or sunk in gales. Lieutenant Colonel William Gomm of the 9th Foot, on the staff as an Acting Quarter Master General, feared that a few of his letters had been lost this way.

Arbonne 15 January 1814
Your two last letters confirmed my suspicions that two of mine, written shortly after the passage of the Nivelle must have been lost in the packet that was taken some time ago.

A change in the rules also prevented him from sending his mail home in the official bag, saving postage costs.

> Arbonne 3 February 1814
> I find we are no longer suffered to frank letters at the Quartermaster General's office; and in addition to this grievance, I have just learnt that poor Major O'Neale, to whom I addressed all my packets for you, is dead. I am therefore, under the necessity of sending you this by the direct post.

Even when the packet ships arrived safely, there were stories of parts of the mail being held back. Lieutenant George Woodberry of the 18th Hussars complained that:

> Camp near [Santa] Cecilia [del Acor], Sunday 6 June.
> The English mail arrived the day before yesterday. Lord Wellington only allowed the letters to be delivered to the officers, reserving the newspapers till a future time, thinking if the officers got them now; they would be reading the news instead of attending to their duties and we're so close to the enemy.

Sometimes the letters were chasing around the country after officers, Henry Johnson, an aide de camp to the Prince of Orange, moaning that:

> Freineda 13 January 1813
> No new mails, my dear mother, and my letters by the two last [packets] still wandering with either Lord W[ellington] or the P[rince] of neither of whom have we for some days had any intelligence.

Another problem was misdirection, such as Lieutenant Edward Fox Fitzgerald of the 10th Hussars mentioned.

> Tafalla 19 August 1813
> Tell Pam always to put on the direction '10th Hussars' as one of her former letters was opened by Lieutenant Fitzgerald 20th Foot.

Or an unfortunate accident occurred to the post, as described by Major Edward Charles Cocks of the 16th Light Dragoons.

> 24 November 1811 La Puebla de Azava
> We have been an unparalleled time, 57 days, without mail from England when the arrival of three was announced. Everyone was on

the alert for their letters and papers, when, alas! The dragoon who was conveying the bag for the cavalry fell in the night, lost his horse and lost his bag. . . . for some days we gave up all hopes of recovering the mail but I believe nearly the whole has since been found, though how I do not know.

But far more frequent were the voices of bitter disappointment as mails arrived without a letter for them. George Woodberry felt thoroughly neglected.

Camp near [Santa] Cecilia [del Acor], Sunday 6 June.
Alas I have no letters from England; I am quite forgot, I shall be soon tired of this country if I do not hear from my friends, particularly those most dear to me.

Major Alexander Gordon of the 3rd Foot Guards, aide de camp to the Duke of Wellington, had an ongoing issue with a lack of regular correspondence, showing his anger over the failure of his family to write to him, although he apparently was not perfect himself on this score: indeed, arguments vied back and fore throughout the years. He started by excusing the loss of a letter from himself:

Pero Negro 20 October 1810
I have just heard that the packet in which my letter of the 20th of last month, was obliged to throw her mail overboard . . .

However, he was not happy that he was not receiving any mail.

Pero Negro 10 November 1810
Another packet has arrived and no letter from you! Unless I hear by the next, this is the last letter I shall write.

A reply showed that the family were not very good correspondents either, but promised to do better.

Brighton 17 November 1810
As to my not writing which I assure you, so far from being owing to any neglect, arose from an excess of anxiety about the result of an event to which I looked with such mingled sentiments of fear and interest on your account. However, I now faithfully promise to write you regularly once every fortnight.

However, a year later he was again complaining.

> Freineda 20 November 1811
> Although we have received late accounts from England I have not heard from you since August. You cannot expect that I will continue to write you when you take so little trouble about writing to me.

Another year later he was admonishing them once again.

> Ciudad Rodrigo 19 November 1812
> I have no time to write more, or indeed ought, as you never write to me in return, I therefore shall cease my correspondence and write oftener to those who more desire it and who do not think it too much trouble to answer me in return.

It is presumed that they finally did correspond more regularly after this, but Gordon was not alone. Colonel John Keane was particularly unhappy with his wife for her extended silence.

> 10 January 1812
> How many months have now elapsed without one line from you. Packet after packet have I expected an acknowledgement of some one of the many communications which I have made and after the strong assurances I received from you at our last meeting, disappointment is the least I can feel. However, it is a consolation to know that I have scrupulously kept my word though I have had more difficulties to encounter and less time to spare than you have had.

Others admonished, only to be criticised in reply for a similar lack of correspondence. Lieutenant William Bragge of the 3rd Dragoons found himself in this awkward situation and turned on the weather instead.

> Falques 24 January 1812
> It is a literal fact that I yesterday morning wrote you a letter complaining heavily of the neglect and idleness of all my correspondents, but having in the course of the day received one from you and another from Lucy making the same charge against me, I was induced to destroy my former epistle with a determination to blame the winds and waves in future, who certainly are most execrable post masters.

Young officer and servant set out to join his regiment, from Rowlandson's *Johnny Newcome*.

On the march in the rains, by St Clair.

Muleteers near Irun, by Batty.

Light dragoon outpost, by William Wollen.

A young officer learns how to smoke and drink, from Rowlandson's *Johnny Newcome*.

Soldiers on the march, by Thomas Rowlandson.

10th Hussars in camp at Morales, by Denis Dighton.

Cavalry stabling in a church.

Bivouac at Vilha Velha 1811, by St Clair.

Spanish camp in the Pyrenees, by Batty.

Officer on the Sick List, from Rowlandson's *Johnny Newcome*.

The troops advance – note the soldier stripping the dead in the foreground – from Rowlandson's *Johnny Newcome*.

Battle of Albuera, by William Wollen.

Marching the French prisoners into Salamanca, by Edward Orme.

Storming a fortress.

Collecting the dead after Talavera, by Lady Butler.

Some were a little more sympathetic, Life Guardsman Henry Willis writing home to his sister that:

> Vitoria, 28 June 1813
> Having received no answer to my last dated March, I do not conceive it any neglect of yours or Miss Slater's, I think it must have been detained on its way, or by some means miscarried.

A few covered over the issue by stating that they surely would be happy to hear simply that he was safe. Captain Frederick Philips of the 15th Hussars wrote:

> Puylaurens 20 April [1814]
> You will begin to think me idle my dearest mother, for not having written a line since the Battle of Toulouse, but you will have seen by the Gazette that we are all safe.

Many chose to blame the distance from Lisbon for causing serious delays. Major Thomas Brotherton of the 14th Light Dragoons did so in a letter to his wife.

> Madrid 24 August 1812
> My dearest love,
> I am much surprised to find that you have not received my several letters. As I was aware that you would be uneasy, I wrote oftener than usual and in the letter enclosed you a draft for £23 which I hope you received. . . . We are now so far advanced into Spain & so distant from Lisbon that the correspondence is very uncertain. I have received altogether three letters from you & have written five to you, one immediately after my wound. . . . Take great care of yourself. Believe it is not my fault if you want for anything.

Lieutenant George Barlow of the 52nd Foot wrote further on the difficulties with the post, but added a sting in the tail.

> Camp near Vitoria, 20 June 1813
> There exists no such thing as an established post in these parts and no means of forwarding letters except through the medium of the Adjutant General, who thus concisely sends round to officers *'Letters for England must be sent to my office in half an hour'*. It behoves me therefore to keep something in hand ready prepared & I will now write in perfect ignorance whether it may go off tomorrow or three weeks hence and only trust that my epistle though slow, come sure to

hand at last. I sent *two letters* from Lisbon, *one from Abrantes, one from Castelo Branco,* one from [Fuente]*Guinaldo,* one from *Aldea Nueva,* one from near Palencia & concluded near Burgos. Referring to those in your possession, you will see if any have missed from shipwreck, the enemy, or any other mischance. At present not a line from any of you has reached me since leaving Streatham.

A lack of sufficient paper, or simply wishing to avoid paying more postage, often caused them to fill the pages and then continue writing, by turning the paper 90 degrees and writing across the sheet on the other axis. This often made reading the letter very difficult, as this author can verify, and led to numerous complaints from home. Orlando Bridgeman was one of those required to apologise.

Irun, Saturday 23 October 1813
I am annoyed at your having had so much difficulty in reading my letters, for some of the reasons you give I will endeavour to rectify, for instance the cross lines, I have written this small & close in order to prevent them being necessary, but my hand shakes so today, that it is with the greatest difficulty I can write at all. My only reason for crossing my letters was to prevent double postage, darker ink I fear more difficult to remedy, as English ink is difficult to pick up & the generality of the ink in this country is very bad; but I will do all I can, & I think this I am writing with now is pretty good, how to account for the worn state of my letters I know not, yours do not reach me so, but then, to be sure, they always come in large brown paper bundles with other letters, when I write from camp the paper naturally will be damp, but most of my letters have been written lately from this house, & despatched perfectly dry. Your letters have indeed been themselves again lately, & the pleasure they have given me is not to be described, & to be sure when you are in spirits there is nobody who writes so pleasantly as you.

Besides complaining about the lack of post, the trials they underwent to get anything written at all were regularly described. Ensign Robert Garrett of the 2nd Foot explained how lucky they were to get anything from him.

Camp near Alfaiates 10 June 1812
I have not had time to sit down to write a single line to you till now, nor should I have attempted it today, having arrived here just now after a march of twenty miles which we began at two o'clock this morning

Captain Henry Dawson of the 52nd Foot complained of the excessive heat.

> Castello de Vide 28 May 1812
> It is so confounded hot I can hardly write, the very goose quill hisses.

Henry Johnson also wrote to his mother of the problems of writing in the heat.

> Palacio d'Asuna, Madrid, 25 August
> Raking until nearly six this morning; not the best weather possible for such doings you will say when I add that the heat has so dried my inkstand and split my pens that I fear my patience will be quite exhausted before I reach the bottom of this page . . . My patience is nearly exhausted. My ink being in lumps not in the power of water to dissolve, not nearly but quite – therefore, my love to my father.

Lieutenant George Barlow of the 52nd Foot excused how he wrote scraps as and when he could and went on to describe his novel writing equipment and the sudden rush to finish.

> 13 June 1813, Camp in front of Burgos three leagues,
> You see I am obliged to write this in scraps as we keep constantly and rapidly moving. It is now past five o'clock, we are but this moment come in from a long march and the adjutant has just sent us a message that the letters for England must be sent to the orderly tent in half an hour and there is no alternative. I write the present *in a ditch* leaning against the bank for *a table*, in the middle of a wheat field . . .

Even generals had such inconveniences sometimes. Major General Frederick Robinson described his writing office.

> Camp before San Sebastian 31 July 1813
> Yesterday I had my writing case upon a large flat, high stone in a goatherd's hovel on the summit of the highest of the Pyrenees in these parts (Monte La Sain) . . . I did all in my power to make a room habitable but every effort was defeated by long established filth and myriads of fleas . . .

Major Edward Cocks, now serving with the 79th Foot, described the difficulties of writing on sloping ground and with all the cacophony of noise from a camp all around.

27 September 1812 Camp before Burgos
In what a different situation do I write and you read this letter. I am sitting in a very small bad tent, on a box which feels very hard to the part applied to it. My table is rickety, one leg being too short, and whenever the stone slips away, which I shove under to keep it steady, down rolls the ink. The said table is covered by a blanket instead of green baize, which identical blanket, in the course of half an hour with an addition of a bear skin and a cloak will form my bed, bedstead and bedding. So much for the inside. Outside three mules belonging to my nearest neighbour are occasionally whinnying.

The whinny of mules is between the bray of an ass and the neigh of a horse, more un-harmonious than either. A little further some drunken Portuguese have got some music and are singing, playing and huzzaing, much to their satisfaction. Further still is heard the continual firing of the siege and if I chance to look out, the chances are I see a shell or two in the air; all round are campfires. The most magnificent part of my writing equipage is my wax candle in a silver candlestick.

Lieutenant James Crummer of the 28th Foot also wrote of the noise levels.

Camp near Gallisteo 16 May 1813
. . . Were you to have a view of our present situation, you would give me every credit, for my attempt to write, for with drums beating, sounds of bugles, asses braying, horses neighing and other occurrences equally annoying & troublesome, I can hardly keep my few ideas from scattering.

Staff Surgeon George Morse, serving with the Portuguese army, recorded similar discordant scenes.

16 July 1810
. . . We are now in a camp under the shelter of chestnut trees & several of us mess together, have a number of servants & live very well indeed, I am now surrounded by mules, baggage horses, saddles & soldiers & am writing on my medicine chest in company with a young cadet whom I have given some paper to & the use of my ink to write to his mamma . . .

Captain George Widdrington of the 34th Foot complained that it was so cold that he could barely hold the quill, but he could still impart warm words.

Almeirim 1 January 1811
The weather has set in very cold and from not having fires in the rooms in Portugal, I can hardly guide my quill from numbness, but however frigid the fingers may be, my heart's warm and dilates with pleasure as I trace these characters to you.

The sudden short notice of a mail going off seems to be a consistent complaint, as William Gomm struggled to rush off a Christmas message.

Bidart Christmas Day 1813
The mail is made up earlier this week than usual and I am taken by surprise. Scarcely time to wish you all as merry a Christmas as we mean to pass and to express my regret that I am not able to pass it with you all, but I trust there are still many such in reserve.

Henry Johnson also wrote of receiving very short notice of a mail going off.

Headquarters, Huarte, near Pamplona, 2 July 1813
After dinner. The mail I find certainly starts this evening and I have to copy a lengthy dispatch of Graham's for it, so I shall only have time to write scraps while I wait the [ink] drying for a turnover [of the page]. . . .
It is raining like England and very cold. For light's sake I must stick to a window *sans* glass.
Thank heaven I have closed Sir Thomas ['s dispatch], my wrist being quite stiff.

Obviously much of the correspondence was on family matters of every conceivable issue, but this letter from Lieutenant Colonel Sir Henry Murray commanding the 18th Hussars commemorating his third wedding anniversary, wrote about ensuring that his son had been inoculated for smallpox and his wife's singing.

Palencia 2 July 1813
As you were not here I could only *renew my vows* in presence of your dear picture, with ever more affection than in 1810. I hope you have had dear Frederick *carefully* inoculated for the cow pox. I feel certain that your recovery from your lying in by the sea side has not cost you any of your fine tresses. Pray practise your singing for which purpose I send you '*Die Liebe*' wretchedly misspelt I dare say, therefore don't show it anybody but learn it by heart & lock it up. When I went near the enemy I

burnt every letter that I had that in case my baggage by any chance fell in their hands they might not amuse themselves by publishing my secrets.

Only a few officer's wives actually came out to the peninsula to join their husbands and far fewer actually left Lisbon and marched with the army. Henry Murray sent a typical reply when his wife suggested coming out to join him.

> 25 August 1813
> I shudder at the idea you expressed of coming out to me, if there is anything on earth that could make me completely miserable it is your undertaking a scheme in which you would be exposed to every sort of insult & outrage & could only leave ten thousand anxieties upon me without being able to afford me a single comfort. I trust that *you will never* let such a scheme enter your head, though I have too good an opinion of your sense to think that it could have done more than passed through your imagination & been forgotten.

Staff Surgeon Morse with the Portuguese army also discussed the option of his wife coming out to Portugal at great length, particularly as she might be pregnant.

> 10 April 1811
> . . . upon my word my love I do not know seriously what to say about your coming to Portugal. Could I continue at Lisbon it would be productive of much gratification & probably be less expensive for I do not find things by any means so dear in Lisbon as I expected: but if you was to come out I should no doubt be gone from Lisbon & if not, I shall go soon afterwards & it would be impossible to take you up to the army of Lord W[ellington] where my brigade now is. In fact, nothing there would be procured & you would suffer every hardship & privation besides the oppressive heat of the climate which you would not be able to bear particularly *if the fruits of my late visit to you should not be blighted*. I can only say my love, that if you should come . . . I will do everything in my power to make your situation comfortable & about the dear children, what is to be done for them? You would not like to leave them & it would be madness to bring them to this country.

Family correspondence also unfortunately brought unwelcome news from home. Major Edwin Griffith wrote to his sister having learnt of the death of his mother, exactly two years to the day after the death of their father, both parents dying on 18 June – Edwin was to join them on 18 June 1815!

Elcano near Pamplona 2 August 1813

To Charlotte [his sister]
  Since the arrival of Morgan's [his brother in law] letter of the 23rd of June you have never been out of my thoughts . . . Alas my dear girls this blow has deprived us of our only parent & a most heart breaking one it is; but we must bow with resignation to the will of heaven; . . .

Alexander Gordon, aide de camp to the Duke of Wellington, received the melancholy news that his sister-in-law had lost a baby as a still birth.

Brighton 1 December 1810
  I write now to inform you of the unfortunate accident that has happened to us. Lady A[berdeen] without any cause whatever was suddenly taken in labour, a month before her time, and brought to bed of a boy. It died in about half an hour after its birth. You may believe this is a great disappointment. She bears it however with the greatest possible composure and is getting well . . .

More often the news was serious rather than final, Surgeon George Morse was typical, with his concerns for his wife's health after a simple cough had deteriorated significantly. The delay of post taking on average two weeks each way, left him anxious for better news.

Elvas 23 September 1809
  With the most poignant grief is my heart hurried in consequence of the information your letter of the 28th August conveyed to me. Little did I think that from the letter received a few days before, wherein you mentioned having a cough & cold I should have so early received a more unfavourable account of your health. I trust in God that your apprehensions have made you imagine your case to be worse than it really is, but from the symptoms which you so fully & so feelingly enumerate I fear I have too much reason to dread an unhappy result. I trust however that before this reaches you by the kind care of Dr Wallers you will have so far recovered as to be able to give me the fullest assurances of it . . .

George Widdrington wrote of his marriage prospects, assuming that he had plenty of time to settle down, but he did apparently have someone in mind.

Almeirim 1 January 1811
  I am greatly formed for domestic life, the charms of those joys I envy, but not the hum drum life of Darby and Joan; still must sometimes

amuse me and therefore I must look for a wife with considerable fortune. Elen Allardice would be the wife of my choice, her mind is improved, her figure interesting, and her fortune estimable. Do not think that I mean to sacrifice my heart's affections to money but without *I may love* but cannot marry. When I am a Field Officer my chance will be better for settling in life, but here I am sacrificing the best part of my manhood without being of any great use to my country.

Lieutenant William Freer of the 43rd Foot discussed his mother's provisions for his sisters in the event of her death, reassuring her that their brothers would not abandon them.

7 December 1810

Frequently my dear mother, do I think of what privations you have undergone for our sakes and through your exertions have three of us been comfortably set up in the world, what do we not owe you. Can our gratitude be shown sufficiently to the best of parents. Excuse me my dear mother but it is love to my sisters & regard for you that makes me mention what I trust will be long, long ere it is necessary. I have often heard you mention that your property is to be divided among your children. The shares that would fall to the lot of Edward & myself we give up to our sisters. This is what my brother John proposed and I follow his example & give our dear parents the satisfaction of knowing their daughters are not deserted. I hope my dear mother knows all the sentiments of her sons too well ever to doubt their daughters being friendless.

The sister of Andrew Barnard simply wrote of the love his family had for him and their desperate wish to see him come home.

Berkeley Square 8 September 1811

Long, long is it my dearest Andrew since you have heard from me, but I seem to have resumed the exertions of my pen for a fortunate moment when I have nothing to communicate to pain you & many things to please you. The first & best of things is the assurance that absence is not curing any of us of our affection for you. On the contrary your being so highly prized where you are would give you even more value amongst us here if any more was necessary but tis needless to be more than beloved & respected & wished for home again.

Private James Dilley of the 40th Foot wrote home during the rains and urged his brother not to be lured into the idea of becoming a soldier. His misery drips from the page.

> Galegos 5 November 1811 amid torrents
>   For now we are laying against a northern garrison town cald [called] Aldrega [Almeida] but I hope it will not prove as bad as Baryoys [Badajoz], but thanks be to God I bear it up with a good hart & I hope by the blessing of God that I shall live to see you onse moor. I hope to God that my brother will never think of gouing for a solder, for I cannot express the sufferings in the compass of a solder that we undergo in this distressed country. I should be glad if you would send whear any of the young ones his [has] moved. I have nothing moor to had [add] but remember me to every one of my frends.

Perhaps the most poignant letters of all are those from their children at home and their responses. His son Charles wrote to General Robert Craufurd of the Light Division in his best handwriting and was clearly helped by his mother.

> My dear Papa,
>   I am very glad you asked me to write to you because it seems as if you like to read my letters. I should not have doubted the buttons were silver if Mama had not thought so, so pray Papa do not be affronted with me. Mama received a letter from you a few days ago, it gave her very great pleasure and I was very much obliged to you for the little bit which you sent to me. Mama says that the day after she is settled, she will send to the tailor and order jackets to be made for our buttons. Bob and I are very impatient to wear them, but much more so to have you see us wear them. Al is very much grown since you was at home, I wish you could see how much. I love you very much and am your affectionate son C[harles] H[enry] Craufurd.

His father sent him a personal reply addressed 'To Charles Henry Craufurd from his father in Portugal' and dated 1 April [1810?]:

> My very dear Car,
>   I was very much pleased at receiving your letter & I assure you that you cannot wish to see me more than I wish to be with you, and your dear Mama and my nice little Boody & Lou and little Al, whom I hardly know. I think I shall be quite surprised when I come home & find him

walking about. I have got a poney [*sic*] but he is rather too large and too frisky and jumps too much for you. But if I cannot get a very nice one here, I certainly will buy one when I come to England for you. It shall be yours and dear Boody shall have a *Donty*. And what shall we give to our nice little Lou? I believe a very pretty *Tap*. As for Al, he will be easily suited, I suppose he will prefer some barley sugar to anything else. But is a pity he should wait so long for it and therefore tell your dear mother that I beg she will give you five shillings to make a feast. I think we shall have some fine games and hide & seek next winter.

God bless you my dearest Car. I love you all very very much. I cannot possibly tell you how much. I am and shall always be, your most affectionate father, Robert Craufurd.

Besides such family business, the letters home are filled with requests for family members to carry out various commissions for them while they were in the peninsula. The most common was for new uniforms, shoes, swords or even money to be sent. These parcels were shipped to Lisbon where they often lay for some time, until either they could be claimed or could be transported up to the army, as they could not take too many mules away from the vital supply work. Typical of these was this request sent to his sister from Colonel Andrew Barnard of the 95th Rifles.

Saint Jean de Luz, 9 December 1813
I am going to trouble you with commissions without end. Two or three dozen shirt buttons according to the pattern which I send. A box of Spence's toothpowder, and some medal ribbon to enable to carry the late honours conferred upon me. The cross is really very handsome, I hope to show it to you one of these days. If the toothpowder is folded in papers the whole of these might come under cover through Torrens, if they do not I shall not probably receive them for three, four, five or six months.

Captain Henry Mellish of the 87th Foot ordered shirts.

Lisbon 22 October 1809
I wish you would get me two dozen shirts made. I like the frills tolerably deep & of fine cambric & the shirts of good, strong but fine linen. I find the calico shirts I have worn lately after a few times washing, tear like paper.

Captain Henry Packe of the 1st Foot Guards also wanted shirts and stockings.

Camp, Comvases near Astorga, 28 November 1808

I shall be much obliged to you if you find that we are likely to remain out of England and that you have an opportunity of sending anything to me, if you will get a dozen pair of *short* worsted stockings of the Loughboro[ugh] patent manufactory, to wear with pantaloons drawers and as many calico shirts, for at present I have only two pair of worsted stockings and my shirts are *walking* off very fast.

Sergeant William Smith (actually serving under a pseudonym, his real name being Simonds) of Captain Elphinstone's troop of the 7th Hussars wrote of his survival in a number of engagements but added some needs and news of his promotion.

St Nicholas France 5 May 1814

Thank my good God that he has preserved me from several dangerous engagements that we have met with since we left England, that kind providence who has protected me I have heard has taken our dear mother, which I hope & trust is for the best, had it pleased God to have spared her life I should have been very happy to have seen her once more, but as it is I hope its for the best, although so far away, in spite of all my fortitude a tear or two will start from my eyes now and then, yet I have some consolation to think that she is happy.

My kind love to Mrs Fisher & tell her I am much indebted to her for the kindness she did me in sending me a couple of flannel shirts since I have worn them I have not any aches or pains.

I have made some little progress in point of promotion being made sergeant, of course I have less duty to do only to see that duty is done. I have now a man to clean my horse and clothes &c

Edward Cocks also wrote home with a very specific list of commissions to his brother.

22 December 1810

I am now going to trouble you with a few commissions, for the length of this campaign has made great havoc with my equipage. First, Egerton the bookseller; Gilbert bootmaker, Old Bond Street and Cunningham hosier, corner of St James's Street, Picadilly; I should be much obliged to you to settle with.

Second, would you order me a new hussar saddle with accoutrements from Whippy. There is a new hussar saddle at my father's in Cavendish Square; I should ask this to be fitted up and sent out at the same time . . .

Third, would you order a new helmet from Hawkes, I wish it to be very light and low . . .

Fourth, a new sabre and belt from Prosser. It should be roomy in the handle and not too heavy at the point. Will you be so good as to have it proved. . . . I do not like the handle roughed with fish skin.

Fifth, four pairs of new hussar boots, not open, from Gilbert, three pairs of laced half boots with spurs to them all. All these will make a pretty good package . . . The only thing I want more are a few books, [he lists 9 volumes] of course, pocket editions where they can be procured and all bound as they take up less room.

However, the following year he wrote home with a complaint.

12 July 1811
By the bye, . . . the sword you sent me broke to pieces the first time I had it in my hand and I discovered a flaw about 22 inches from the handle.

Some supplies were even sent without having to be requested. Andrew Barnard received from his sister such an unsolicited, but undoubtedly welcome, package.

Berkeley Square 14 October 1812
. . . . I know not how I can better prove the desire I have to keep you in this world than by sending you a suit of fleecy hosiery to wear for my sake when winter comes on and the frost begins to punish the noble regions. There is trousers, shirt, night cap and gloves & stock if I can get one; they go by a friend of mine who you may talk in a friendly manner to if he falls in your way.

He received another to help with the theatrical productions.

Espeja 19 April 1813
Many thanks my dear Sarah for your songs, they have arrived at too late a period for the theatrical campaign of 1812-13, yet they may serve for the ensuing season should we again take the boards.

John Blackman of the Coldstream Guards was delighted to hear that two pairs of shoes were on route, but now came up with a further list of requests.

31 January 1813
I am happy to hear you have ordered me 2 pairs of shoes, as I stand much in need of them. At present, I am not in want of more overalls, but

I should like a pair of dark pepper and salt trousers and a blue waistcoat, with our regimental buttons, and I do assure you I am *very much* in want of a blue great coat, we wear nothing else in cantonment, except on parade, in short we never wear our redcoat except on parade, or on the march. I should like it single breasted, strait collar and the Coldstream buttons. The one I brought out I had turned some time ago and it is now quite worn out. If you would also send me a plain blue foraging cap, with a little velvet round it, I should be extremely obliged to you.

Alexander Gordon also requested that his clothes trunks held in storage could be opened and some of it sent out to him.

10 July 1810
PS I will be very much obliged to you to cause my trunks to be opened and take a pair of new boots by Meyers (there are two pair beside) and pack them up and send them to me as fast as possible to the care of Mr Smith Falmouth [where the packets sailed from] as I find my servant has brought but one pair with me.

Edward Cocks sent home a more unusual request.

10 June 1812 Camp near Puebla de Azava
I have taken a servant whom I like, his wife lives by washing in number 9 North Row, Park Lane. Her name is Churchill. If you can do anything for her in the way of getting her washing I will be obliged to you.

Captain Henry Dawson confirmed the arrival of his packages in Lisbon.

Village near Castelo Branco 28 April 1812
My packages from London I have just heard are arrived [in] Lisbon. I anticipate their arrival with the army with much pleasure.

He also explained how they got newspapers far more regularly than their post.

Burgos 27 September 1812
The latest papers we have are of the 1st of September. A packet goes twice a week from Corunna but I believe the mails still go by way of Lisbon.

A few requests also went the other way, with Alexander Gordon confirming the shipment of a pipe of port, which held 1,008 pints! He also had hopes of getting other items.

> Badajoz 9 September 1809
> I have bought you a pipe of the very best port possible, it is some of the true wine, without any brandy in it . . . .I have also got some few Merino sheep for the best kind. I am also in hopes of getting some of the finest La Mancha wine.

However, a year later his brother was writing to ask again for the sheep.

> Argyll House 25 July 1810
> If you have any communication with anyone near Badajoz, or wherever good Merinos are to be had, I wish very much that you could get me a couple of rams and half a dozen ewes of a good kind.

Within two months Alexander replied with good news.

> Gouveia 13 September 1810
> Your sheep . . . I believe are now on the road to Lisbon.

An item requested from Captain Charles Lennox, The Earl of March, of the 52nd Foot but serving as an aide de camp to the Duke of Wellington, was too fragile to put in the post.

> Headquarters Amusco, 9 June 1813
> I will get you a guitar & send it by the first opportunity but we have nobody going home now.

Andrew Barnard had received a similar request from his sister but was able to find someone who was going home to take it.

> Isla 26 March 1811
> Captain Lambert of the Guards who is going home in the *Bulwark* will take charge of your guitar . . . I hope it may not be injured by the journey as it is a really superior instrument.

Another cause of lengthy discussions in their correspondence was the continual machinations seemingly necessary to gain advancement in the regiment. When a vacancy arose by an officer retiring or quitting the service, the rank would be offered to the most senior officer in the regiment of the rank below, but to do so, it was necessary that the regulation purchase price (or more) was already in the hands of the Army Agents previously. If they declined or could not afford to purchase, the next in seniority was offered it, although sometimes Horse

Guards would offer it outside of the regiment. Officers killed in action allowed the most senior of the next rank to gain the position without purchase, a much more appealing prospect, although caused by the death of a colleague. The system was therefore fraught with hidden dangers, twists and turns and this caused much angst for aspiring young officers, often reflected in their letters home, particularly to their fathers or wealthy patrons, in the hope that they would put up the purchase money and deposit it with the agents. Major Alexander Gordon was cheered by his rapid rise in the regiment while on active service.

> Villayerna 3 miles from Burgos 18 October 1812
> It must be allowed that war, or rather service, is a famous thing for promotion. I was twelfth lieutenant when I landed at Lisbon; am now fifth and shall probably be first for purchase by the time I have served the regular period as more of our captains and subalterns are heartily sick of the business.

This sentiment was also echoed by Ensign John Blackman of the Coldstream Guards.

> 31 October 1812, Camp near Tordesillas
> Ensign Bradshaw has given in his resignation and is gone home, I have now only 5 ensigns before me, in these events you behold 'la fortune de guerre'.

However, positions often went for much higher amounts than the regulations stated, causing some officers to bide their time, as Captain Henry Packe of the 1st Foot Guards did. He still did get his lieutenant colonelcy by the April of that year.

> Viseu, Tuesday 5 January 1813
> Macdonald is to give six thousand guineas for Sam Anson's company, taking upon himself the sale of the lieutenancy and ensigncy, it is certainly too large a sum to give, and would not answer to me to give so much particularly as circumstances stand at present, as I understand there are two more companies going very soon for a more reasonable price.

It was also frustrating when an officer transferred out of the regiment and then promptly resigned. Lieutenant Charles Lennox, Earl of March, when previously in the 13th Light Dragoons showed his frustration:

> Gallegos 8 January 1811
> I am very glad to hear Bouverie has quitted the army if he had done so before he exchanged so often out of regiments going on service I should have liked him better.

Another fear was that they would be exchanged into another battalion in the regiment which was stationed at home where the chances of promotion by the loss of officers was infinitely less likely. Lieutenant Benjamin Ball of the 39th Foot hoped to avoid this.

> Albuquerque, 15 November 1811
> Our first battalion arrived at Lisbon sometime since from Sicily & is shortly expected at Portalegre. I do not however suppose the transfer will take place between the two battalions before the 24th December. At present there is great canvassing in the regiment for who is to go home & who to stays, a question which time only can resolve.

One route to advancement was to transfer into the Portuguese service, where officers received a brevet promotion to their next rank up, but unfortunately James Crummer of the 28th Foot had been persuaded not to do so and was now clearly regretting it.

> Camp near Gallisteo 16 May 1813
> I should undoubtedly have had a majority in that service had I entered it [at] the time of my application . . .

Captain Henry Mellish of the 87th Foot was enraged by abuses of the system, allowing others to break the rules.

> Tomar 7 June 1809
> . . . You see what has been done for Lord Burgersh by the exertion of his friends. He has not only got his majority *against* rule, but in *four days* afterwards has lieutenant colonelcy, although an order has been established that no person shall be competent to hold a Lieutenant colonelcy until he has been *two years* a major. This is a most flagrant case & has given great offence to the army. I could hardly wish to be promoted in so unfair a way. I only ask for what I am by the regulations entitled to. But there is nothing to be got in the army but by g[reat exertion] & if any of one's friends have interest, it [must be fully] exerted & made a point of.

It was also possible for senior non-commissioned officers to purchase a commission, often as a Paymaster. Sergeant William Ross of the 74th Foot wrote requesting the money to do so.

> Albergaria 27 April 1812
> One thing I request and I beg you will not be offended at my boldness, I have not money to purchase a commission, but I am sensible that you

could obtain me one by interest and for so dowing [*sic*] I will give you fifty pounds sterling for your troubles. One thing that hurts the service very much at this present time, our regiment had no less than two cadets or volunteers, which hurts all the non commissioned officers as well as the Sergeant Major of the regiment in regard of getting forward, if you will have the goodness to write me. I will be glad to have your opinion on this subject.

Colonel John Keane of the 60th Foot, commanding a brigade in the 3rd Division, found it difficult to live on his allowances, having signed over his pay to his wife and children at home, he therefore needed a staff appointment to survive:

> 11 January 1813
> . . . To you who have felt for me, I do not hesitate to state particulars, enviable as is my situation and command in this country, unless I am shortly put upon the Staff, which entitles me to the allowances *I must cut*. On leaving England, I gave up my Lt Colonel's pay to support my wife, three children and maid, on less they could not exist. There then remains for me to support the character of brigadier, one hundred pounds a year as bat & forage and three shillings a day as commanding a regiment. . . .

Lieutenant Colonel Henry Murray of the 18th Hussars gave a moving account of one of his officers desperately pleading for him to support his application for promotion so that he could feed his family.

> 25 August 1813
> Poor Russel [sent in] a memorial, a copy of which he sent me, which almost or perhaps quite drew my iron tears. He had looked forward to this promotion as the only means of providing comfortably for his family, who are hard struggling with poverty, a wife & six children on five shillings a day, all he can allow them & at the moment he thought this promotion within his grasp it is snatched from him. I have written in his favour tolerably strongly to Lord Wellington, all I have said is very true but I am afraid it will be of little use, but I could not have slept comfortably if I had not done everything in my power to serve this poor man.

As the war drew to an end in early 1814, the threat of being put on half pay for years if not decades loomed, an unpleasant prospect for many. Lieutenant George Young of the 38th Foot was one.

Camp near Bayonne, April 28th, 1814

I have now to inform you that the Articles of Peace are signed. This morning the garrison of Bayonne hoisted the white flag and joined the common cause under a Royal salute, which was returned by us with three cheers. I think it likely we will return to England immediately; it is the general opinion here we will be home in three months at farthest. I am sorry it is over so soon as I am not yet out of the break and fear I will be sent on half pay, which would not answer me at this time. However, I must content myself to fate and hope for the best. There are three yet before me, so I think I have but little chance if the reduction takes place immediately on our return to England; however I must content myself with it. The half pay is about forty pounds a year so I may get some place to trust [thrust] my head for it. . .

Others feared a distant posting or an unhealthy climate more. Lieutenant James Crummer of the 28th Foot was certainly one of those.

4 June 1814 Bordeaux

I need not say how uncomfortable we have been in the uncertainty of our destination which I believe, as I trust, is settled for England. The troops destined for a *Particular Service* [North America], have embarked this day. The 28th was the first regiment to have gone in the last brigade sent off, but being deficient of clothing, we were counter ordered, as has been the 40th & 60th Rifle Corps. You may challenge my esprit, but the dread of being sent to do duty in a West Indian island (perhaps for seven or ten years) damps any wish I should otherwise have of seeing more service. Nothing would give me greater pleasure than a campaign in America, yet these considerations operate too strongly to allow of my wishing a visit to that quarter of the globe.

A short spell with the army also convinced some that it was not for them. James the brother of Major Edward Charles Cocks of the 79th Foot had clearly come out to Spain to see what it was like and he wrote a note giving his decision at the bottom of his brother's letter,

10 June 1812 Camp near Puebla de Azava

Charles is quite well, the French were completely defeated yesterday evening. They are flying and Lord W continues the pursuit today. Everyone is in high spirits; the loss of the French is great, ours comparatively small. My decision is in favour of the Church as to my own profession.

Major Alexander Gordon, aide de camp to the Duke of Wellington, had a similar issue with his brother Charles in the 3rd Foot Guards. In this case it was too late and Charles stayed in the army.

> Celorico 15 August 1810
> I really think that not only Charles's constitution, but his inclinations & habits of life are ill suited to a military profession. Under these circumstances I cannot help suggesting to you a wish for his quitting it, if you think there will be a probability of providing for Charles in the church, if it is not yet too late.

Clearly the war and operations were also discussed, leading to much sensitive material being sent, at a time when there was no censorship of mail. This was a dangerous habit, with the threat of capture or even the very great possibility of someone publishing it in the English newspapers, which Napoleon regularly read! Being attached to headquarters, Alexander Gordon was well aware of this and warned his family.

> Freineda 13 November 1811
> I must beg of you to be very careful to whom you show my letters and opinions, as of late things have got about which we do not like and which may do harm to the cause and the more so as you must be aware that I frequently inform you of movements & plans before they are decidedly fixed upon . . .

As can be seen, correspondence with Britain was usually quite regular, although obviously affected by contrary winds, and it covered the whole gamut of personal, family and career issues. Indeed, it appears to be very similar to the mail we are more cognisant with in the two World Wars and even more modern times. Perhaps this is not so surprising, as human nature is pretty much a constant. What may be a little more surprising was the vast amount of supplies being requested to be shipped out to the peninsula and their ability to apparently get it to them relatively efficiently.

Chapter 11

Discipline and Punishment

The discipline of the troops was a regular theme in correspondence home and consequently the legal system and the punishment regime was also. Many officers' diaries are simply littered with a seemingly continuous cycle of offences, court martials and punishment parades. The official returns show that around 600 general court martials were held during the six years of the Peninsular War of both officers and men. For the officers these generally related to breaches of discipline or duty; whereas for the ranks, it was generally for desertion or plundering and theft. However, below this, thousands of regimental court martials dealt with things 'in-house' thereby often not appearing in official disciplinary returns and even seeing unofficial ad hoc punishments meted out. This all points to an army with a serious disciplinary problem. Soon after his arrival in Portugal, Lieutenant George Woodberry of the 18th Hussars recorded in his journal his strong reasons for worrying about the discipline of his men and his determination to get them under control.

> Quinta near Cartaxo, Good Friday, 16 April 1813
> I am plagued to death with the troop; the men are going on very bad. Two men were punished this morning by their comrades, and I was compelled to send another, George Carr to Cartaxo to be tried by Court Martial. I am now determined to work them right and left, till I bring the fellows to a true sense of duty.

In a previous case two weeks before, he and all the other officers had tried vainly to get the punishment reduced on another soldier.

> Luz, Friday 2 April. At eight o'clock this morning the right wing of the regiment marched to Sacavem. I was sitting on a Court Martial all this day, tried 4 men at Benfica, Corporal Thompson, punished this morning, received 100 lashes and reduced, this man was particularly well recommended, as to character, few in the regiment bore a better. All the officers interceded for him, yet Colonel Murray would not pardon him. His poor wife was within hearing of her husband's sufferings, and [I] must say, I was never so much affected, more by her sobs than her

husband's cries; I wanted to be one hundred miles away. His crime was drunkenness and striking Sergeant Williams.

Within two weeks he realized that he faced a much bigger challenge than he had at first thought and he hoped that the punishments meted out would deter future problems.

> Barquinha, Thursday 29 April 1813
> What a villainous troop I belong to; one of the men confesses he was accessory to a murder, which has never been found out, for want of an informer; and then was caught in the act of a crime, which nature shudders at in Cartaxo. The whole troop have broken open several wine houses since we have been here and committed numberless depredations. However, the punishment inflicted upon Sergeant Eyres and Corporal Boughtflower and three privates tomorrow morning, for breaking open the wine house at Quinta de Cardiga will, I sincerely hope, deter the troop from committing the like again.

Lieutenant James Crummer of the 28th Foot understood that many regiments had a large number of bad characters. He found that watching a hanging was an unpleasant experience, but he did not condemn the practice.

> Coria 2 March 1813
> [We . . .] have like many regiments many conspicuous bad characters in its ranks, we have had four men sentenced to death for robbery, three of who were executed by hanging before the troops paraded for that purpose, it was the first hanging sight I ever witnessed, it was truly awful. I am sorry alas to add that three more are to be tried for desertion and attempt at murder by wounding one Spaniard in the leg with a ball and stabbing another when pursued. They will also suffer. I am ashamed to add they claim Ireland as their birthplace, indeed their language and appearance confirms it.

Theft was a common problem and it was often difficult, if not impossible, to identify the culprits. Lieutenant George Woodberry's experience was not untypical.

> Olite, Monday 16 August
> What a dammed unlucky fellow I am, the rascally servants robbed me last night, my desk was broke open, and sixty-eight pounds[1] taken out

---

1. About £3,500 in today's terms.

of it, not a farthing of it shall I ever touch again, it was in doubloons, seventeen of them, and although there was also valuable jewellery the villains never took a thing but the paper of money; alas I am born to misfortunes.

Band Master John Westcott recorded an instance of a threat of a court martial being used to control the men, although on this occasion it probably wasn't necessary.

22 July 1811
The commanding officer gave positive orders that any man detected breaking into the gardens or orchards of the inhabitants, will be confined and immediately brought to a court martial, this order was only as a caution as no soldier has the smallest occasion to plunder the gardens having more than sufficient of fruit, from the inhabitants where they quartered.

However, Major General Frederick Robinson saw faults in all of the Allied armies.

Camp before San Sebastian 31 July 1813
The Portuguese are an army of thieves, the Spaniards have no feeling for their countrymen & our soldiers would be worse than either were it not for the severe discipline in use . . .

Interestingly, there was little correspondence regarding the morality of the punishments meted out, nor much comment on the form of punishment or its severity; it would appear to have largely been simply accepted. The question of the morality of the use of the lash would appear to have only been a phenomenon of post-war Britain. An example of this straightforward acceptance of the need to flog miscreants is provided by Lieutenant George Barlow of the 52nd Foot.

Celorico 26 October 1811
[We were] sometimes impelled [torn – making?] detachments to go foraging for what they could find, as it necessarily was for every regiment in the army, some black sheep of course found their way into it. Our commandant however most properly kept up his discipline and bringing them instantly to a court martial at the drum head when caught in the act, they were flogged & several examples of that sort were at first found necessary to produce good order & regularity.

Lieutenant William Bragge of the 3rd Dragoons also felt that floggings were necessary to curb the soldiers.

> 9 January 1812 Castelo Branco
> Our men have taken a great fancy to the forage corn belonging to the horses and in order to put a stop to such ravenous appetites we have been under necessity of flogging every Irishman and many twice and three times over.

Ensign John Carter of the 30th Foot was sure his man deserved the punishment.

> 6 January 1812
> . . . in the afternoon we had a drum head court martial on a man for stealing flour, he was found guilty & received 200 lashes when stript [sic] you might perceive that he was exceptionally lousy, he had one of the toughest hides I ever saw. When he went to the hospital the doctor was under the necessity of burning all his clothing.

George Woodberry did have a strong repulsion towards corporal punishment, but hoped that it would curb the troops' excesses.

> Luz, Monday 8 February.
> Sat on a Court Martial this morning for the first time, on two men for un-soldier like behaviour to their officers, they were both punished this afternoon before the regiment. No one can detest corporal punishment more than I do, but subordination must be kept up or we shall all soon go to the dogs. I am very much afraid some of our men will get themselves into serious trouble when we join Lord Wellington's army, for if they go on with any of their drunken tricks there, Lord Wellington may perhaps shoot some of them, which I should be extremely sorry for.

The Portuguese and Spanish civilians generally held a strong detestation of floggings and either tried to prevent them or left the scene in disgust. It wasn't unknown to see them cut down and burn the trees that had been used in floggings or hangings. First Lieutenant William Swabey of the Royal Horse Artillery tried to obscure a punishment parade from the populace, but was interrupted by a priest.

> 16 October 1812
> I was under the necessity of putting in execution the sentence of a court martial, on a man who merited his punishment. Though I contrived

to have it in a yard . . . still a priest succeeded in getting in and putting himself in the way, begged and prayed my forgiveness . . . as he was a thief, this could not be granted. Then he threw down his cloak, a proceeding which I understand in the country of priestcraft, is enough to stop the execution of justice. No wonder that vice should predominate over virtue in such a country.

Ensign Orlando Bridgeman of the 1st Foot Guards records an incident when General Trant, a British officer serving with the Portuguese army, tried to deal with a group of drunken soldiers, but it did not go to plan:

Oporto Tuesday 29 June 1813
. . . on Sunday night, General Trant, the governor of Oporto found three of our men in the streets drunk, & making a great riot, upon which he went up to them, & desired them to go home, an English soldier when he is drunk will obey nobody but an officer of his own regiment & General Trant being dressed in the Portuguese uniform, was to them a nobody, however he told them he was an English officer in the Portuguese service, & governor of the town & desired them deliver up their side arms & consider themselves as prisoners, upon which our men were very impertinent & two of them drew their bayonets. The governor then drew his sword, & made a lunge at the foremost soldier, his sword however struck the breast plate & did no harm, the Portuguese guard took this opportunity of disarming our men & they were marched up as prisoners. A brigade court martial sat upon them yesterday & sentenced the two men who had drawn their bayonets to receive eight hundred lashes each, & the third man who was by no means so riotous as the others to receive three hundred.

At the request of the governor this punishment was to take place in a public a manner as possible. The whole of the Portuguese troops attended & the square was formed in front of our barracks, the crowds of people that were collected together to see this unpleasant sight was immense, but they appeared astonished at the severity of the punishment, the day was intensely hot & consequently the men could not receive anything near the number of lashes that they were sentenced to, the man who was the least riotous of the three being tied up to the halberds was taken down before he received any lashes at the request of the governor.

Some floggings evinced mixed reactions, however, as witnessed by Henry Johnson, aide de camp to the Prince of Orange. This was probably because it was carried out on Spaniards.

Fuenteguinaldo 10 May 1812
   [On the] 11th Just as I closed yesterday I was attracted to the market place by sundry wails and found the muchachas crying and the muchachos laughing at a brace of Payanos whose backs the Provost's cat was clawing in high style for mule stealing; a third is to be hung.

Lieutenant Charles Crowe, now with the 27th Foot, the Inniskillings, found that the French civilians were also horrified by the floggings.

2 May 1814
   This morning, at sunrise, one of our drummers received desserts of his good behaviour; according to the sentence of a general court martial. One thousand lashes was his award but he escaped with only eight hundred. This event also excited the curiosity of the inhabitants; but very few waited for the end. They were much shocked at the severity of our punishments; but admitted the good effect; not a single complaint having been made against any man, since we entered the town which would not have [been] the case with their own soldiers. The drummer's misdemeanour had been committed long before we came hither. The daughter of the gentleman where Major Thomas was quartered, a very fine woman about 26 years of age, and very high spirited, intimated her desire to witness the punishment. The major flattered himself that his strong remonstrances had prevailed: but the young lady crept to the scene just as the blood was trickling down the culprits back but was quickly carried home, totally insensible.

George Woodberry similarly watched the execution of a murderer without comment.

Luz, Friday 5 March 1813
   A soldier of the 32nd Regiment was hung this morning at Belem, for stabbing the mate of the transport he was on, and attempting to murder his officer, he looked a very fine fellow and behaved with a deal of fortitude and exhorted his hearers not to be guilty of the like offence, acknowledging the justice of his punishment.

Lieutenant James Gairdner of the 95th Rifles recorded watching the death of some British soldiers who were guilty of desertion to the enemy and fighting with the French during the storming of Ciudad Rodrigo. He does not appear to have been moved by it, presumably believing their crime could not be pardoned.

25 February 1812

We remained all this time at [Fuente]Guinaldo and lived very well, the weather was for the most of the time fine and frosty. We had no marching or bother. The only time that we marched out of the place was one day that the division was ordered to assemble at Ituero [de Azaba] to be present at the execution of 9 men who had deserted to the enemy from this division and who were condemned to be shot.[2] They were taken in Ciudad Rodrigo on the 19th of January.

Desertion to the enemy by British soldiers was not commonplace, but certainly happened irregularly. The desertion of officers was excessively rare, and indeed there is only one recorded occasion that this happened during the Peninsular War. Alexander Gordon, aide de camp to the Duke of Wellington, recording his horror at hearing that:

Cartaxo 2 March 1811

. . . an officer of the 45th Regiment [Lieutenant Richard Burke] has deserted to the enemy, as a circumstance unknown in the British army before, unparalleled, most disgraceful. He was an Irishman and a Roman Catholic.

Despite the broad hint that he was guilty because he was an Irish Catholic, which was a clear attack on his loyalty to the Crown, it has to be said that many Catholics served as officers and many more as ordinary soldiers and served the king well. The French left Burke behind when they retreated from Portugal and he was recaptured, but was found to be insane and was quietly discharged from the army.

Not all offences were dealt with officially, however. Many who deserted but returned to their regiments later were not court-martialled, but instead were punished for absence at a regimental level and were therefore not included in the official returns to avoid too many questions from on high. Band Master Westcott of the Cameronians, records another local and quite novel punishment.

---

2. Privates William Mills, Miles Hodgson and Malcolm McInnes of the 95th, Corporal Robert Fuller, Privates James Cummins, William Robinson, Patrick O'Neil and John Maloney of the 52nd and Private Thomas Price of the 43rd were found guilty of desertion. Nine others from other divisions were also tried and found guilty. Costello (*Costello, the True Story of a Peninsular War Rifleman*, Eileen Hathaway, Swanage, 1997), records that two deserters were pardoned before the execution, one being 'Hodgson of the 95th . . . The other was a corporal of the 52nd Regiment, called Cummins.'

30th July 1811
    The men were ordered on no account to cut olive or other valuable fruit trees, the three soldiers who were found guilty of stealing honey, are to have their wine allowance stopped and it gave [*sic*] to the women of the regiment until the 14th of August, and at all times when wine or spirit is deducted as a punishment from the men, the women are to have it divided equally among them.

Lieutenant William Swabey of the Royal Artillery understandably took matters into his own hands on one occasion, but his methods cannot be condoned.

7 December 1812
    I caught an infamous Portuguese bullock driver, the lowest coward perhaps in creation, beating with a stick an unfortunate wounded soldier who had spilt his blood for the villain at Burgos, because he was too helpless to dismount from the car to walk up the hill. I actually beat him till I could not stand over him.

Henry Johnson also recalled a strange request from a local official to carry out a punishment for them.

Fuente Guinaldo 11 May 1812
    The commanding officer of the horse artillery was yesterday paid a visit by the padrone [local leader] of Puebla d'Azava, who after the usual compliments, proceeded to state that two of his villagers having taken a notorious bandit the night before, he requested the loan of two of the guard for half an hour merely to march him about half a mile from the town and there shoot him, adding that sending him to the justices was no good as he would certainly escape.
    NB [he] was much astonished at the refusal.

Of course, officers could also fall out amongst themselves, resulting in a challenge and a duel. They were strictly prohibited from doing so, but that did not stop them. Lieutenant George Woodberry recorded one major incident and how it was finally dealt with 'in house'.

Olite, Sunday 11 July
    Captain Burke and Lieutenant Dolbel have a dispute of honour, which must be settled in some way, in a few days, I shall, therefore, forebear from saying more upon it now . . . .

Olite, Monday 12 July

I have just returned from Major Hughes', where the officers of the regiment had assembled, by order, to investigate the dispute between Captain Burke and Mr Dolbel; when after deliberately and maturely weighing the whole affair, came to the unanimous resolution, that they ought to be requested to resign immediately. But Major Hughes recommended a milder course and proposed that they should be reprimanded in the most strongest manner, before the officers of the regiment, which was accordingly done, by both being instantly called into the meeting. Major Hughes told them of the sentiments of the officers, and though want of courage is not proved against either, yet the language made use of by both, was such, which ought to have gentlemen to have had immediate recourse to arms and that death alone ought to have settled it between them, and that it ought never to have been referred to him. However, as commanding officer, he now strictly forbids them proceeding to any but conciliatory arrangements; they immediately begged each other's pardon. Their dispute began a few days ago: Burke told Dolbel he was the most quarrelsome fellow in the regiment, and if he said anything to him, he would cut him down; this was in front of the squadron. Dolbel, told Burke in answer, to his remarks of being the most quarrelsome, that he Burke was a dammed liar. These proud men spoke first of fight, but they soon subsided, and they wished that the affair was forgotten when the officer corps seized on it.

Band Master John Westcott recorded a number of rules put into place by General Orders to the Army in an attempt to control the worst abuses.

22 July 1811

The Commander in Chief has been in the constant habit of allowing soldiers who make any capture from the enemy to receive the value of their capture, but he has received several reports from the General officers, that this indulgence has had the effect of inducing some of the soldiers to look for and secure captures rather than to engage and destroy the enemy, and he is induced therefore to give the following orders. All horses &c captured from the enemy not purchased by the commissary must be sold by public auction at headquarters or such other place as the commander of the forces may select, as that in which it is most likely to bring the largest price, the value of any animal taken from the enemy, the contents of baggage, knapsacks, saddlebags, shall be divided amongst those present at the capture, whoever may be the individual who happens to make it any man or number of men who secure and bring in any number of prisoners or capture horses, shall not be allowed to share in this benefit unless he or they shall have been ordered by the officer under whose immediate command they are serving to secure the prisoners or horses captured. Any man who leaves his ranks in order to secure prisoners or horses or other articles captured without orders from their commanding officer must be brought before a court martial on the charge of disobedience of orders, when before the enemy. These orders must be read to every regiment in the army at two different parades and afterwards at the same periods with the Articles of War.

Westcott was clearly not in favour of this regulation.

If this were the rules of the French army there would not be such singular acts of individual bravery, but a British soldier were he to take a general from the enemy prisoner would be liable (according to the General Orders of the army) to be punished in the most ignominious manner, if he acted without orders.

Further orders were set in place regarding the women accompanying the regiments.

8 August 1811
... The general officer commanding the division desires the women of the division, may not be allowed to go before the column on a march and enter the villages, the Provost Marshal has received the general's directions to proceed before the column and punish women he may find disobeying the above order. . . . This order was certainly necessary for the women were fully as much given to plunder as any men in the army and had always a better opportunity as they could absent themselves at any time from their regiments without being missed while the men could on no account leave their camp quarters without leave from their commanding officer.

Another order issued on 23 August 1811 insisted that:

As there seems no other mode of keeping the soldiers from straggling from the camp, the commanding officer is sorry to be under the necessity of ordering that the rolls of each regiment of the brigade be called every half hour, till eight o'clock at night, the officers of companies attending, and that the names of all absentees be reported by the commanding officers of regiments, to the commanding officer, of the brigade.

He also recorded that General Stopford called all of the non-commissioned officers of the regiment together on 15 September 1811.

> The whole of the non-commissioned officers of the regiments present, paraded before Major General Stopford, who spoke a considerable time to them, particularly desiring of them never to strike or use any improper language to any soldiers whatever, as there was other methods to be taken if a soldier committed a fault. He also told them that if a man had the spirit of a soldier, he could not stand to be insulted in such a degrading manner, and therefore he requested that no such unsoldier-like customs would ever appear in the brigade he had the honour to command. What occasioned the general speaking to the non-commissioned officer in this manner I can't say, unless he thought they might copy it from some of the Portuguese regiments, who still continued that degrading custom. I never heard of the custom of striking being in any British regiment in Portugal, a non-commissioned officer would be reduced for the like in the Cameronians.

General Sir Thomas Graham also ordered strict obedience to his restrictions.

> 1 October 1811
> This is a season when if protected, the poor peasants may provide subsistence for their families by the produce of the vintage, and of the harvest of the Indian corn, millet, and potatoes. Let it not be said that His Majesty's soldiers are plundering those whose distresses the liberality of his subjects has been endeavouring to relieve, as at all times, it is better to prevent, than to punish excesses. Lieutenant General Graham, recommends that every precautionary measure may be resorted to, rolls must be called frequently and sentries must be posted in such numbers as may be necessary, and limits must be set beyond which no soldiers is to go from his cantonments, besides the corporal punishment that the case may require, all soldiers found committing depredations of any kind shall be deprived of the allowance of wine or spirit, which the soldiers of the army receive by indulgence, but which forms no part of the regulation rations. Brigade orders during the time the brigade is in cantonments the whole allowance of spirit is to be issued to the men at once. The soldiers detected this day by Major General Stopford in the act of plundering, must not receive their allowance of wine or spirit which however will be drawn and distributed amongst the good men of the respective companies.

However, it is at best doubtful how well all of these orders were obeyed and discipline was maintained. Colonel Andrew Barnard recorded in a letter from Mont Marsan dated as late as 2 March 1814.

> William Napier, the 43rd his regiment being absent for its clothing followed the division in rear but being unattached he took up his quarters on the night of the 24th at a village at a short distance from the army but unoccupied by any other officer. At night a crowd of plunderers, British and Portuguese, attacked the houses and were committing outrages of every description. Napier went to the [mayor?] collected a set of the peasants armed and attacked the robbers, killed two and two prisoners, one a Portuguese escaped through the roof of the prison but the other a British soldier (31st Foot) was hung the next day by order of Lord Wellington. This circumstance had a great effect on the neighbourhood where it took place. It showed the people that we were in earnest in our propositions of kind treatment and that none were guilty of bad conduct but when out of sight of their officers.

Pride and a maintenance of honour were paramount to Spanish men. They always carried a stiletto knife and were not afraid to use it if they felt their honour being questioned. Many British soldiers suffered stabbings because they had offended a Spaniard and as these were seen as 'honour killings', little was done by the Spanish authorities to bring the perpetrators to justice. Lieutenant George Woodberry's account of the murder of a hussar is very typical.

> Olite, Friday 9 July.
> It is with extreme sorrow I have to notice a most daring outrage, and murder, committed near the south gate, last night on a private of the 15th Hussars, he was found with his brains knocked out, and his mouth stuffed full of rags, which I presume were put in to stifle his voice. A few days back, two men of the town were stabbed, but by their own townsmen. These were the occasion of jealousy. One died after a few hours afterwards, but no enquiry was made after the murderer.

Discipline often broke down in the aftermath of sieges and on retreats and these have been dealt with under their respective chapters. However, one other infamous occasion where the troops became uncontrollable because of plunder was immediately following the defeat of the French army at Vitoria, when the troops discovered a huge park of abandoned vehicles full of all manner of riches. Lieutenant George Barlow of the 52nd Foot described the scene.

174   Marching, Fighting, Dying

> Camp in sight of Pamplona, 24 June 1813
> Words cannot paint the scene of confusion which pervaded the roads leading from the field of battle. Had there been permission or time, I could have furnished myself with a complete fit out for a campaign. Here lay a broken-down waggon stocked with claret and champaign [sic], but which as officers we could not touch, being moreover ordered to prevent the soldiery from doing the same. In another were hams, tongues, plenty of bread flower [sic] and other most tantalizing objects to hungry soldiers who had fasted nearly a whole day. Portmanteau's full of linen clothes, shoes, casks full of capital brandy, kicking about in all directions and not a few full of money, which the women and followers of the army plundered. Flocks of sheep & numbers of horses and mules were seen to invite a pillagers hand, whilst lots of books & papers excited the attention of the curious and bestrewed our route in all directions. It is inconceivable the quantity of papers be-spread over the face of the country, such indefatigable scribblers are the French. Doubtless many a cheating commissary or swindling paymaster blesses the result of the 21st of June, which has buried in oblivion all traces of his former rogueries. His lordship, without allowing the fugitives a moment's breath, pursued them in the direction of this city, before which I am now writing.

Whilst his regiment did not halt and dissolve into a plundering rabble, others certainly did. Lieutenant Charles Crowe of the 27th Foot recorded that he saw pillaging and was not personally above taking some small advantage.

> 22 June 1813.
> We noticed the soldiers busily employed in examining their various booty. One man came to us and offered a silver fork and spoon for a dollar which was then equal to six [shillings] and six pence. I bought them and still preserve them as mementos of the day and scene.
> A soldier of the 5th company requested his captain, Frank Bignall to accept a heavy tea caddy. Frank instantly broke it open by aid of the soldiers' bayonet and to the astonishment of both, found it filled with doubloons, at that time worth £3/12s/0d each.[3] Frank frankly gave the money to the soldier, retaining the caddy as the original present. It was estimated that full three thousand dollars, besides plate, regimentals,

---

3. Each coin was worth the equivalent of about £190 today.

swords, fowling pieces etc etc were secured by our regiment alone,[4] whatever fell to others of the brigade.

There was an official auction or 'Cant'[5] which he goes on to describe.

> A Cant, or auction of French baggage was proclaimed and proved to be a most amusing and extraordinary scene. I really think it would have defied even Hogarth's graphical pencil. The Provost Marshal proved he was quite an adept as auctioneer and made very appropriate remarks on Marshal Soult's stock of wigs. There was a scratch, or everyday wig, a court wig, a Brutus, and I know not what. But many a broad joke was cracked when the Marshal's black velvet breeches were exhibited, which were purchased by a drum major. My fifer's wife purchased Madame Soult's satin slippers, no doubt but that this worthless woman made a good market of these trophies in her marauding excursions.
>
> I had the proud satisfaction of smoking one of Marshal Soult's cigars,[6] but it was only the refuse of his baggage sent to a Cant, for the pages of history prove that it had been overhauled . . .

Lieutenant George Woodberry of the 18th Hussars was horrified to record that the Duke of Wellington had named his regiment as the worst offenders for plundering and had threatened to send them all home in disgrace.

> Villava Atarrabia left of Pamplona, Saturday 26 June 1813
>
> Colonel Grant ordered the officers of the 18th Hussars before him today, and informed us he has Lord Wellington's authority to inform us that his lordship was very much displeased with the insubordination of the regiment, particularly of the conduct of the men in Vitoria on the 21st instant, numbers of them he saw plundering on the streets, he was likewise very much displeased with several of our officers who were there plundering, instead of being in the field. And to finish he had to inform us that his lordship was determined if he heard any complaint against the regiment, he would immediately dismount us, and march the

---

4. The silver gilt stand which forms the base of the centrepiece of the dinner table of the officers' mess was apparently looted from King Joseph's baggage.
5. Cant – probably from the old French 'encant' or auction, denoted a sale of officer's goods after they were killed, to raise funds for dependants.
6. This presumably was the word around camp, but Marshal Soult and his wife were not in Spain at this period.

regiment to the nearest sea port town, and embark us for England, and at the same time send the Commander in Chief (the Duke of York) remarks on the subject. O God has it come to this! I want language to express the grief I feel on this occasion, to think I should have come out with a regiment who have contrary to all expectations, acted so differently.

The incident caused the internal discipline of the regimental officers' mess to collapse for a significant period. Woodberry, however, was happy to record that he was innocent of any charge.

Olite, Wednesday 14 July 1813
Good God, how the regiment has fallen off since then, now half the officers are implicated, so I was informed last night, in an unfortunate affair respecting the plunder and remaining in the town of Vitoria, and will be obliged to exchange, resign, or perhaps [before] either can be done, they may be cashiered. Their names are Major Hughes, Captain Bolton, and Burke, Lieutenant Conolly and Dolbel, Adjutant Waldie; these are the men, Lord Wellington has on his blacklist. The whole may not suffer, but I think it likely the whole may leave. That brute of a fellow Dolbel, has charges against Bolton and Burke, which would supersede them, no one yet knows how he will act. The regiment it is plainly to be seen has gone to the devil; God send, I was out of it, but I must now stop and see the end of it. I feel more than happy when I think of that day, and of my not going into town, during the plundering.

His commanding officer, Henry Murray wrote privately to his wife, confirming the problem with his men and made an astonishing attack on one of his captains.

25 April 1814
. . . the men behave past endurance ill . . . . The officers are idle with some few exceptions & the men the worst in the army. I do not dislike Captain Grant, he is either stark staring mad, or might as well be so, he is forever a paroxysm of rage or good humour, invectives or smiles he is either excessively angry or excessively pleased, he has much volubility, some cleverness & the loudest voice that ever shook a cathedral or hailed a prize.

Some senior officers, such as Colonel George Bingham, chose to turn a blind eye, however.

Camp near Pamplona 25 June 1813
   The quartermaster of the 53rd . . . contrived to stow away fifteen hundred dollars in it and came to me: I advised him to keep his own counsel, so he saved the whole.

As has been seen, indiscipline was frequent and the staple punishment was invariably the lash. Following the war, attitudes towards flogging turned very much against it and later memoirs capture this mood, with frequent demands for an end to the practice. What is less clear, is that there was any sizeable groundswell of opinion against the lash during the actual campaigns. Clearly some officers evince a clear unease over the use of flogging, but there is no strong evidence for a clear and outright repugnance for the practice at the time. What is more obvious, is a consistent downgrading of offences, with regiments often mitigating the charges, such as desertion, down to absence from duty, even before a trial was deemed necessary and therefore allowing the regiment to deal with their own, without it appearing on official returns and hence making the regiments look much better disciplined than their true record would indicate.

Chapter 12

The Enemy

British attitudes towards the French were complex. The French Army had gained a fearsome reputation after its resounding successes against Austria, Prussia and Russia between 1805 and 1807. The British Army had in stark contrast seen little success on the continent of Europe, although the army had gained great success in the West Indies and many other parts of the world, wherever in fact the Royal Navy – which had achieved global ascendancy of the seas after 1805 – could actively support them. However, many of the failures on the continent were largely due to the small size of their army against the great masses available to the Emperor Napoleon, forcing them to rely on allies who regularly failed to stand for long against the French. On the few occasions where British and French forces met on relatively even terms, however, the British were most often the victor and therefore the soldiers arrived in Portugal, confident of success against equal numbers. The fact that France had vastly superior forces in the peninsula was countered by the belief that the Spanish armies which had risen against the invasion of their country would even up the odds. But it has already been seen that these initial hopes were soon dashed when they first encountered Portuguese troops and further experience showed the inadequacy of the Spanish troops, despite their initial good showing, indeed flattering to deceive.

As to the French themselves, they were seen by the British as very much the vanguard of the Revolution and their extremely harsh treatment of the Portuguese people simply confirmed their view of them as little more than irreligious murderers and vandals simply despoiling the country for their own gain. The horrors the British soldiers witnessed which had been perpetrated by the French soldiery on the Portuguese people shocked and disgusted them. Yet the relationship between the British and the French soldiery at all levels remained strangely aloof from these dreadful atrocities, both sides scrupulously caring for prisoners and the sick who chanced to fall into their hands, while they continued to perpetrate such despicable acts on Portuguese civilians at the same time. It was rather a strange attitude, of preserving professional courtesy towards each other, while everything else sank around them to the base level of almost a war of extermination. It will, however, become clear that the French attitudes towards

Portugal and Spain were also very different in reality, their treatment of much of Spain being very different indeed.

Initial reactions to the ravages enacted by the French in Portugal in 1808, 1809 and 1810 was complete shock: they appalled the British troops who witnessed them. Typical is this by Lieutenant Colonel George Bingham of the 53rd Foot at Coimbra on 28 May 1809.

> It is not possible to describe the horrors committed by the French during the four days the place was given up to pillage; the unfortunate inhabitants of this opulent town were left to the mercy of the most brutal soldiery in the world, the most wanton barbarities were committed. Women with infants at their breasts were shot in the streets in the open face of day . . .

Captain Henry Mellish of the 87th Foot wrote of the horrors of the French retreat two days before the Battle of Talavera. Like many others, he could not forgive the French brutality to their mules:

> Talavera de la Reyna 25 July 1809
>
> The horrors of the French retreat are not to be described. At every hundred yards dead men & horses, parties of sick remaining behind to surrender themselves being totally unable to proceed farther. Numbers of these unfortunate wretches murdered by the Portuguese, whose cruelty can scarcely be blamed when one reflects on what they have suffered at their hands. Having destroyed all their artillery & ammunition, the French proceeded with their baggage, plunder & musket ammunition on mules & horses. This however they were obliged to give up & to their eternal disgrace, when they found it necessary to destroy them, instead of killing them, they cut their ham strings & left them in that state. We put the poor animals out of their misery by shooting them . . .

Rumours of the terrible treatment of the Portuguese by the French as they advanced in 1810 was confirmed by the large number of refugees which Lieutenant Charles Madden of the 4th Dragoons saw fleeing before them.

> 7 August 1810
>
> The inhabitants continued to flock through this place from the part adjacent to the French, as they committed all kinds of depredations in the village they entered.

As the French then retreated from Portugal, having failed to breach the Lines of Torres Vedras, the British troops followed in their wake and were horrified at the terrible devastation they left behind them. Madden again recorded that:

> 16 November 1810
> Marched at 4 a.m. by Frarea [Feligueira?] through Sobral [de Monte Agraco] and were quartered in some quintas near a large town called Alenquer, which we found full of troops; this was an unusual long march, being nine leagues, with the roads very bad and constant torrents of rain; our move was in consequence of the French having fallen back. We could see near Sobral their camp, which they had left a few hours before, and their camps and positions on each side of the road as we marched along; the roads were offensive with the stench of dead horses and beasts of burden. I think on a moderate calculation we did not march 500 yards without seeing one lying on the road, and as they had mostly died when the French first marched towards Lisbon, which was near a month ago, they were quite putrid. We saw several dead bodies of the French lying in houses and on the road, who had been removed when sick, and died on the march. There were also two bodies of Portuguese, who had been murdered by the French and had lain on the road just as they fell. The houses the French occupied were left in a most filthy state.

Captain John Ewart of the 52nd Foot recorded another instance of French brutality to their horses.

> 20 March 1811
> Marched to near Ponte de Mucela, five leagues, bad road, passing by Foz de Arouce, where a sharp skirmish had taken place on the evening of the 18th instant, when the rearguard of the French were completely surprised by the Light Division, and, by a bridge blowing up sooner than was intended, above 100 of the French were drowned in attempting to ford the river, . . . The artillery on both sides had done much execution here, four men of Captain Douglas's Company 52nd being struck at once; great part of the road was strewed with dead horses, mules and donkeys, many of which had been hamstrung to prevent them being of service to us, and left in that terrible state by the French, who had also burnt every village near this . . .

Lieutenant Henry Dawson of the 52nd Foot was concerned for the welfare of the Portuguese people.

Martiago, 11 August 1811

The country people are extremely glad to [see] us. It is too evident how cruelly the French have treated them. Burnt every village, collected all the grain, compelled the inhabitants to thresh it by taking some of the principal people prisoners as hostage for its being done & levied contributions to a considerable amount.

Lieutenant George Brown was struck with how crowded Lisbon was and how expensive basic commodities had become:

Valle 14 December 1810

When we were in the lines I went down for a day to Lisbon, they are under no apprehension there for the French, but the town is very crowded, every house having two or three families in it. God knows what is to become of the unfortunate inhabitants if the business is protracted much longer, they are already in a most wretched condition, bread that formerly cost 3d now costs 1/- here.

We have not heard anything of the Militia since we have been here but they are round the enemy in every direction, in fact no one can account for them having subsisted so long.

Captain George Westcott of the 77th Foot was particularly horrified by the sacrilege.

20 July 1811

Golega is but a small town with very few inhabitants remaining in it. The regiment quartered in the chapel and other vacant houses, we were shown by the inhabitants the very coffins laying uncovered which the French took out of the graves in search of plunder, on their retreat from the lines of Torres Vedras. I never would have believed any civilised Europeans would have been guilty of such savage tricks, had I not have seen the graves open and the coffins laying out myself, I must say I never thought a great deal of them taking, through necessity the useless riches out of the Portuguese chapels which were lying for centuries of no use to mankind but to gaze at, but to open the graves, the savages in Africa or America, would scarcely be guilty of the like. Perhaps the Portuguese in some instances may have hid their riches in such places thinking the grave would be held inviolable, but they found to their grief, that the French army paid no respect to either the dead or the living, the French army must certainly have gained a vast deal of plunder in Portugal, for not a spot that could ever be thought of by man, but what they searched, the chapels and most of the houses of this town were in ruins, and nothing but misery, and sickness appeared in the few survivors of the inhabitants . . .

Captain John Ewart of the 52nd Foot almost felt sorry for the French as they retreated back into Spain, emaciated and drawn after their terrible experiences, while unconsciously congratulating himself on their own good fortune.

23 March 1811
A great many French prisoners passed us daily, mostly stragglers, badly clothed and seemingly worse fed. We now got rations of bread and meat regular.

Captain James Gubbins of the 13th Light Dragoons wrote of the French depredations and the terrible Spanish vengeance.

Machacon 2 leagues from Salamanca 28 May 1813
Rapine and cruelty to the poor Spaniards mask the steps of the French, but woe to the Frenchman who falls into their hands, they always strip the dying and the dead, but they have brought it upon themselves, the[y] slaughter the Spaniards in the most wanton manner.

The French treatment of much of Spain was, however, markedly different, as Major William Gomm of the 9th Foot realized.

Nave d'Haver 8 April 1811
They [the French] stormed like a hurricane through Portugal, but they are observing a different policy already with Spain. A proclamation was issued the moment they passed the frontier that no further outrages should be permitted . . . and the first, I dare say the only, offender was instantly punished with death, and left hanging upon the high road *pour encourager les autres.*

Indeed Edward Cocks of the 16th Light Dragoons understood that Spanish fraternization with the French had been so accepted that at Salamanca on 19 June 1812 that he wrote:

The French officers individually appear to have behaved well. They say 300 married here.

Lieutenant James Gairdner of the 95th Rifles thought that the inhabitants of Valladolid were very content under French rule.

> 30 July Valladolid
> The French having been here so long, the place is completely Frenchified and the inhabitants did not seem over glad to see the English. There are good shops & coffee houses here, the latter of course established by the French for I never saw any in the country before except at Badajoz which place also the French had possession of for a long time.

Indeed Major General Frederick Robinson agreed fully in a letter to his wife, believing that the Allies brought much greater destruction with them.

> Camp before San Sebastian 31 July 1813
> We paint the conduct of the French in this country in very strong and harsh colours, but be assured we injure the people much more than they do, and all in the name of friendship. The French demand heavy contributions which fall on the wealthier class only, but they punish plundering in the most severe manner except where it is intended as a punishment for fruitless resistance. Wherever we move devastation marks our steps. . . . The beauty and fertility of Gloucestershire is trifling compared to what the country for miles around this house was when we arrived. Where you have one apple tree here there is a hundred, and where you have one apple there is a thousand. Corn and vegetables were in greater abundance than I ever saw before, the former has been cut for the horses & mules of the army, and the latter has long ago been consumed in the camp kettles of the Portuguese. The face of the country is at this moment like a sandy desert, with the exception that the apple trees remain, deprived of half their branches.

This, however, was not always true of the French, especially when they required materials to construct a camp. Lieutenant Charles Madden of the 4th Dragoons saw this wanton destruction at first hand.

> 11 April 1811
> Marched at 11 a.m. near Albuera, a small village (three leagues). We found the village compleately [*sic*] destitute of inhabitants, and the houses nearly pulled to the ground, scarce a roof was left standing. Near the town was the remains of a large cavalry encampment of the French, which had been occupied the day before; the huts were small but built with a great deal of trouble and ingenuity.

184 Marching, Fighting, Dying

However, Lieutenant Colonel Henry Murray of the 18th Hussars makes quite an interesting comment with regard to how the Spanish upper classes heartily welcomed the French into their homes, while the Spanish peasantry were actively planning to massacre them all.

> Plasencia 24 July 1813
> 1,200 French prisoners marched in here yesterday, some of the rich people went out to meet the French officers & took them into their houses. But the guard was turned out in the night or the common people would not have left a Frenchman alive.

This war of extermination was designed to frighten and deter resistance, punishing harshly any resistance to their rule, while placid obedience was rewarded. Meanwhile the war they waged against an established European army, such as the British, was looked upon as completely different, each treating the other with respect, looking after the sick and wounded that were captured and treating their prisoners well. It was a gentlemanly war, conducted very much in the style of the wars of Marlborough nearly a century earlier, and this ease between two warring forces lying so close to each other, was often mentioned in letters home. Private Richard Smith of the 3rd Foot wrote of it in his imperfect English.

> January 1811
> We lye within a mile of the French but at moment we are respectable hear [sic] as you are there at home, for they never interrupt us nor we them. I believe the French very bad off for provisions, for I hear that they seldom get any bread, but are obliged to get Indian corn and boile it and beat it between tow [sic] stones and so they gets every sort of corn or rubbidge and make burgue [burgoo] with it, and that is the only way they have. I believe they are very short of meat and I hear they are obliged to kill their horses for their men to heat [sic] and indeed I hear that they are very misrabell [sic] of everything and I really think, they often some thinks that they will give themselves up as prisoners of war and if they do not, we shall have a very sharp battall sum wuerr [sic] about Abrantes in the course of 3 or 4 months, when the wether gets so that men can lye out of doors.

Ensign Robert Garrett of the 2nd Foot also spoke of this ease between them and their foe.

> Camp between Rueda and Tor de Sillas 9 July 1812
> When our light companies were down at the river our people & the men of the advanced posts of the French used to get water at the same

time out of the Douro & while filling their canteens & kettles used to talk to one another.

Discourse between British and French officers at the picquet line was a regular feature of this war although the Duke of Wellington actively sought to discourage it. Ensign Orlando Bridgeman of the 1st Foot Guards mentioned this happening during the siege of Cadiz, although the Spaniards were very unhappy about it.

> 12 June 1812
> Our out picquet which mounts every night at six o'clock at a bridge called the Suazo is close to the French & our sentries & theirs are divided by a very narrow river, but they never hurt one another & at night the officer walks about without the least fear. Of a clear night it is the custom for the French & English officers to pull off their hats to one another, they used to talk, but the Spaniards are so jealous that they spoke to the general about it & we have received an order not to do it in future.

Ensign John Mills of the Coldstream Guards mentions a pleasant conversation whilst burying the dead after the Battle of Fuentes de Oñoro.

> Fuentes de Onoro 8 May 1811
> I had some conversation yesterday with some French officers who came out to me as I was employed in burying the dead. They were extremely polite, talked much of their own cavalry and lamented their being obliged to leave Salamanca, where they said the women were so beautiful.

Lieutenant George Barlow of the 52nd Foot wrote regarding how close the enemy camp was and how easy it would be to upset them with a few shots, but of course the point was that they wouldn't dream of doing so,

> Vera, 16 July 1813
> We are encamped upon the side of some very steep hills, at the bottom of which runs a steep ravine, whilst opposite rises a corresponding chain of heights occupied by the French troops within half cannon shot of our position, so near that we could upset their dinners, or spoil their slumbers with a few shots whenever we please.

He wrote again to describe how close they were, but living in perfect harmony, despite the best efforts of the Spanish.

186   *Marching, Fighting, Dying*

> Undated [supposed August]
> Our present state of inactivity however offers little to fill up the remainder of this sheet, and I may therefore be pardoned for mounting afresh my favoured hobby horse, within cannon shot of the formidable pass of Vera and staring Messieurs les Francois in the face, whose advanced sentries and our own are posted within two hundred yards of each other, along a little valley through which runs the stream of the Bidassoa and dividing the ridge of our position from that on which theirs is situated. Every drum and trumpet may be distinguished from either camp, and should the foe possess a spy glass, he may perceive me in the door of the tent sitting down to the table just as clearly as I have frequently observed them cooking, washing or employed in their various occupations. The greatest politeness is maintained on both sides, although the Spaniards & Longa's guerrillas are frequently apt to break through the laws of this belligerent etiquette and which specimen of ill breeding the French resent against *them* alone by the exchange of partial shots.

Captain Edward Cocks had a conversation with a French officer, confident he would not be fired on.

> 9 July 1810
> We are on very good terms with the French. The night before they attacked us at Gallegos I had a long conversation with a French officer, a little brook only divided us. Both parties made a point of never firing on single officers in this way without calling to them first.

Lieutenant William Bragge of the 3rd Dragoons recorded that the French were perfectly happy for the British to water their horses and even bathe in the stream that divided them in full trust.

> Pollos 18 July 1812
> The French are very civil and allow us to water horses and bathe in the river; the latter experiment I have not tried although hundreds do every day.

Lieutenant James Gairdner of the 95th Rifles mentions the unexpected hospitality of the French.

> 15 December 1813
> One of the enemy's sentries opposite my picquet deserted from his post today about 3 o'clock to the picquet on my right. While I was at my

dinner a man came up & told me that the officer of the French picquet wanted to speak to me, I accordingly went down & passed the abattis. Two officers of the 55th [French] Regiment came to meet me, we shook hands very cordially & when I asked them if they wanted anything, they produced a keg of brandy & said they only came to drink my health & chat a little, which after doing we parted, they were very civil.

A few days later he mentions the ease with which he passed over correspondence to a captured officer.

18 December 1813
Rainy night, fine day, I went in to the French picquet today to take a letter for the officer of ours [2nd Lieutenant James Church] who was taken on the 10th.

Private John Insley of the Royal Dragoons was struck by a kind gesture of the French.

26 December 1810
A remarkable instance of good nature, in one of our men losing his cloak, which was found by the enemy and returned back to the owner.

Lieutenant George Woodberry of the 18th Hussars recorded an occasion of an officer being granted parole to return to his friends, on the understanding that he did not serve with the army until formally exchanged.

Pedrosa del Rey, Thursday 3 June 1813
The enemy left this place last night, and left Captain Lloyd of the 10th Hussars, who is severely wounded on his parole of honour, they likewise left my old bat man, Morris, who was taken prisoner and wounded yesterday.

Two months later he wrote of an incident that summed up the relations between the French and British troops perfectly.

Battle before Pamplona, Thursday 29 July 1813
Last evening I saw a sight that pleased me much, while with the regiment was on our position, we saw in front of us, near the rivulet, some of the 95th Riflemen, about a dozen, skirmishing with the enemy, they were at it till near dusk, when they left off. Three of the Frenchmen advanced, and next several of the 95th, each without arms, had entered

into a conversation, shook hands, and after a short time withdrew to their post; where they are today, looking at each other, but not fighting.

Charles Madden of the 4th Dragoons recorded the outcome of a parley with two French officers.

> 26 March 1811
> ... On their near approach I took up another position about an equal distance from them, and drew my sword, on seeing which one of them sounded a trumpet which proved them a flag of truce. I rode up to the officer, who very civilly saluted me and informed me he came with a letter for General Beresford. As he spoke Spanish very well, and Portuguese tolerably, we were able to keep up a pretty good conversation. He informed me he came to inquire after his brother, who was colonel of the same regiment (the 26th Dragoons) and was seen to fall off his horse in a charge. On our coming towards the place where the charge was made the trumpeter pointed the place out, and shortly after we discovered a body lying quite naked on its face, which they both recognised to be he. The colonel's brother got off his horse and wept over the body for a considerable time. As it would be improper to allow the flag of truce to approach our lines, so as to be able to make any observations, I requested them to halt till I went forward with information of their being on hand, which I brought to General Cole, commanding in Campo Maior, on which two of his staff accompanied me back again. As I understood my regiment had marched, I took off my hat to wish the French officer good day, on which he came up to me, and giving his hand, requested me if by any chance I became a prisoner in General Mortier's Army, I should consider I had a friend in the Lieutenant Colonel of the 26th Dragoons.

By early 1814, this cordial relationship has grown so well that George Woodberry felt very comfortable placing an order with the French. Indeed he became very jealous of the French officer!

> Piquet at Bonloc, Sunday, January 23
> This evening I sent a peasant to the picquet line of the enemy cavalry, to ask the officer to send me some good wine which was for sale in the village: he did and also refused the money that the peasant offered to pay him. French officers take what they please without a thought; I find this very evil is even allowed in their own country, but I would like Lord Wellington to allow us to do the same.

French prisoners were treated with humanity but Charles Crowe was appalled by the state the prisoners left the church where they had been held temporarily.

> 10 November 1813
> The French prisoners were marched off this morning by an officer of the Quarter Master General's Staff. The church is opened for ventilation; and unfortunately the wind is in the south and blows the stench up to my quarters, rendering my room insufferable. I was compelled to walk out for fresh air; curiosity induced me to go up to the church door, in spite of my olfactory nerves; the floor was really ankle deep with filth! I never witnessed such a sight and the street on the south side of the church was like an open sewer!! I never saw such an accumulation of filth!! I was obliged to wander beyond the bridge to relieve my miserable head.

After the dreadful carnage at the storming of Badajoz, the French prisoners were protected and well looked after, unlike the civilian population. When the prisoners, including the governor General de Division Armand Philippon arrived at Lisbon castle, they were feted by the British officers. Band Master John Westcott was there with his regiment as the garrison. He recorded their treatment in his diary.

> 13 April 1812 – General Philippon the late French governor of Badajoz, three colonels, and two aide-de-camps, were escorted by a party of the Third Portuguese Light Dragoons to an inn, in the city.

> 14 April – One sergeant, and twenty-one ranks and file, of the Cameronians, went to assist the police of the city, in escorting the French governor and staff, through the city up to the castle. As they rode through the city General Philippon was in front upon a fine horse highly caparisoned with an aide-de camp, on each side of him mounted the other French officers, followed mounted also, upon fine horses. They had a deal of baggage which their servants carried, behind them, in the centre of the guard the crowd of people were very great in all the streets they passed through, but particularly at the Rossio Square shouting and abusing the French general has [sic] he passed, but notwithstanding the immense multitude that assembled in this square, he betrayed no symptoms of fear, but rather looked down upon the crowd, with an air of disdain. . . . When they arrived at the castle, they sold all their horses to the English officers, three of the Cameronian officers, who knew the French language superintended in their affairs and paid them every respect and attention, which were due to their rank, and which certainly

ought to be the duty of every soldier to a brave prisoner. Most of the French officers taken at Badajoz and Rodrigo were in this castle . . .

17 April – General Philippon, the commissary general, and the principal French officers taken at Ciudad Rodrigo and Badajoz dined with the officers of the Cameronians at the mess room in the castle, the night was spent with the greatest agreeableness and very convivial until a late hour. The most soldier-like hospitality were shown them by the Cameronians, on every occasion during their stay in Lisbon which General Philippon and the rest of the French officers, acknowledged in the most polite manner on leaving the Cameronians in the castle.

19 April – General Philippon and forty of the principal French officers left the castle to embark for England they were escorted to the Commercial Square where they embarked, by one ensign two sergeants, and forty rank & file of the Cameronians, their baggage were carried by the soldiers of the Cameronians, to the boats, another division of about fourteen hundred French prisoners, landed at the Commercial Square, having come down the Tagus, from Abrantes.

21 April – Another division of the French officers were escorted by the Cameronians from the castle to the boats at the steps. To see our officers and the French shaking hands on parting, would occasion an idea that those brave men could never oppose each other, but for the ambition of a few.

British prisoners of war also fared well. Major Thomas Brotherton of the 14th Light Dragoons was captured in 1813 and was still able to write home to confirm that he was in good health.

25 December 1813
My dearest Elizabeth,
I could not before tell you of my misfortune, I was wounded & taken. I remain a prisoner, unfortunate indeed! Address your letters through the Agents. Adieu dear love. Yours TW Brotherton, I have not time to say more.

Tarbes South of France, 29 December
My dearest love,
My exchange has not taken place & I am sent into the interior of France, but I am well & still entertain hopes of seeing you soon.

My wounds, which were slight are nearly well and I have been well treated. I trust you are well, yours TW Brotherton

Obviously, not every officer or indeed soldier was cared for so well as these staff officers, but it shows that the chivalric code was still very much in action. A defeated enemy was to be well treated at all times. Another guarantee of good treatment was also very evident at this time; this was membership of the international brotherhood of Freemasons. Many officers and even some rankers belonged to this organization, indeed many regiments abroad established branches. Evidence of this does appear relatively often in soldier's accounts and this account by Major William Brooke of the 48th Foot who was captured during the Battle of Albuera provides a perfect example.

15 July 1811

We had been but a few days in the Inquisition Prison when the Grand Master of the French Freemasons Lodge discovered that I and Captain Allman were brother masons. He waited on me and told me that both their Lodge room and his own private quarters were in this same vast building where we were confined . . . From this dreary place the Grand Master took me to his own quarters on the first floor of the front of the prison. They were most elegantly furnished and he showed me many pictures of immense value. He introduced me to his lady and her sister, who gave me cake, wine, and French liqueur. He requested his wife to bring me half a dozen of his own shirts and as many pairs of stockings, which he wished to give me as a brother mason. I refused them with thanks, but accepted half a dozen bottles of choice wine, which he sent to the room of our confinement. A few days later he called, in company with a deputation from his lodge, on Captain Allman and myself, to ask whether they could serve us in any way; he assured us that even if we wanted a thousand dollars the masons could get it for us. Being already provided with money, we did not accept this kind offer. But next morning we wrote a polite note to thank the Master and Lodge for their attention to our welfare, and requested it might be read to the Lodge at its first meeting. We said that we should not fail to represent their conduct to our brethren in England. Captain Allman delivered this note in person to the Grand Master.

It is clear that the French and the British soldiery of all ranks understood that they were all professional soldiers, who fought hard for their cause, but beyond the fighting there was no need to be constantly at each other's throats. Parleys were regularly practised, allowing the wounded to be evacuated to be cared for and the dead to be buried. *La Petite Guerre* (Small War) was left to the Portuguese and Spanish guerrillas, who were vehemently detested by the French and a bitter war without mercy was waged alongside the gentlemanly war with the British. In this war, sentries patrolled without fear of having their throats cut and attacks were announced minutes before they were launched, allowing the picquets to retire to the main body. The loss of individual lives in such brutal warfare was seen as pointless in the grand scheme of things, far too many would die of wounds on the battlefield and fevers off it to make such '*petite guerre*' irrelevant. War on the grand scale was still a gentlemanly pursuit.

Chapter 13

Girls, Women and Nuns

One eternal fascination for young servicemen in any age has always been the excitement and curiosity engendered by foreign women. It is clear that during periods when cantoned in towns or villages for any appreciable length of time that there would be increased fraternization between the soldiers and local women, some so young that we would now class them as teenage children, although in Spain at this time it was quite normal for girls to be married off as young as 14 years old. Despite strict controls being maintained by Spanish fathers on their eligible daughters and jealous husbands closely controlling their wives, opportunities did arise for liaisons and it would appear that both sexes were willing to ignore the social conventions. Some officers prudishly criticised the vulgarity of the Spanish women and unfavourably compared them with the women at home, but was this said more for the home audience than truthfully? There is certainly some hint of this. Ensign Orlando Bridgeman of the 1st Foot Guards claims to be not too fussed, but his civilian brother then touring the peninsula thought very differently.

> 12 June 1812
> I cannot say I like the Spaniards in general, the women are very nearly pretty well vulgar looking, the best of them looking not too well, as an English ladies maid, their manners *extremely* forward & disgusting, & few good figures, but Charles swears by them, he is in love, but certainly his taste is good.

Lieutenant Hugh Mallett of the Royal Horse Artillery found the genteel accomplishments of the ladies in his billet a very pleasant distraction despite the fact that it made him melancholy.

> Lisbon 26 August 1810
> . . . I have drunk tea twice with them, & find it so agreeable a way of passing an evening, that I shall invite myself there very frequently: what makes it more pleasant to me is that one of the family, (a sister of the lady of the house) speaks English tolerably well, & also plays on the piano forte, she has many English tunes & country dances in her

collection, and when I sit listening to her, I almost forget where I am, it reminds me so strongly of days that are passed: nothing brings to our recollection more forcibly scenes of former happiness than hearing tunes played which we have once been accustomed to hear. This young lady is about 20 & though she has no pretensions to beauty, yet she is very good natured and agreeable . . .

General Sir Thomas Picton wrote of his delight with the beautiful Spanish women.

20 April 1814

The people are particularly civil and obliging to us, and the ladies, who are particularly fascinating and beautiful, manifest by no means an indifferent feeling towards '*Los trepas Inglesias*' [the tall English]. For myself, I am lodged comfortably, and very respectably quartered with a widow, who prides herself in the enviable possession of a beautiful daughter, Maria Antonia Pi'ol, a perfect Venus de Medici, with the advantage of a pair of most languishing dark eyes, and jet black hair, equal in profusion to that of the celebrated 'Eve', in the Palais Pitti gallery at Florence. Heigh-ho! I almost regret having seen her; being already [married] I know not how to describe the sensation.

A month later, back in Britain, he compared British women unfavourably in some respects, but ultimately preferred them.

21 May 1814

The women do not walk so well as the Spanish women, nor, *perhaps*, so well as the French; nor are their feet so small as those of the former: nor are they, in most instances, so neatly 'calzadas' . It is true, that the Spanish style of walking, in some degree, approaches to a 'demarche flére', as the French would say; but still it shows off the figure of a fine woman to advantage, and which is certainly to be admired in preference to the French *petit pas* quick march. I wish herein, however, to make no allusion whatever to our ladies who have received an education.

I anticipated to have seen every countenance insipid, or difficult in expression, after the 'piercing black eyes' I had been accustomed to sigh to; but the contrary was the case; every woman, although, in fact, but of the middling class, I thought well-looking. The ruddy complexions and blue eyes of the fairest 'Catalanas', I now perceived, fell far short of the delicate complexions and soft winning blue eyes of my fair countrywomen. They appear coarse in comparison, and the same may be said of the 'Viscaynas'; another circumstance also forcibly struck me, the fine, delicate, and *truly effeminate* soft tone of the voice in both old and young, while I found them, in comparison, taller than the 'Espanolas'.

The soldiers soon had eyes on the women, but also quickly became aware of the dangers, Cornet Charles Madden of the 4th Dragoons was typical.

28 April 1809
Rode into Lisbon; . . . the women in general walk with a hood drawn over the head which covers the face as much as a bonnet. If two or three of the family walk out, they always walk one before the other, with a string of servants more or less according to their quality. This is principally the policy of the men, who are very jealous of the women, and when married have always a spy on their wives.

Madden also noted some significant differences with Spanish women.

11 September 1809
Marched to Badajoz, a frontier town of Spain, the women dress mostly in dark silk and satins (I mean the higher class) with a great deal of silk lace; being constantly braced up from their infancy they have generally very fine figures. They have generally a shawl or lace over their heads. They have much advantage of the Portuguese women.

Captain James Gubbins of the 13th Light Dragoons was also wary of these 'Sirens'.

Ribera eight leagues from Merida 19 April 1812
The Spaniards are a fine race of people in general, beautifully made, muscular, with small ankles hands and feet and some of the women are beautiful, there is one of the daughters of Don Ignacio, in whose house I am, quite beautiful with a fair complexion and such eyes that one may say with the song '*from the glance of her eye, shun danger and fly for fatal the glance* &c'.

George Woodberry of the 18th Hussars regularly waxed lyrically over his love for his Amelia in Britain, but also constantly wrote notes on his observations of the Portuguese and Spanish ladies.

Luz, Tuesday 30 March 1813
The women wear a kind of boot made very like our hussar boots, these are usually worn by those who have thick legs.

Ibeisua, near Pamplona, Sunday 8 August 1813

The Spanish women carry everything on their heads; I met one just now carrying a bucket of water. I attempted to lift it, and was much surprised to the weight, but she instantly put it on her head again and walked off, as if she had only a light head dress on.

It soon became clear, however, that he was becoming more enamoured with these women.

Olite, Tuesday 17 August 1813

The little doctor called, Pulsford and I had another visit from my female acquaintances, six of them, the doctor played the flute, and we danced. The doctor . . . was drunk, and created much mirth, the ladies got him on the ground, and nearly tickled him to death, the little man had a completely black face and I was obliged to drive them away from him. Spanish ladies have a charm that is dangerous even to describe: as a young Englishman, gracious and polite, full of chivalric considerations, I am wary from the memory of a friend that has since left the country, that he must close his heart against these beautiful repositories of his first oaths, with their perfect oval faces, beautiful light brown hair, big black eyes, mouths full of grace and modest attitudes, with simple clothes that often remind us of the sweet simplicity of Greek beauty, an outfit full of sensitivity and vivacity . . .

Soon he found the constant attention and jealousies of his women very trying indeed and refused to become romantically attached to them.

Olite, Saturday 21 August. Hang the women, they plague me to death, the weather is so excessively hot, I am unable to ride out, and have to stay at home and be plagued by two nice girls, one telling me of my faults, the other accusing me of falseness, '*Voodvurry mucha falsa*'. I find they are in love, but it will not do, I say no, no and I see no right way.

His constant need for female companionship continued into France.

Hasparren, Monday, 17 January 1814

I was at the town of Hasparren, to visit many of our dancers [from last night], with Hesse. We found that one of the most beautiful was the servant of an old chap who appeared to be little charmed by our presence. Two others were serving in their shops; one of them gave us each a piece of sugar and she at the same time put one in her mouth. I think that it was a great honour, in the fashion of her country, but we could not help bursting out laughing.

However, his true attitude regarding these women is betrayed in a candid diary entry.

> La Bastide Clairence, Sunday, 13 February 1814
> I've been at the house at the outposts and I saw the beautiful Maria, who seemed very sad and very abandoned. She asked if she could come with me and follow me during the campaign but I replied 'Marry me? No, Maria. With you I want fun and to play, I really want to embrace you, but hang me, for a wife!'

Henry Murray of the 18th Hussars claimed to his wife that he had not seen any great beauties (he would say that, of course) and mentioned one who was particularly striking in other ways.

> Palencia 18 August
> On my duties I have not been struck with the beauties of the fair sex & the only one worthy of notice was a woman about 40 or upwards, whose hair stuck out like gorgons & really appeared never either to have been cut or combed since the day of her birth, I don't think I ever saw anything so terrific.

Lieutenant Henry Hough of the Royal Artillery recorded how readily they would get up a dance even after a long march.

> 1 August 1812
> In the evening we got the bands of the 2nd Regiment & 61st Regiment who were marching for the army & knocked up a dance. We had a very fine assemblage of beauty & kept it up till 12 o'clock, having English and Spanish country dances, with lots of waltzing. I lay down for 3 hours and then marched for Mojados.

Lieutenant Colonel George Bingham commanding the 53rd Foot also wrote of dances and beautiful women, but was critical of their evening wear.

> Arevalo 2 September 1812
> We have been very gay here; balls almost every night. The ladies have learnt English country dances and perform very well. There is one very pretty girl here, and only one. The Spanish ladies look more to

advantage in the morning, and in their native dress. Of an evening they are dressed in the French fashion and in white which does not become their complexion.

Andrew Barnard commanding the 1st Battalion 95th Rifles wrote to his sister of their merriments.

> El Bodon 5 November 1811
> We also have balls almost every night but the Castilian paysanas fare in beauty and grace to my Gaditanians – but as Mrs Downing used wisely to remark 'for want of company welcome trumpery'.

However, the Spanish ladies knew it was wrong, as Lieutenant George Woodberry noted.

> Olite, Friday, 20 August 1813
> The Spanish ladies all say that the English would be perfect if they were Christians, and they generally get absolution the next morning for having danced with us the night before . . .

Lieutenant William Freer of the 43rd Foot sought to ingratiate himself with the locals by joining a wedding party but made the age-old mistake of showing too much interest in the bride!

> Arzinhal 25 February 1810
> We had last Monday a wedding in a house & about 10 at night we persuaded the fair couple & their friends to come to our room & dance a fandango, which they condescended to do & for clod hoppers I assure you they danced with considerable taste, but the exertions they made applauded, some of them now & then opened the wind passages & left in the room (which was small & full, we having that day a large party to dinner) perfumes agreeable to none but themselves. I, unfortunately touched with the juice of the grape, became somewhat amorous with the fair bride, which the groom observing & who played the guitar, by which instrument they danced continually, played out of tune.

This was, however, a very dangerous game, as Spanish men were infamous for their intense jealousies and their rigid honour code, causing them all too often to seek revenge with the thin-bladed knives which every Spaniard carried. Lieutenant George Woodberry recording one incident.

Olite, Friday, 20 August 1813

I have just heard that Lieutenant Fitzclarence [10th Hussars] was wounded in the thigh at Tafalla yesterday; that he with others had been playing tricks with some Spaniards and they stabbed him, it is not a dangerous wound I understand.

He also had a close call himself.

Quinta near Cartaxo, Good Friday, 16 April 1813

I am never out of danger, the militia captain, he spoke to one of the sergeants last night saying that he threatened to stab me or cut my throat on account of his sister, who he said I came on purpose to seduce; what a villain, he is worse than his father, who took the poor girl to Santarem, he went there himself this morning, and when he returns I will teach him to threaten an English Hussar's life.

Surgeon Thomas Maynard of the Coldstream Guards wrote of a much more serious incident which ended in the death of an officer.

14 January 1814, St Jean de Luz

A most horrible outrage occurred about a month ago at Vitoria, in the murder of Captain Gore,[1] the circumstances are these. Captain Gore had taken into keeping a girl of notorious character, who had lived with several French officers, while they occupied the town, so that there was no violent breach of morals as far as the character of the female and her family. The connection between them, however created great jealousy and uproar in the town and on the evening of his death Captain Gore, supposing there would be some attempt made to take her from him by force, left her privately in the protection of a friend, at another house and returned to his own quarter.

At midnight a party of Spanish soldiers came to his room and demanded the lady, he said she was not there, they then threatened to search the house immediately. This he resisted, saying he was regularly in possession of his quarters and without proper authority he would never submit to being searched. The soldiers, for I believe, there was no commissioned officer with the party, grew insolent and a scuffle ensued, and Captain

---

1. Captain Saunders Gore of the 94th Foot. The circumstances of his death are repeated in many memoirs and all agree in their basic details.

Gore, assisted by his secretary, succeeded in pushing them all out of the room and [then?] returned to it. Then while endeavouring to fasten the door against them, he received several balls in his body, fired through the door, and soon after died. At present no notice has been taken of this affair and it is the general opinion there will not. This needs no comment, but if we compare it to cases in which the British have been grievous against the natives of Spain or Portugal in a much more mitigated degree, we shall see a difference, not in accordance with sheer justice. Nay, in a case where a British officer ordered a sentinel to fire on a mob at Abrantes, who were threatening his life and his man's, all protection was refused him, and an offer was made of delivering the officer up to the civil power of the country. At a court martial this officer was fully acquitted. How shall we harmonise these instances, or what will the family of Captain Gore say?

A number of officers did take the risk, however, and formed a relationship with a local woman, many eventually choosing to remain with their man and follow the army. When the British army eventually sailed home in 1814, Judge Advocate Larpent estimated that over 700 abandoned women were given money to return to Spain alone. A number of soldiers are known to have deserted to stay with their women while other women were surreptitiously smuggled onto the transports conveying the regiments home. George Woodberry records meeting one such officer with his lady friend, but he was not impressed with his choice!

Ibeisua, near Pamplona, Thursday 5 August 1813
I met Lieutenant Newland[2] and his lady, not his wife, I don't admire his choice, he might certainly have got a prettier girl to have accompanied him, but what very much surprises me, he appears so fond and attentive to her! Her constancy may deserve it, but if I kept a lady, I would have a handsome one, and run the risk of her being inconstant; sent the letters by Mr. Foster's servant, to England. The company of a woman, particularly a woman of our country, would be here delicious and I often wished to have the happiness of a pleasant companion, because I think like Lord Bacon, that in youth, women are our mistresses, in middle age, our companions, in old age, our sick care, and in all ages, our friends.

One consistent fascination were the numerous convents full of unobtainable nuns. Whether it was the fabled beauty of so many young virgins, isolated from the world that enraptured them, but their letters and diaries abound with their

---

2. This is Lieutenant Robert Newland of E Troop Royal Horse Artillery.

attempts at fraternization at the iron grills. Lieutenant Colonel George Bingham went to one but he was not impressed.

> Guarda 13 January 1810
> They appeared about fifty in number. As the grating of the windows was large, we had a good view of their persons, but none appeared handsome.

Lieutenant George Woodberry of the 18th Hussars was very much a womaniser, but found little to appeal to him initially amongst the nuns.

> Olite, Saturday 3 July 1813
> Opposite to my quarters is a convent and in it are twenty-two nuns. I was talking to several last evening through a thin partition of wood. This morning I was allowed to see them through a grating, there were several young women amongst them, but none handsome, one had been in the convent for thirty-two years, was the most engaging of the whole. She entered it very young, and her countenance bespeaks she was once beautiful. I asked them if they would like to live in a casa, instead of the convent, which was answered immediately by the Lady Abbess in the negative. They appeared particularly happy in the sight of an Englishman, and though I could not talk much to them, I made them comprehend that I was a hussar, and that in England we are the pride of the fair sex, which they were not at all astonished at. They said they liked us better than those they had seen from their windows in red coats.

It did not take him long to find an easier target for his affections and in describing his attempts to woo her, he admits that one nun had taken his fancy.

> Olite, Sunday 25 July.
> Last night Kennedy and I met two nice girls walking; we dismounted and walked with them for some time, and then came to their house, we were able to convince them that we would like to have more knowledge of the two women than we should and found we had got acquainted with two of the most respectable ladies in the town. Kennedy who is more brazen than me, walked into the house with them, of course I followed, and was introduced to Mrs Murphy, of Irish origin, who entertained us some time with wine and cake. On our departure we begged very hard to walk with the young ladies tomorrow, but the mother would not consent at all to it, however, I believe we shall have the pleasure of their company today, in spite of mother; we were not such new hands as to believe her,

I shall give up the nun, no more my religious fair, shall you see me at your grate.

Others were invited in to take refreshments with the nuns but were rarely graced with a beauty amongst them. George Barlow of the 52nd Foot visited a convent in Spain and found it difficult to maintain the solemnity of the occasion.

> Camp near Subijana [- Morillas], four leagues from Vitoria, 20 June 1813
> It has been observed that for the first time I entered within the hallowed precincts of a nunnery, a most liberal intercourse with the rest of the world, has and will continue to do away with much of the superstition of the peninsula & has already removed much of that impenetrable secrecy which was thrown around these mansions & their inmates when a packet of British heretics were allowed to behold & converse with the spouses of God. We were ushered into a neat little apartment, in which, behind an iron grating resembling that of the jewellery in the Tower of London, were ranged a dozen of those vestal virgins; our nation & the circumstances attending their entry occasioned us a welcome reception. Cakes were handed around and upon us expressing our wish for some bouquets, one of them went into the garden and plucked some nice bunches of roses. In the course of conversation, we made a request which the usual gallantry of our cloth prompts us to beg of this sex. Stop now, do not be alarmed, it was all innocence itself, in asking them to sing. The toothless grins of the majority however at this proposal soon convinced me that all hope of success in our petition lay in one or two whose mouths & features bore less traces of antiquity. After many hums and hangs and such like full ruminary, clearing of pipes, one of the younger sisters began a doleful quivering ditty as to require the utmost possible compression of the risible muscles to avoid giving offence. The sister however soon found that she had undertaken a task above her power and sinking in the middle of the strain released the audience to their no small satisfaction from so severe a trial upon their gravity & decorum.

Major Edwin Griffith of the 15th Hussars chose to decline the opportunity to visit a convent, but he was honest as to why he was disappointed not to go.

> 15 September 1813
> There are also two noble convents & gardens adjoining this walk which contain (I was told) some pretty nuns. I was sorry not to have time enough to visit them, as all the nuns I had every yet seen were old & by no means pretty.

Captain John Ewart of the 52nd Foot found out the hard way the truth about nuns.

> 28 July 1812
> Marched at 3 am three leagues to Olmedo, an old walled town, with the ruins of a castle and some old convents; five are still inhabited. We went to a nunnery, and were at once admitted into an ante room, but only eight old women appeared, who produced some bad wine and biscuits.

Some, however, even received visits from the nuns. Second Lieutenant James Gairdner of the 95th Rifles was not impressed.

> 10-14 April 1812
> We remained here until the 15th doing very well. There were 12 nuns in the house who came daily to see us, they were however almost all of them *ancient* . . .

However, Colonel George Bingham undoubtedly comes up with the most unusual time to hold a conversation with the local women in France in 1813.

> Ascain 20 November 1813
> Being exposed to a cannonade from the heights I got my battalion in column behind the largest house in the place waiting further operations; in this house had assembled all the better description of women of the village and whilst the cannonade was destroying the back part of the building and offices in the rear, we were chattering with the ladies in front, whose tongues ran faster than the roll of musketry on every side of us.

It is clear that both men and officers spent much of their idle time chatting up the local women, despite the threat to their lives, and in many cases this relationship passed well beyond mere friendship and became sexual, even amongst a number of the married men. However, there is a very significant difference between the attitudes of the rank and file in comparison to the officers regarding these liaisons. For many ordinary soldiers there was no stigma in courting a Portuguese or Spanish woman and for many this became a full and lasting relationship, with a significant number either formally marrying or forming an enduring partnership. For officers, however, married or not, flirtatious dalliances with these ladies was seen as having fun, without any thought of these relationships outlasting the war. The higher echelons of British society would look with disdain on any young gentleman officer marrying a Portuguese or Spanish girl, unless perhaps they were titled and brought a sizeable dowry with them. The honest and brutal reaction recorded by Lieutenant George Woodberry above was typical of this attitude: it was fine to sew wild oats in a foreign country, but very much another thing to take them home with them. The well-known example of Harry Smith marrying Juanita and having a very successful marriage together, with her being fully accepted into society, was very much the exception rather than the rule.

Chapter 14

The Experience of Battle

Readers may well be conversant with numerous tales of 'derring do' as recounted in many recollections of events in the Peninsular War, but these were written many years later and often with the sole purpose of selling books. There is therefore a great deal of hyperbole, long descriptive passges and even the blatant theft of stories already recounted by others. The question posed here is how much of the experience of combat was actually related to those at home at the time. Cornet James Wedderburn Webster of the 10th Hussars had promised his uncle he would write about his first action.

> 3 December 1808 Astorga
>
> I believe I promised to write to you after our *first* action, would that I could, as of the result of such an event I entertain *no* doubt, as in my opinion England is not easily beaten, on any ground. Here we are in miserable villages after a most distressing march of 35 leagues from La Corunna, the point of disembarkation. I have suffered much in horses as you will suppose. I have now though the *worst* task to tell you, our army are retreating as fast as possible. The communication between the armies of Sir J Moore and Sir D Baird (so much to be desired) is entirely cut off, the French are at least 3 to 1 in point of numbers & as they march infinitely *lighter* than our troops & of course *must* be both in better health & spirits.

Major Gregory Way of the 29th Foot wrote of his delight in being mentioned in dispatches after an affair before the Battle of Oporto on 12 May 1809.

> 24 June 1809
>
> Sir Arthur had thanked me after the business of the 12th in General Orders, but [I] had no idea of [it] being announced to the world in the Gazette, until I read it with my own eyes & repose in the satisfaction it would give my dear Mater & friends. Our affair (which is the present military term of French adoption) in the pine wood on the 11th was I assure you no joke. My light troops who I was advancing in 4 tiered order though their eagerness got us into a battalion of Frenchmen, who

were concealed in the grass upon their hands & knees & as they practise all kinds of pranks, enticed our men still further by calling to them in Portuguese and in the same uniform could not be distinguished till they opened their fire and assumed a more heel posture. Not a moment was to be lost for fear of being surrounded; 2 volleys & forward with the bayonet made them take to their heels without loss of time, but confess I never expected to come out with an entire skin & mounted upon rather an unmanageable charger, such are the singular chances & escapes in the day of battle. This and the heights of Rolica, the 17 August [1808], convince me not half the balls fired take effect upon these occasions.

Private John Bald of the 91st Regiment only wrote home to his parents in Dunfermline from his garrison at Southampton to report what he had been doing for the best part of the last two years. He spoke particularly of the Battle of Talavera fought on 27–28 July 1809.

Southampton, 15 November 1809
. . . Then we commenced our march to Spain with our brave commander Sir Arthur Wellesley. We marched on for several days till we came to Talavera, where we engaged the French for two days. The French lost fifteen thousand men. This battle was very dreadful. Both armies left off where they began. Not one made an inch of ground upon another but they retreated in the morning early. We had only 25,000 men and they had 54,000. We stood our ground two days after they went away, then we had to retreat for want of provisions . . . Our regiment lost 300 men. Our company of the 91st Regiment was 80 strong going into battle, and we had twelve killed, twenty wounded, one lieutenant killed and our good captain taken prisoner.

Some particularly focussed on the horrors of war. Private George Woolger of the 16th Light Dragoons wrote of the Battle of Talavera and was shocked by the sights he saw in the aftermath.

Villaviega, 26 October 1809 Portugal
. . . By this time our infantry had formed the line, the British on the left, ye Spanish on the right. A little before sunset the battle became very hot, which continued till nearly 12 pm, the remaining part of the night was employed in arranging cannon on 2 hills which we took possession of, which if the French had gained, would have turned our army.
As soon as light appeared on the 28th the battle was renewed with a most tremendous cannonade from the contending armies, which

continued for some hours without intermission. Our infantry was sharply put to it, our regiment suffered much, we lost 8 men and 21 horses in about 15 minutes, besides what we lost the day before. About 2pm the battle became dreadful, all this large plain was all in a smoake from cannon and musketry, and when the French give [sic] way their dead & wounded lay in almost whole ranks. The French stormed the 2 hills 6 times & were as often drove back with great slaughter till both hill were covered with killed and wounded. Too much praise can't be given of the 29th, 31st, Guards, 48th Foot, in short every regiment did their duty, they staid [sic] like stone walls disdaining to flinch, dispersing their numbers, although they were 3 to one & we had had scarcely any bread or water these two trying days, excessive heat and hard fighting still & found none grumble . . . The battle continued till dark till neither side could see where to fire a shot. The British remained on the field of battle all night, the French retreated during the night & left 20 guns behind them. We remained on the field till 10 am 29 July, but no enemy appeared to renew the actions. We were then ordered to our old camp ground, it was shocking to see the killed & wounded on both sides, some with both legs off, others both arms or one arm off, in short wounded in all parts. Men & horses lay together mangled in a shocking manner. All the houses in Talavera are filled with English, French & Spanish wounded, many die with loss of blood, some with there wounds.

Lieutenant Henry Dawson of the 52nd Foot wrote hurriedly to squash rumours that he had been captured.

Celorico 29 July 1810
I hope that you will have received the letter which I wrote you on the 25th as it will have relieved you from any reports which may have reached you respecting myself, as I know several of the officers wrote to England mentioning that I had been taken prisoner.

Lieutenant John Brumwell of the 43rd Foot wrote a postscript to his brother challenging fate. He was killed 18 months later at Ciudad Rodrigo.

Valdesaras 15 August 1810
Write to Gregson, tell him I am in good health and spirits and I hope to live to see you all again. But there is no saying what a piece of lead or cannonball may do. After the scenes that I saw the other day, both men and officers shot on each side of me, I am now beginning to think that the

ball is not yet cast that is intended for me, but there is no saying for the chances of war.

Near misses often got a mention, no matter how brief. Lieutenant William Freer of the 43rd Foot nonchalantly recorded:

24 August 1810
I had two shot hit me, one on the sole of my shoe, the other went through the sleeve of my jacket, gave me a smart rap.

Lieutenant Charles Madden of the 4th Dragoons described more of the plunder gained and of the terrible sights after the fighting rather than the fighting itself.

25 March 1811
The enemy left in the road seven tumbrils, two forge carts, one howitzer, and all the plunder from Campo Maior which they could not get off quick enough, such as sacks of corn, bread, cloathes of all kinds, besides a great deal of camp equipage and personal baggage. There were in the charges made against the enemy, as well in the rere [*sic*] of their column, number [*sic*] of horses and mules taken. When we were ordered to halt we were about 200 yards from their column, but sustained little injury as they reserved all their fire for our charge. In the evening we returned to our camp ground near Campo Major. It was both a distressing and singular sight to see the different objects which presented themselves to us on the road back to the town, both friends and foes lying alongside of each other as they fell. In one group lay six Frenchmen who had been killed at the same instant by a shell, and some of the most dreadful gashes that could be inflicted on the human body by a sword. The brutality of the scene was heightened greatly by the Portuguese, who cut and mangled all the unfortunate wretches who came within their reach. I had the satisfaction of preventing a Portuguese Dragoon from destroying a wounded Frenchman with his carbine as he lay on his back in some bushes with his hands stretched out imploring to be spared.

A few weeks later, he wrote a more matter-of-fact account of another action.

16 April 1811
Marched at 2 in the morning with the division of cavalry and a division of infantry for Zafra, five leagues, when we came near a town called Los Santos, half a league from Zafra. We got information that two regiments of French cavalry were near the town, the 2nd and

10th Hussars; that they had ordered 1,000 rations of bread, meat, and wine, and were waiting for the bread to be baked. The cavalry instantly advanced at a quick trot, and on our passing the town a small distance we saw them drawn up in column ready to receive us; the 13th [Light Dragoons] was in the centre, and the heavy brigade on the right flanks. The French charged the right squadron of the 13th on our advancing near them, which was returned. We then went up to charge them on the flanks, on which they went about and galloped off as fast as they could. We pursued them for about two leagues, most part of which time the French were compleatly dispersed, and as their horses brushed up we picked them up. We took on the whole 107 prisoners, two officers and about 200 horses. We should have destroyed most part of them had we not come off a march of five leagues, without corn, and the French having in the head of their column a considerable start of us.

Henry Dawson's brother Lieutenant Charles Dawson, also of the 52nd, wrote hurriedly of his first experience of combat.

Albergueria 8 April 1811
We had a few shots flying near us but did not lose a single man killed or wounded. As it was the first engagement I had witnessed, several of us after the affair was over, walked over the field of battle, the sight was horrid in the extreme.

A month later he wrote of another first, being fired at by cannon at the Battle of Fuentes de Oñoro.

Gallegos 12 May 1811
Their shot went rather close over our heads. This having been the first time I had stood to be shot at by cannon, I must confess that I did not much relish it, but after a few shots had passed, it became more familiar to me.

Private James Dilley of the 40th Foot wrote a brief comment on his experiences at the Battle of Albuera which was fought on 16 May 1811.

We was first to leave Badajoz to the French & march to the plains of Alverder [Albuera] where the severest action tooked place that ever was fought. The ded [*sic*] covered the ground for a long way round & now I think on the old saying 'A solder [*sic*] is alike a game cock, if he gens [*sic* gains] one battal [*sic*] he is sure to be tried again'. . . . But thanks be to God I bear it up with a good hart [*sic*] & I hope by the blessing of God that I shall live to see you once moor [*sic*].

Lieutenant Charles Madden of the 4th Dragoons recorded what he saw of the battle.

16 May 1811

The 3rd Dragoon Guards were drawn up in front of the ford, and charged the head of the column, on which the enemy retired across the river; this attack seems to have been intended as a feint, as their serious attack was aimed at our right. They advanced against that point in three immense columns, with about 3,000 cavalry on their left flank, so as to turn our right; they came on with such rapidity that they had gained the height our first division was to have been formed upon, before it had been compleatly formed, and began to pour down on us like an immense torrent; at this instance nothing but British steadiness and bravery could stand; the 1st Brigade of the 2nd division, consisting of the 3rd, 48th and 66th, formed up, and after several tremendous vollies on both sides the British charged them at the point of the bayonet. The French being strongly supported stood firm, and a more awful scene was never witnessed; it was a perfect carnage on both sides, bayonet against bayonet for near half an hour; as the brigade which at that time was principally engaged had pushed rapidly forward, they were a considerable distance in front of their support, which the enemy seeing, they moved a large column down on either flank, and surrounded them, at the same time a large body of cavalry commenced a charge on them, as they began to retire, and cut them down in all directions, the whole brigade, 3rd, 48th and 66th, became prisoners, when the right wing of the 4th Dragoons got orders to charge their cavalry, which they obliged to retire leaving a great number of their prisoners. The enemy continued to push forward their columns through the interval where the brigade stood. When a part of General Cole's division came up a tremendous cannonade, and fire of small arms, continued for several hours, in some instances at ten paces asunder; each party charged with the greatest bravery, and the day was for a length of time bearing an awful unfavourable appearance. Had their cavalry, which was three to one of ours, charged round our right flank, which they might have done, and so came in our rere [*sic*], the day was lost. They attempted it, but was checked by a brigade of Horse Artillery, which mowed them down in six and ten at a time; however, had they pushed forward we could have shown them no opposition. After a determined contest for about four hours, in which all our infantry was engaged, with most of the Spanish and Portuguese, the enemy began to give way, when an immense cannonade was opened on them as they descended the hill, and they retired in considerable confusion. Had we a sufficient body of cavalry to charge them as they fell back, they must have been entirely cut up, but as the attack still continued on our left, we were obliged to keep a large portion of our cavalry to keep in check a column which menaced that part, and seemed determined to force the bridge. I was stationed near the bridge with the left wing of my regiment, and a squadron and a half of the 13th [Light Dragoons], to cover some guns and defend the ford against a column of cavalry in our front. We had a brigade of Portuguese cavalry in our rere as our support. The enemy moved forward with the intention of attacking us, on which we advanced near the ford, when an immense fire of artillery was opened on us, every shot told; however, our advances had the effect of checking their cavalry. We remained for five hours exposed to a heavy fire of artillery and musketry. We had nine guns playing from the church over the bridge, which did great execution. We had also near us a brigade of German rifle men. The uproar and confusion was dreadful, each party cheered when they came to the charge, and every inch that was gained could easily be discovered on which side it went by the immense shout of the parties engaged. They were like an immense body of water ebbing and flowing. Had a man time to reflect, one's situation must have been dreadful, but each man had his point to watch, which took up his whole attention. Wretched objects in all shapes and descriptions were to be seen in every direction, some creeping on their hands and knees, with both their legs shot off, and others in equally a distressing situation. . . . The French were supposed to have lost between 7,000 and 8,000 men, with two generals killed and three wounded. We had in the charge of the right wing of the 4th two captains and one lieutenant taken, and one captain and one lieutenant severely wounded, with a great proportion of men and horses killed and wounded. In the left wing three men dangerously wounded, one having his thigh shot off, with eight or nine horses killed. The charge of our right wing was made against a brigade of Polish cavalry, very large men, well-mounted; the front rank armed with long spears, with flags on them, which they flourish about, so as to frighten our horses, and thence either pulled our men off their horses or ran them through. They were perfect barbarians and gave no quarter when they could possibly avoid. However, they confess to have lost 300 men.

He also described the melancholy aspect of the battlefield the next day.

> 17 May 1811
> I rode over the field of battle, where lay between 5 and 6,000 dead and wounded, most of whom were compleatly naked; in some places they lay so thick, a person could have supposed they had been collected for the purpose of being buried. The wounded met one's eyes entreating assistance, many of whom lay covered with mud and wet for ten hours without their wounds being dressed. British officers lay mortally wounded, in many instances stripped of their cloathes for hours before they were dead. This piece of inhumanity was to be attributed to the Spaniards who plundered the whole of the night after the battle, without respect to rank or persons. The different attitudes of the dead could not fail striking a man's eyes. The British universally lay with their arms in the position of charging, and the countenances of both parties, even in death, bespoke a fixed determination to conquer or fall. On an average, two-thirds of the British officers were either killed, wounded, or prisoners. The Buffs [3rd Foot], which went in 600 strong, could only muster 40. The 48th and 66th about the same. The two latter lost their Colours.

He returned one month later and described the scene again:

> 16 June 1811
> Turned out at 3 a.m. and marched to Albuera, the ground was covered with the remains of the bodies which had been burned by the peasantry, who were sent from all parts for that purpose. I went within a few hundred yards of the ground where I was stationed on the 16th. I also rode over the spot where the French guns were stationed, which saluted us the whole of the day; they had two 9-pounders and two 6-pounders and a howitzer which threw 24 pound shells. The effects of our guns which played on them was manifest; two mules and three horses and several human bodies lay on the spot. That spot occupied my particular attention on the 16th, as I could see every shot that was directed at us, and their ammunition waggons arriving several times in the course of the day with fresh supplies; bodies lay in every direction, half roasted, and the trees were covered with eagles and birds of prey.

Captain John Hill of the 23rd Foot also wrote briefly of Albuera to his mother.

> 18 May 1811
> Thank the Almighty that he has again saved your son unhurt in the tremendous battle of the 16th, the papers will give you the details.

Our regiment went into the field, counting the men with the mules in the rear, about 560; our return of killed, wounded and 16 missing, the latter of whom we have all now accounted for, amounted to 310 which included 14 officers . . . .

In the early part of the day I thought everything was going against us. A portion of the British infantry was put into confusion by a charge of cavalry after some of the regiments had made a 2nd charge on the French infantry. The Spanish infantry, regulars, behaved very well; the Portuguese in our division were as steady as rocks.

Lieutenant George Crompton of the 66th Foot wrote in a little more detail of the disaster at Albuera, but he ended on a high note.

20 May 1811

I think it was about 10 o'clock am when the French menaced an attack on our left; we immediately moved to support it. It proved however, to be a feint, and the right of the line was destined to be the spot (oh never to be effaced from my mind) where Britons were to be repulsed; 3 solid columns attacked our regiment alone. We fought them till we were hardly a regiment. The commanding officer was shot dead and the two officers carrying the Colours close by my side received their mortal wounds. In this shattered state, our brigade moved forward to charge. Madness alone would dictate such a thing, and at this critical period cavalry appeared in our rear. It was then that our men began to waver, and for the first time (and God knows I hope the last) I saw the backs of the English soldiers turned upon the French. Our regiment once rallied, but to what avail! We were independent of infantry; outnumbered with cavalry. I was taken prisoner, but retaken by the Spanish cavalry.

Oh what a day was that. The worst of the story I have not related. Our Colours were taken. I told you before that the two ensigns were shot under them; two sergeants shared the same fate. A lieutenant seized a musket to defend them and he was shot to the heart; what could be done against cavalry.

A miserable lieutenant of the unfortunate 66th Regiment.

The Fusilier Brigade afterwards came on, also the other brigades in the division with some Spaniards and Portuguese, we beat back the French and gained a complete victory.

Lieutenant William Woods of the 48th Foot wrote at length on the terrible battle in which he was made a prisoner, but eventually escaped.

Almandralejo 29 May 1811

... At daybreak on the 16th the picquets were skirmishing and at 8 o'clock there was a heavy cannonade. At this time the rain began to descend in torrents, and in a great measure obscured the distant prospect. The enemy forded the river two miles below the town. Already they had occupied some commanding heights and were attempting to secure another on which almost the fate of the day depended. The First Brigade consisting of the Buffs, 48th, 66th and 34th Regiments were ordered to check them. We advanced rapidly, under a most unparalleled fire of grape, musketry and 12 lb shot. At the foot of my hill my worthy captain was shot through the thigh and the command of the company devolved upon me. As well as I could amidst an incessant roar of artillery, I entreated the men to be firm and steady. They however, needed no caution. We were soon halted and began a brisk fire, but trifling compared to that of the enemy. In a few minutes the drum beat for it to cease and General Stewart ordered us to charge. The men huzzaed and advanced with the greatest spirit. A column of grenadiers of gigantic stature, rendered hideous by the huge fur caps and enormous beards and mustachios which they wore, were opposed to us. When within a few feet of them, the bayonets so terrified these formidable heroes that numbers dropped their arms and attempted to fly. Our men made dreadful havoc amongst them. This column was completely routed and two others were giving way. Had another brigade been near to support us at this juncture, the fate of the day would in a few minutes have been decided. But alas! No support was immediately near. The French general saw it and got a regiment of hussars and a new species of troops armed with lances and mounted, amongst us. At this time more than half the brigade were either killed or wounded and I found myself left with only four men of the company, surrounded on all sides. In a minute after, I was struck smartly on the right leg by a ball which had rebounded from the ground and the next minute a number of hussars came upon us and rode me and the four men all down together. Before I could get up a French officer came, I called out in French 'I am an English officer'. The scoundrel made no reply but spurred his horse violently to get him over me. He was followed by several dragoons and I was trampled upon and bruised in several places, but not half so severely as I expected. I got up as soon as I could and was cut at by two dragoons in all directions. I evaded many cuts and expected to have got away, as some of our dragoons were coming up the hill, when someone gave me a blow on the back of my neck which brought me down again. At this instance a French officer came up and saved my life. The two villains with horrid imprecations robbed me of everything, pockets and all. I was then taken to the rear where to my regrets and horror, I found Major Brook, 2 captains and 5 subalterns with a number of our men prisoners, besides about 17 officers of other regiments, all but about three wounded. They used us most cruelly, many of my brother officers could not get their wounds dressed, they were completely drenched in blood, which was still fast flowing from the deep cuts of the sabres. . . . My whole thoughts were bent upon getting away, and . . . Some of the wounded officers had permission to sleep in the town and partly from these circumstances, Captain Spedding of the 4th Dragoons and myself arranged a plan of escape . . . In our two battalions [of the 48th] we had 50 officers present and all, with the exception of eight were either killed or wounded. After the action, the 2nd Battalion out of 413 men had only 25 fit for duty; we now muster 7 officers and 120 men. ..In a few days I hope my wound will be healed I have now command of a company consisting of only eight men, the poor remains of more than fifty fine soldiers . . .

Captain William Bragge of the 3rd Dragoons was very complimentary as to the phlegm shown by a senior officer who rarely receives a good press.

Belem 6 September 1811
    No one stands shot and shell with greater phlegm than General Slade and I hear he was in conversation with Colonel Hervey when a spent shot struck the latter's sabretache, which together with the shot and a volume of *Tristram Shandy* lodged in the horse's side and was afterwards cut out.

The melancholy remnants of battles past drew a thoughtful response from Band Master John Westcott, when the 26th Foot marched over the battlefield of Bussaco, some 18 months afterwards.

27 February 1812
    . . . to a certainty Massena although [more] numerous, must have had great confidence in his troops to attempt to force a British army, in such a noble position. The mere marching up those hills, without an army to encounter at the top, was sufficient to tire any men in Europe. We saw several men's skulls laying by the side of the road, as we ascended, which had been laying ever since the Battle of Bussaco. When we arrived at the top of those hills, the regiment halted, for about three quarters of an hour, in order to rest themselves, after the fatiguing mountains they

ascended, . . . The regiment halting on this celebrated hill of Bussaco, we had a little time to walk about it and take a view of the spot that once was guarded by a British army which defied one of the ablest marshals of France with an army far superior in numbers of tried soldiers . . . I took up a skull which had been perforated through, its owner, had been killed by a musket ball through the head, we saw several skeletons of men who had perhaps died of their wounds in some unfrequented part of the mountain, and had not been buried as the British army retreated shortly after the battle . . . many a poor fellow was left dangerously wounded on parts of those hills where their comrades could not find, at the moment, such as riflemen who's situation often require them to be separated from the main body of the army, and in that forlorn condition died on some solitary rock without help. What must be the dying thoughts, of a poor soldier in this dejected dismal situation, absent from every human being and breathing his last in the recesses of some desolate mountain or dreary heath, his friends receiving no other satisfaction than perhaps hearing of him being returned amongst the missing of his regiment. The advocates of war, who knows nothing of its miseries little considers upon the short life of a soldier, to see him leaving his friends and country, in the bloom of his youth going on a harassing campaign, where most likely either by the sword or fatigue, he never will return again, to either, friends or country, perhaps to breath his last in the most agonising pain, on some dreary mountain left alone, through necessity like at Bussaco and perhaps without a drop of water to quench his dying thirst, or a human being to convey his melancholy fate, to his friends.

Brevet Major Edward Cocks of the 16th Light Dragoons mentioned a small tussle with a Frenchman at close quarters.

15 April Ribeira 1812
[Villa Garcia] I had no personal adventure except that in coming in contact with a French hussar we rolled over each other. I was on my legs first and with a coup de sabre invited him to surrender.

Lieutenant George Woodberry of the 18th Hussars likewise recorded a close personal combat, but was also struck by the terrible consequences afterwards.

Morales de Toro, Wednesday 2 June 1813
I had a cut at one man myself, who made point at me which I parried. I spoilt his beauty, if I did not take his life, for I gave him a most severe cut across the eyes and cheek and must have cut them out, however in

the scene of confusion when the enemy fired their first shot, he and many other prisoners made their escape. The ball from their second fire fell within a foot of my horse, and nearly smothered me with dust, but as the saying goes, every bullet has its billet! And there were none for me. We in our turn were obliged to retreat, back out of the range of their artillery, which after firing about a dozen times, and throwing two bombs [shells], they retreated.

Out of the numbers of prisoners we took 35, hardly one was to be perceived without some dreadful cuts on their head and body. I never saw men so mad for action as the hussars were before and after the skirmishing, and all appeared disappointed when ordered to march into this place and take up their quarters.

Lieutenant Charles Crowe of the 27th Foot witnessed some of the terrible injuries suffered by the French prisoners that he came across in the town of Toro.

2 June 1813

We went into the fort, or citadel, on the south west side of the town, and found many Staff surgeons employed dressing the wounds of the prisoners taken this morning, many of which were very ghastly, and all on the heads and shoulders. I was utterly astonished in noticing the third prisoner, waiting for his twin to be dressed and directed my chum's attention to him . . . A remarkably fine and handsome fellow, he stood upright and undaunted with his arms folded and returned our looks of compassion with haughty frowns of defiance. The long gash on the upper part of his head gaped horribly and his shoulders were covered with coagulated blood. The lobe or lower part of the ear was clean cut off and gone, but the extremity of the lower jaw bone hung down over his collar.

However, Lieutenant Edward Fox Fitzgerald of the 10th Hussars was quite bombastic in his letter to his grandmother.

Camp, one league beyond Burgos 13 June 1813

The letter I wrote you after the engagement at Morales I find was lost, so that you will have been in a dreadful fright lest I should have kicked the bucket on that day! That day proved the British cavalry to be the finest in the world. Our regiment charged thirteen squadrons of the corps d'elite of gendarmes; killed, wounded and took nearly five hundred of them. The prisoners amounted to two hundred and fifty with three officers. The corps of French cavalry was commanded by General Dijon, who was nearly taken. The French retired in great disorder to the batteries on the heights, from which they peppered us with grape shot and shells. We lost one captain taken prisoner, four men killed and ten wounded; and poor Cottin, the lieutenant, killed. . . . Our regiment was the only one engaged at Morales.

Captain Duncan Robertson of the 88th Foot was keen to reassure everyone that he was safe and well, but also to give some detail of his part in the Battle of Vitoria.

Vitoria 23 June 1813
Aware of the anxiety you will feel on my account when you hear of our doings for the last two or three days, I lose not a moment in acquainting you that I am safe and sound and never in better health after all our fatigues and dangers than I am at this instant . . .
. . . our division (the 3rd) under Sir Thomas Picton crossed the river in the face of the enemy by a bridge which our brigade forced about half past 12 o'clock, we crossed with such rapidity that although the French had cannon placed to scour it, and sharpshooters beyond calculation lining the whole opposite bank, we lost only a few men. Had the British been placed in the situation the French were to defend it no human power could have forced this bridge, the first success put us all in high spirits, however the grand thing was yet to come, our brigade the 45th, 74th & 88th formed in three separate columns the moment we crossed the bridge and moved as quickly as possible to attack a round steep hill in front of us about 500 yards, the enemy had a body of cavalry at the foot of it and a strong column of infantry hid behind the brink of it, but our advance was so rapid and determined that the enemy's cavalry first gave way and then the infantry without daring to show their faces, the 88th being the centre regiment, was posted opposite the middle of the steep hill where tremendous opposition was expected, however we were not long getting to the top of it, I had the honour to command the leading company of the regiment up this hill, when we go to the top we turned to our left where we saw the enemy's grand line of battle formed about half a mile off ready to receive us, a few moments after Lord Wellington came up from a height upon which he had stood in the rear and passed at full gallop to the left of the 88th where he stopped to view the enemy's line, he had hardly looked at them when he ordered the 88th which was the nearest regiment to him to form a line and advance to attack a strong body of the enemy formed in close column about 100 yards only in front

of us, this column was covering the centre of the enemy's principal line and seemed determined to make a hot stand. The moment we advanced it opened a tremendous fire upon us, but at the same time began to waver and some even to run away, we gave them a volley and intended to charge immediately after but the fellows did not wait for us and ran like a flock of sheep into a small straggling village something like Pitlochry, we followed them to the end of the village when our general ordered us to halt and wait the arrival of the other divisions of the army which were intended to form on the right and left of us, for at this moment we were quite alone and within 150 yards of the centre of the enemy's main line which opened a truly tremendous fire of shot and shell upon us to drive us back from the village and the fellows who ran away picked up a little courage when we halted and annoyed us very much from behind walls and houses, the 74th very soon came up to support us and charged with a wing of the 88th through the village out of which we drove the enemy in an instant and occupied the whole of it, if our general [Brisbane] had not halted us, we would have driven the enemy out of this village at once without giving him time to do us any mischief, the 74th and us continued in this village in spite of the enemy's efforts to drive us out of it until our line was complete and advanced to the village, when it came up to us we rushed forward and occupied our place in the general line of battle. This moment was the most interesting of the day, it is impossible to give an idea of the steadiness and rapidity with which the British line advanced not heeding the enemy's fire though vollies of cannon were fired at us, the enemy's line very soon began to break and by the time we got fairly within about a hundred yards of its centre, the whole gave way and ran for it, we followed as quickly as possible, . . . the enemy fired incessantly at us during this little halt but we never fired a shot in return nor took any notice of him as we wished to preserve our means of destruction until we should be close up with him, when we were ordered to advance and charge the line on the hill, the fire from the enemy became extremely hot indeed and as we were quite exposed we lost a great number of men, however this did not in the smallest degree check our progress, on the contrary we advanced all the quicker, when we were within 150 yards, the enemy's line gave way and fled as usual, we pursued almost out of breath, a good number of the French were killed here, this hill being forced the whole of the enemy's third line fled, at this moment Lord Wellington galloped past to the front of our brigade to view the state of the enemy, here he beheld one of the most gratifying sights he ever saw, the whole of the enemy's army flying away in the greatest confusion, cavalry, artillery and infantry all mixed, our cavalry was now ordered to the front to complete the work of destruction, we rushed on as fast as our legs could carry us to support them, from that moment there was nothing but prisoners, the enemy abandoning artillery, baggage to facilitate his escape, night alone put an end to the pursuit, our division halted for the night about a league beyond the city, the fruits of the victory are the taking of 151 pieces of cannon, 415 ammunition wagons, the whole of King Joseph's carriages and baggage and cows and mules loaded with the plunder and baggage of his officers beyond all calculation, besides the military chest with a great deal of treasure, I was ordered here on duty the day after the action to pick up the wounded and to assist protecting the captured cannon and this gave the opportunity of seeing the extent of the enemy's loss, the number of prisoners we have taken is by no means as great in proportion as the ordnance, their killed and wounded are numerous and so are ours as you will observe by the gazette account, the 88th lost nearly 250 men in killed and wounded, by far the greater part wounded in consequence of the great distance, the enemy took care to keep from us, we have only one officer killed, Ensign Saunders & five wounded; all the Athole lads in this army are safe, . . .

Lieutenant George Barlow of the 52nd Foot wrote to his father also describing the fighting at Vitoria.

Camp in sight of Pamplona, 24 June 1813

The Light Division now advanced in line to carry a village under a heavy fire of cannon & here it sustained almost all its casualties, their artillery being very well served and every shot telling with effect through our ranks. At this instant the two left hand companies of the 52nd were ordered to clear some coppices & woody ground on the left, ours unfortunately was one. A swarm of tirailleurs were driven out of the lanes and enclosures into a field of corn; we followed them closely into the wheat & in getting across a hedge through some broken down gaps, my poor captain (Currie) was shot through the forehead & never spoke another word. This light infantry work is very sharp, more especially for the officers, who are much exposed in skirmishing through covered countries. Our company sustained a loss of one sergeant & eight men in casualties & I have to mourn the death of one who whether as a friend or an officer I think had not his equal in the regiment.

Life Guard Henry Willis wrote of his experiences in the same battle.

> Vitoria 28 June 1813
> ... They made a stand, took up their position, we advanced, a general engagement began about eight in the morning of the 21st of June, both sides fought with a determined resolution of gaining the victory for several hours, cannonading were never brisker. They said we could never move their position if we were ten times stronger. We showed them British play, our cannon kept a continual fire upon them, at last we moved their guns, we begun to advance upon them, numbers of lives were lost [&] we came in sight of the town about ½ past 5 o'clock in the evening. Captain J[ohn] Davis were ordered to march one squadron of the Life Guards and take possession of the town, the French kept retreating and fighting till dark at night. Next day we pursued them, they flew into the mountains and dispersed in such a manner we have not met with them yet. On that glorious day I understand we took upwards of 300 pieces of cannon, what prisoners I cannot learn, you will have the particulars in the papers. I think we are now in a fair way of clearing this country of the French ...

In another letter George Barlow described a very near miss.

> Vera, 24 September 1813
> In the affair which ensued I happened to attend by rotation on General Skerrett, to carry about his orders and accompanied him to a part of the position which the enemy were smartly cannonading and very nearly had my head broke by the explosion of a shell which burst close to my horses' feet before I could say *Jack Robinson*,[1] whilst I beheld the *arm of a soldier* as high as the elbow come flying by me through the air.

Captain Charles Lennox, Earl of March, now in the 52nd Foot, wrote of the experiences of his friend Lieutenant Francis Russell of the 7th Foot.

> Lesaca 19 August 1813
> I suppose you think me very fond of fighting, as you hear of it so often now. My friend Francis Russell was very lucky & only hit in his cap, he carried the Colours of his regiment, the Royal Fusileers & in the

---

1. A phrase denoting a very short period of time. Its origins are unclear, but it was in use by 1778 and is recorded in the *Dictionary of the Vulgar Tongue* of 1811.

first charge made by that regiment he & the other lieutenant carrying the Colours leapt over a wall which the French were standing behind before any of the men could follow them and knocked down the two French officers standing in front of their men. You may conceive that warm hun then began, his regiment lost 215 men & 12 officers & I am sorry to say, the officer who jumped the wall with him.

Lieutenant James Gairdner of the 95th Rifles described in detail the fighting around Arcangues church during the action on the River Nivelle. He was angry at the pointless waste of lives.

10 November 1813

About two hours after day break the enemy in great force attacked and drove in our picquets & those of General Hope's corps on whom they made a desperate attack, with us then was a terrible confusion, and though the picquets had observed the enemy's force collecting in their front for some time, yet when the[y] did attack, they took some of them completely by surprise. When our company arrived at the Chateau d'Arcangues we were ordered to halt there for that the division was to maintain that position, the rest of the battalion came in by companies as the[y] could, but our company was sent out from the chateau to reoccupy the ridge in front of it in order to support the 3rd Battalion who were actually *retiring from the ridge when we received the order to occupy it to support them.* This was mentioned to the commandant who however had not sense to comprehend that it was not only useless but dangerous to send one company up to occupy a ridge on which we were not able to communicate right & left.

However we were ordered to go, leaving a subdivision at the house below the chateau; Hopwood & myself went up with the advanced subdivision and felt our way to the top of the ridge with a few men, the enemy had not yet occupied it but were close to it and immediately after we arrived there, one ball went through the heads of both Hopwood & Sergeant Brotherwood (thus died uselessly two as brave soldiers as ever stepped [out], I have since heard our commandant attempt to maintain that it was not his intention we should occupy this place, that however I will always assert whenever I hear the subject mentioned, to be false. Both Hopwood & myself were too well aware of the useless danger we were going to meet, to run into it without an order, I said and always shall say that Hopwood lost his life through the ignorance of the commanding officer and if Colonel Barnard had commanded the regiment this day poor Hopwood, Brotherwood and the other sufferers of the company this day could have been spared). I went up to Hopwood as soon as I saw him fall, took him by the hand and called him by his name, he half opened his eyes which were closed but never spoke, his brains were knocked out of the wound. This melancholy event left me in command of the company, as I was under the eyes of the commanding officer and so situated that it was in his power by sound of bugle to order me to retire when he thought proper, I (though I knew that every moment I remained there hazarded the loss of the whole subdivision which I had there, for we could not see ten yards before us, and as we were advanced considerably out of the line of skirmishers, the enemy were on our right & left in our rear, I confess I never expected to return with a sound skin) determined not to quit this place until I was either driven from it or ordered from it, the former of which happened very soon for the enemy seeing we were unsupported and out of our place, sent some men who came through the hedge on our left & fired into us, we ran into the road & retired to the house the other subdivision was at and I certainly never ran quicker in my life, a help of that kind gives a man a wonderful agility. We kept the house, beyond which we ought never to have advanced & were relieved at dark by another company. This house is established as a picquet house & the line drawn from it right & left is a very good one, when relieved we returned to the chateau.

Ensign James Rutherford of the 94th Foot wrote at some length of one encounter with the French.

Hasparren 13 January 1814
We had been badly annoyed by the cowardly rascals always showing force and as soon as they had given us the trouble of turning out and standing to our alarm posts they retired laughing at us. This determined our chief to give them a thrashing and accordingly on the morning of the 6th instant our division got under arms at daylight and moved towards a hill occupied by them. We drew up behind a rising ground to conceal our force and at eleven a bugle was to sound as the signal to attack, but owing to the 4th Division not coming up in time, the attack was put off till three. By this time the enemy had given up any idea of our coming up on them, the day being far advanced and they began to cook, when our signal was given and our light company marched on supported by the Brigade and attacked. As the hill was high and steep, before they could recollect themselves we were in the midst of them. They stood a few minutes and gave a few volleys but our men began to close and they gave way and took a run. I never in my life saw cavalry, infantry [&] their Staff

and officers trying who could play the last foot and our light company cheering and calling them all the names they could invent while four six pounders at this moment of confusion came up and opened an obnoxious fire upon them, they left the ground and the arms and accoutrements which they had no time to put on their kettles, went all upset on the fires and every enemy encampment smoking with half cooked dinners. Night came on and put an end to our pursuit . . .

In all wars, however, there are also moments of complete farce. Lieutenant William Swabey of the Royal Horse Artillery described one such incident in his diary.

26 March 1811
Our guns came into action by General Graham's order, at a dark wall, supposed to be an enemy's column; we fired nine rounds before the general would be convinced of his mistake.

As can be seen, they usually wrote of themselves and their friends and close colleagues, and detailed their actions in the battles, rather than attempting to describe the battle in total, much of which they could not have witnessed anyway. This personal detail was what their families and friends wanted and there is a really refreshing honesty to their writing. They also, of course, wrote of their wounds and looked to reassure their families back home of their survival and cheerful determination to rapidly recover and return to their units. Their letters were full of light-hearted banter and simply sought to calm the fears of those left at home as to their rapid recovery.

Chapter 15

Sieges

Without question, soldiers of every nationality saw siege work as the most difficult, arduous and downright dangerous duty they ever had to perform. This was exacerbated further for the British in the peninsula by the Duke of Wellington's need to capture fortresses quickly, before superior French forces could amass and drive him away. This caused the premature storming of incomplete breaches and terrible loss of life. For all of these reasons, sieges feature heavily in the correspondence home and it is patently clear from these letters that conditions in the trenches were often atrocious and that the terrible attacks and their aftermath had a deep psychological impact on those who witnessed it.

Their first experience of siegecraft was actually in the summer of 1810, for the few Allied troops vainly watching the French capture of the fortress of Badajoz and the subsequent sudden surrender of Almeida following a devastating explosion in the main ammunition store, destroying half of the town and damaging a large part of the defences and cannon. Ensign Robert Garrett of the 2nd Foot had to oversee work parties to repair the defences which the French had further destroyed when they abandoned it.

> Almeida 24 October 1811
>
> I have been on duty this last two days keeping the men to their work [repairing bastions]. We have two days more to remain here when our party will be relieved by the 61st . . .

Band Master John Westcott of the Cameronians also witnessed the devastation of Almeida a year after the explosion.

> 30 November 1811
>
> . . . We passed under the walls of Almeida, which garrison is situated on rising ground, on the plain, we passed on the Spanish side of that garrison a great part of its works were destroyed by the explosion of its magazine which occasioned that part of the works near the magazine to be almost totally destroyed. A great quantity of stone some of a very large size was blown from the works of the garrison to a considerable distance on the plain. It was before this explosion a capital fine fortification. It

had six royal bastions of stone and six ravelins or half-moon batteries, the one fronting the river Coa, which runs at the distance of a mile, is of a noble extent, and furnished with a cavalier,[1] for the purpose of commanding the circumjacent country. Nearly in the centre of the town on a lofty mount stands a castle famous for its strength, and before the late accident its magazine was deemed bombproof, within its walls are wells and at a small distance a fine spring of water, it has broad ditches with portcullises like Portsmouth or Plymouth garrison, but there is rising ground on the plain if mounted with cannon, convenient to it that I think might annoy it. We saw a number of Portuguese soldiers in the ditches repairing its works, this garrison must always be keeped [sic] in a state of defence as its one of the Portuguese chief fortifications, and so very convenient [to] the Spanish garrison of Ciudad Rodrigo, and also its being on such an extensive plain that's so well adopted for large armies to act upon, will always occasion Almeida, being a principal post,

The first successful siege undertaken by Wellington's army was that of Ciudad Rodrigo in early January 1812 during hard frosts, but at least it remained relatively dry. Lieutenant George Barlow of the 52nd got close to the town, whilst watching it before the siege even began.

Martiago, 3 December 1811

Two or three days since, I went accompanied by a brother officer, both of us well mounted, to take a close ride of [Ciudad] Rodrigo and well knowing that the enemy would not venture beyond their walls, although at the time they had nothing to dread on that score, those of our picquets being then on the plains. We rode up to a large convent within cannon-shot of the works. Here with a good telescope we had a most impressive view of the whole place, of the sentries pacing the works, ramparts, the guns, bridge and in short of anything that was happening in the town. You may form some idea of our distance when I say that we heard all the clocks do the bells chime although there was little or no wind. Although the works are very strong itself, its defence consists in the nature of the soil which is of solid rock & in which trenches and parallels must be cut with much labour and also loss of blood as during the whole night exposed to the fire of the place.

---

1. A cavalier in fortifications is a raised platform within the defences, which is higher than the surrounding walls, allowing the defender to fire over the outer defences at any attacking force.

He wrote again during the early days of the siege with their progress so far.

> El Bodon, 15 January 1812
> The whole division then came up and broke ground within 600 yards of the place. Our company with several others, were sent forward to cover them, whilst employed in working. Here we lay on the glacis within four hundred yards of their works, on our bellies, in the deepest silence, to be ready for a sortie, and remained there from eight in the evening till five the next morning. The night was terribly cold and frosty, accompanied with dreadful thick dews and we had neither coats nor blankets, as all those encumbrances had been left behind on being ordered with the storming party. The enemy as soon as they heard us digging, opened the whole of their fire and continued it during the whole of the night; throwing their shells with great correctness, our people however nearly completed the covert [covered] way and by morning, when we were withdrawn were pretty well protected.

Lieutenant Colonel Andrew Barnard of the 95th Rifles commented on the siege to his sister.

> Pastores 15 January 1812
> Our 24 pounders are banging away merrily and I trust we shall get into the place tomorrow night.

Major General Sir Charles Colville was also in the trenches that night.

> Salices 15 January 1812
> I am this moment returned with fingers cramped with the morning's frost from my second twenty-four hours' duty in the trenches before Ciudad Rodrigo.

First Lieutenant James Macleod of the Royal Artillery arrived at the front just in time to view the siege of Ciudad Rodrigo, where two of his brothers were already serving.

> Gallegos 15 January 1811
> We arrived here yesterday to witness the siege of Ciudad Rodrigo. The batteries opened for a few rounds last night & since daylight this morning have kept up a pretty good fire, 25 24-pounders are in the batteries & they have certainly made something like a hole in the wall . . .

George [Royal Engineers] is employed on the siege, I saw him there today & Charles's [43rd Foot] division are on duty tomorrow & I shall then see him. We shall be a jolly party of brothers. I am going to give you the intelligence of the death of poor Ross of the Engineers, he was killed by a shell on the night of the 9th, the shell burst close to him & a splinter drove the loop button of his hat into his head. Mr Skelton of the engineers is also very dangerously wounded, a shot having taken away his arm & part of his hip, he cannot survive but was easy. Mulcaster of the Engineers is slightly wounded by a musket shot, it was in the fleshy part of his thigh but was easily extracted & he has gone on horseback to the rear. Dundas of ours got a blow with a splinter on the hip & Holcombe on the foot.

Captain John Ewart of the 52nd Foot wrote in some detail of the storm on 19 January, but concentrated more on the losses in his own division.

19 January [1812]
Marched from our cantonments at daybreak. The division assembled near La Caridad and cooked there, in the afternoon proceeding to the old ground behind the batteries, where we found the 4th Division, who marched off directly and the 3rd, who we heard were to storm the large breach at dusk. 300 volunteers from the British of the Light Division under Major [George] Napier, 52nd (100 43rd under Captain [James] Fergusson; 100 52nd under Captain [William] Jones; and 100 95th under Captain [Samuel] Mitchell) were selected for the advanced party, of whom 25 (of 1st Battalion 52nd party, being in front) under Lieutenant [John] Gurwood 52nd, were to lead into the small breach, which was now also reported to be practicable. The Light Division about dusk marched to the Convent of San Francisco, where we found Lord Wellington, General Graham, with Marshal Beresford, and nearly all the general officers of the army. The 2nd Battalion 52nd were formed in column of three men in front (the 2nd Battalion close in rear of the 1st, both left in front) with the 43rd Regiment, formed in column of three in front, right in front, upon the right of them; so that the two regiments should enter the breach at the same time, preceded by the 300 men. The 95th Regiment and 3rd Cacadores were ordered to carry ladders and bags filled with wool to enable the troops to get over the ditch easier. At a few minutes past 7 pm the whole moved towards the breach, some delay was occasioned by there not being sufficient ladders and by some of the front party going too much to their right, during which time the column was exposed to a heavy fire of grape and musketry, by which some were

killed and wounded. In entering the breach Captain [Joseph] Dobbs 52nd (who led the battalion) was killed and near the same spot General [Robert] Craufurd with Colonel Colborne and Major G[eorge] Napier (who lost his right arm) were all severely wounded, as was General [John Ormsby] Vandeleur, Captain [James] Fergusson, Lieutenants [John] [*sic*] and [Cooke] Patterson 43rd, Captains [John] Uniacke and [Samuel] Mitchell, Lieutenants [John] Cox and [Walter] Bedell 95th. Lieutenant Gurwood 52nd was slightly wounded when leading on the party. At a quarter of an hour after we had left the convent the whole division were in the town of Ciudad Rodrigo, the French flying and trying to conceal themselves in every direction, except a few who attempted to stand in the great square, but were soon killed or taken (here the colonel of the 34th French was severely wounded) but in consequence of the firing being kept up after having once begun, many accidents occurred, owing also to the Light Division in the square meeting the 3rd who had entered at the large breach, but who had lost a great many officers and men (among them General [Henry] Mackinnon was killed at the head of his brigade) chiefly owing to a magazine of fresh shells and powder blowing up near the breach just as they were getting into it.

During the whole night the soldiers committed many excesses, setting fire to some houses, plundering many, particularly after finding some large stores of very good French brandy, bread, pork &c, and it was impossible to get them into any order for a long time. I was ordered by Colonel [Andrew] Barnard 95th, now commanding the Light Division, to take charge of above 700 prisoners collected in a large dirty barrack with two companies, of whom (till next morning) I could get few. The regiment remained upon the ramparts.

The night the fortress was stormed, he was ordered to keep watch over the prisoners with his troops and was relieved to hand them over to a Portuguese battalion the next day.

20 January [1812]
I remained on guard over these prisoners, making good fires and having got a good cloak from my servant, without which I should have been very cold (as we all stormed in scarlet of course) and this morning the total of the prisoners collected at this place besides many others, amounted to 980, some of whom were wounded, but it was impossible to get them dressed. At noon I was ordered to deliver them over to the 3rd Cacadores, as well as 64 officers who had been collected at the governor's house and I set off after the regiment with my guard for El

Bodon, passing on the road the 5th Division, who had just come up from near Coimbra. Crossed the Agueda by the bridge of Ciudad Rodrigo.

Lieutenant George Barlow of the 52nd Foot wrote in detail of that terrible night.

> El Bodon, 22 January 1812
>
> We entered it about nine at night, consequently until daylight all was a scene of disorder & confusion. Every man had three or four loaves stuck upon the point of his bayonet. A guard was luckily placed over the spirit magazine in time to prevent its seizure. Fifty pipes of good cognac were there found,[2] with a quantity of other commissariat articles; very little booty was however to be gained, inasmuch as the whole town had been deserted by everyone previous to its first occupation by the French, who had pulled down the houses for firewood and our shot has demolished the whole of those nearest the ramparts. The night was moreover miserably cold & our troops crowded into the ruined houses to make fires. These rotten edifices soon caught the flames and the conflagration became dreadful. Yesterday I rode over to Ciudad with the view of taking a more ample view of this wretched place . . .

Ensign George Young of the 38th Foot wrote about the siege more than a month later.

> Ciudad Rodrigo, 27 February 1812
>
> I am rejoiced to find you in good health, which you may see by this that I also enjoy, thanks to the Merciful God of Heaven that brought me through the dangers and hardships which I have been exposed to in this country, and has hitherto preserved me unhurt, though many times in the most eminent [sic] danger. To give you a full detail of all I have witnessed in this country would fill a volume, suffice it for the present to say that in no instance have I witnessed death and destruction in so horrible a light as in the taking of this town, which you have long ere this had an account of. In taking this place we lost about one thousand men killed and wounded. The loss of the enemy in prisoners, killed and wounded, &c., was about one thousand eight hundred, also some warlike stores which we found in the town. We are now very busy in repairing the works and erecting new batteries on a rising ground that commands the town.

---

2. A Portuguese pipe measured 550 litres. Therefore, the store held 27,500 litres or 6,049 gallons of brandy!

Lieutenant Charles Dawson of the 52nd Foot wrote of the dreadful scenes.

> El Bodon 29 January 1812
> The bustle and confusion that was in the town after it was taken is more than my pen can describe, plundering, men getting drunk, setting fire to houses &c. It was wonderful that the whole town & everybody in it, was not blown to atoms. Several of the Portuguese soldiers made a large fire in the great magazine where thousands of pounds of powder, ball & shells were laying & the men quite drunk, it was fortunately discovered soon & the fire extinguished.

His brother Lieutenant Henry Dawson, with him in the 52nd, also wrote about it.

> Fuenteguinaldo 12 February 1812
> The carnage at first was great but luckily did not last long. To describe the scene which took place afterwards is more than I am equal to. Firing into the windows, bursting open doors, setting fire to houses, in fact sacking the town, stripping the inhabitants of their gold chains, earrings, trinkets & valuables of every kind, getting drunk and doing everything that soldiers are capable of after having carried a town by storm.

Ensign John Mills of the Coldstream Guards was deeply shocked by the carnage left after the successful capture of the town.

> Espeja 22 January 1812
> During the whole of the preceding day and yesterday morning, the Spaniards had been employed in burying, but the scene such as it was when I saw it, stripped of half its horrors was beyond all imagination. The contents of the houses emptied into the streets, several of the houses on fire and one continued mass of friends and foes lying dead. Caps, clothes, arms, cannon balls, ammunition, beds, chairs, wearing apparel, legs &c &c filled the streets. Those who saw this scene on the morning after describe it as dreadful beyond expression. Added to all this, the houses near the breaches were knocked to pieces.

In a further letter to his brother one week later, he added a few more details, including the terrible pillaging that had followed.

> 29 January 1812
> Bodies were lying about in all directions and as is always the case, stripped to the skin. The walls were terribly battered, several guns

dismounted and the blood upon the gun carriages testified that our shot had told. I was really afraid of walking about; there were quantities of loose powder and loaded shells and the town was then on fire in several places . . . when the French begun to run, pillage was the order of the day. They thought no more of their enemy, but set about plundering . . . the first thing they seized was a large bag into which they crammed eatables, drinkables, clothes, furniture, fiddles, frying pans, in short anything they could find. When it was full, they got into a corner and drafted the most useless.

Repairing the defences after a siege was always necessary, but extremely unpopular work. Ensign John Carter of the 30th Foot wrote of the soldiers' skulking away from the work and provides a cautionary tale.

26 January 1812

At six o'clock we went to the trenches a very cold misty morning, several of our men who were skulking from this work got into a small shed, & these began to light a fire, this shed was a temporary kind of a magazine, some loose powder took fire & literally blew all the clothes off two or three of them, they were sadly burnt.

The repairs went on slowly, as they were not complete when Lieutenant James Gairdner of the 95th Rifles viewed them nearly six months later.

21 June 1812

Went to Ciudad Rodrigo, drew rations and went on to Sancti Espiritus . . . The breaches of Rodrigo are not half finished nor the forts either. The inhabitants are the sulkiest, most uncivil set I ever saw. Although it is six months since the siege I saw unburied human skulls and bones lying in the streets contiguous to the breaches.

The army had no time to rest on its laurels, however, before it was marching south to take advantage of French difficulties and to launch a swift attack on the fortress of Badajoz. The fortress had been besieged before by Wellington's troops, but they had failed because superior numbers of French troops had arrived in the vicinity. Major General Sir Charles Colville had participated in the earlier attempt, it being his baptism of fire.

28 May 1811

I have had two spells of 24 hours in the trenches. I shall have my third this evening because Generals of Division do not share this duty, but commanders of brigades only, and besides me there is one only of this rank, viz General Hamilton. Being the first siege by regular approach that I ever witnessed, I am glad to be upon this; but otherwise it is a service of no small discomfort, as you must either be exposed without any cover at all the almost incessant fire of shot and shells, or take what cover is offered behind the batteries or in the ditches, at best a partial one and especially for shells and where, in addition to the torrid heat by day and the dews of night, you are half suffocated between the dust kicked up by the afore named visitors and by the effluvia of three or four thousand men, half of them Portuguese, the filthiest nation upon earth.

First Lieutenant James Macleod of the Royal Artillery had also served in the earlier siege and showed his frustration when they could not complete it.

Elvas 13 June 1811
I was in hopes to have dated this letter from Badajoz, but alas after ten days open trenches and a breach in the castle (which when in possession of the place would surrender) nearly if not already practicable . . .

The third siege was to prove to be the worst of the entire war. Ensign George Young of the 38th wrote of the preparations.

27 February 1812
We are to leave this in a few days for the south; it seems to be his Lordship's intention to attack Badajoz, all sorts of preparations are making for the purpose. The Battering Train are moving towards it with numerous quantities of shells and rockets to bombard the town. Our division is mentioned as the storming party. We are completing in shoes and blankets and expect every moment to receive the route. Part of the army are already on their march, we are only waiting to be relieved by the Spaniards that are to garrison this place, which we expect in tomorrow. You may expect to hear of something very soon from this country (I hope it may be good news). The army are in high spirits and are anxious to come in contact with the enemy. . .

Lieutenant George Barlow of the 52nd wrote of the terrible weather and of his experiences in the trenches.

Camp before Badajoz, 19 March 1812
The season at this time of the year is not very pleasant for those who live under canvas; a great deal of rain has lately fallen accompanied with

high & tempestuous winds, the camp is moreover very inconvenient in two most important respects. Water must be fetched from a considerable distance & that not of the best; and which in summer must be particularly unwholesome, from being stagnant. It is a considerable distance to the Guadiana and the whole country around a sandy, barren flat, almost as naked as the palm of my hand and almost destitute of wood for fires & cooking; these are indeed two great inconveniences much felt.

I am very sleepy, not having had any sleep these two last nights of any nature in camp; on the first being attached to the party which opened the trenches and on yesterday, everyone being sent out with a picquet to watch some roads leading to the bridge of Badajoz, where the enemy have a post and from which duty I have only returned this morning.

Lieutenant James Gairdner of the 95th Rifles was in the trenches before the assault on Badajoz, in the attack he was wounded three times.

6 April 1812

Our company was sent to relieve a company of the 52nd on picket near the river at about 12 o'clock, this day. At about 6 o'clock we were ordered to come in and join the regiment at dark as the town is to be stormed tonight. A third breach has been made since yesterday. At about 8 o'clock we paraded in rear of the 52nd and our regiment was directed to put itself under the orders of Lt Colonel [Sir George] Elder who was to command the reserve and who had orders to remain in some quarries till further orders, he however neglected those orders and followed the column to the breach and brought his reserve into action with the main column.

The defence of the garrison is universally allowed to have been very good. I received three wounds early in the attack, viz one in the right leg very slight, one in the left arm and one in the chin and after lying on the ground was at last helped off by a sergeant of our company and with the assistance of some of the 52nd band who were coming with bearers carried to the hospital tent where my wounds were dressed and I was then put into a tent for the reception of wounded officers.[3]

---

3. George Simmons records that Lieutenant Gardiner was wounded at Badajoz, a clear misidentification of our James Gairdner. These two officers are constantly confused.

Soon after the victory Lieutenant Henry Dawson of the 52nd Foot wrote:

Badajoz 8 April 1812
Badajoz is now in our possession, but I am sorry to say with most severe loss on our side. Charles is very slightly wounded in the calf of the leg with a slug & is doing very well. I did not escape, but so trifling the wound, I would not allow myself to return wounded. I sincerely hope this will reach you before any idle reports or even the Gazette.

George Barlow wrote at length of the storm and his wounding.

Badajoz, 18 April 1812
The night was quite dark, which would render the least confusion & certainty of ill success. This presently occurred by the loss of the two engineer officers who alone knew the way and whilst leading on the advanced parties, fell by the very first volley from the enemy. Our column and that of the 4th Division crossed at that unlucky moment and got mixed and in this state both crowded together to the same breach, instead of each taking its own particular one. This great body of men had to descend a steep counterscarp by five or six ladders only, which as you may suppose, took some time, as four only could go down at once on each. We had then to drive them out of a demi-lune,[4] and all this close under the noses of between 2 and 3,000 men the greater part of whom had *three* spare muskets each, with people to load them in their rear, and kept up one of the most rapid and murderous fires, such as our oldest veterans affirm they never before experienced. Aim was unnecessary, we stood so thick and crowded on the glacis, and in the ditch, besides the enemy threw amongst us a number of fire balls which enabled them to see our movements as clear as at noon day. The breach would not admit of more than 13 or 15 men abreast and the storming party made a number of gallant though fruitless attempts to carry it. They repeatedly arrived on the summit, but found the entrance filled up with a massy row of chevaux de frise, which it was impossible either to remove, cut away, or even to get over.[5] The slope of the breaches were covered with planks, full of nails with the sharp ends sticking upwards;

---

4. A detached outwork, usually triangular in shape, which was placed in front of the long curtain wall to protect it from artillery fire.
5. A chevaux-de-frise or 'Frisian horse' was a large beam covered with projecting spikes or blades which formed a hedge of points against cavalry or infantry.

the interior of the bastions were afterwards found to have been traversed in all directions, ditches and pits fifteen feet deep cut everywhere, into which our people might fall like traps during the darkness of the night; and a new fosse with a rampart thrown up in the rear of all these works.[6] In addition to this, shells and grenades were placed in rows along the parapet to be hurled down on the heads of our poor fellows and a new species of destruction fired out of their muskets, called by us *musket grape*, being a number of slugs bound together, and resembling that sort of cannon shot in miniature; in a word every obstacle which the engineer's art or invention could devise, seems to have been put in requisition by our able foe; in this horrible state we remained, excepting myself and one or two others, they all were killed and wounded on the very breach one after another, and in this awful crisis persevered in using their utmost personal exertions, till Lord Wellington, who was on a neighbouring hill, sent us orders to retire, leaving 70 officers in the horrible ditch and nearly 1,000 men. I speak of course only of the transactions of our own division. Nearly three quarters of an hour without being able to retaliate in the least on the enemy . . . As for myself, I was first hit in the thigh when the column approached the glacis;[7] the ball carried away a canteen hanging down my back by cutting in two the leather strap to which it was affixed, and taking a downward direction lodged a little below the right hip bone. A poor fellow at that very moment was shot by my side and I concluded at first that in falling he had struck me off my legs. The pain in a few moments decreased however and about a quarter of an hour afterwards as the column moved forwards, I got over the palisades of the ditch, was shown some ladders a little on the left. I turned half round to the men telling them to follow me thither and waving my cap when the second shot struck my right arm, chapeau dropt quick enough as you may suppose and I not being able to hold out any longer, with great difficulty persuaded a couple of soldiers (Portuguese) to help me off. They wanted me to lay flat on the glacis in company with them till the fire which was very heavy should abate a little. To this I would not agree, feeling myself growing fainter every instant from loss of blood. A British soldier coming past with a bearer[8] at that moment, lifted me into it and carried me to the surgeons. Finding the sword and belt galling me much, I requested my Portuguese friends to take charge of it, by the way and

---

6. In fortification terms, a fosse was a long narrow trench.
7. The earthen bank sloping away from the fortifications.
8. A stretcher.

whilst under the surgeon's hands, they whipped them off and I have seen no more of them as you may imagine.

Sergeant William Ross of the 74th Foot wrote home regarding some incidents during the siege.

> Albergaria 27 April 1812
> At night when Fort Pickroon [Picurina] was stormed by the covering party of the 3rd Division, our regiment suffered much in killed and wounds on that night, the place is much stronger than was expected, with a deep trench, the walls of the fort in most places was thirty feet in height which could not be discovered by the British until the moment of attack, in the place was five hundred men, about three hundred surrendered & prisoners, the rest was put to the bayonet. . . .

As to the storm itself, later in the letter he recalled:

> [The 3rd] Division rushed on and got under their guns, but they greatly annoyed us with their musquetry from off the walls. The men that was employed in carrying the ladders not being able to keep up with their regiments, exposed us for a long time, to the enemy's fire, at last we gained our object in getting possession of the [castle]. The French soldiers stood by their guns until they were put to the bayonet.
> The contest was dreadful and the killed and wounded on both sides dreadful, the 4th & Light Division were repulsed back from the breach with great loss the first time and would never gate [*sic*] possession of Badajoz had it not [been] for our division. The storming of Ciudad Rodrigo was nothing to Badajoz.

Henry Johnson, attached to the Prince of Orange, wrote of the number of cannon balls fired during the siege.

> Fuenteguinaldo 10 May 1812
> The works and repairs at Badajoz are in a very forward state thanks to the exertions of Sir R[ichard] Fletcher . . . The returns now being complete I find that instead of 32,000 rounds, we fired 35,000 [&] odd hundreds in 12 days, the average number of pieces at work 28!! The train will be sent to refit at Gibraltar.

Captain James Gubbins of the 13th Light Dragoons wrote of the achievement:

Ribera eight leagues from Merida 19 April 1812

You will long before you get this letter see the official account of the fall of Badajoz, a conquest of importance, it was gallantly and dearly earned.

Advancing to the city of Salamanca in 1812, the British found that the French had left three strongly-fortified convents in the middle of the city, which required a formal siege to take them. Captain John Ewart wrote at length regarding the forts:

17 June 1812

Under arms before daylight; halted about a mile from the bridge over the Tormes close to Salamanca, found it commanded by a fort erected lately by the French who had left a garrison in it of about 500 men. Some plunder was also reported to be in this fort; a great smoke, apparently from the burning of stores, was seen in some parts of the town . . . The 6th Division (at the head of General Graham's Corps), preceded by the 14th Dragoons, forded the river about half a mile above the town and formed in the square . . . the Light Division and the remainder of General Graham's corps had crossed the Tormes by the ford above the town and were encamped near it about half a mile from the gate of Salamanca, into which most of the British and Portuguese officers went during the day. Several of the best buildings have been destroyed since 1808, but in general the town looked much more flourishing than we expected to find it. Many of the inhabitants and students had left the town; those who remained received us with loud acclamations, particularly the women, waving their handkerchiefs and throwing roses from the windows. They were apparently much rejoiced at our arrival, probably owing to their not having shared the terrible fate of Rodrigo and Badajoz. From the atrocities committed at these places, we find the French had intimidated and irritated the people of Salamanca much against us, but no soldiers of ours except officers' servants and sergeants were allowed to enter, except the three brigades of the 6th Division, and the rest of the division, 2nd, 32nd, 36th, under General Clinton, who had strong guards in many parts of the town, and also were obliged to watch the forts, from which the enemy not only fire round shot at all who approached the bridge, but musketry at everyone who attempted to approach, or out of curiosity got on the tops of houses, chiefly on the roof of the cathedral, which we found as fine as formerly; as we did the Great Square, neither having been destroyed in any way . . . Lord Wellington's headquarters and most of our general officers remained in the town, which at eight o'clock was as quiet and regular as possible; 24 hours before, 7,000 French were in it . . .

Lieutenant Henry Hough of the Royal Artillery was fully engaged in this siege and kept a campaign diary.

June 24 [1812]
   Endeavoured to take the convent by storm but were repulsed (on the evening of the 23rd). Skirmishes took place between the cavalry this day and yesterday.
   25th Was ordered into the batteries. It was intended to fire red-hot shot into the convent but not having any heavy ordnance arrived, it was ordered to be given up, as we found the metal expand so much and the guns so very warm, that it would be impossible to fire many rounds. A slow fire was kept up from the F[rench] fort all night.
   26th Army in same position. Heavy artillery arrives. Lieutenant Elgee ordered to Ciudad [Rodrigo] to bring up 18 and 24 pounder ammunition. Baynes on duty in the town. Remained in charge of Reserve till about 3 o'clock p.m. when I received Colonel [Haylett] Framingham's orders to go into the howitzer battery with 2 N.C. Officers and 20 gunners. Got there about ½ past 4 o'clock pm and commenced firing red-hot shot at the fort & continued till about 12 o'clock Saturday morning. Captain Edward Michell was in the same battery.
   About 8 o'clock Friday evening [26th] we set the roof of the left wing of the fort on fire, which burnt for near 4 hours and then was extinguished, the French batteries playing upon us all the time, their riflemen very troublesome indeed. Kept up a firing all night, they returning us shot for shot, and shell for shell, with plenty of grape into the bargain but thank God with not much effect.
   27th Near abouts 7 o'clock Saturday morning we got it in flames again & had a very hard struggle which should put it out, or which should keep it in, but our batteries cracking shrapnels over their ears and sending plenty more red-hot into the same spot, soon made a fine blaze and made them abandon their batteries, and send out a flag of truce.
   Their offers of giving up two forts, provided we would let them quiet 2 hours, Lord Wellington would not listen to. The officer returned and we rattled away again as hard as we could *lick* at them. This made them send a second flag, which was also refused, and we gave them another taste of the red-hot, the 6th Division (Clinton) storming at the breaches at the same moment. They took the two forts, without any opposition, and then advanced on into the large fort, where all the French garrison had retired. The place was soon filled. I was there a very short time, when I got orders to repair to the small fort and collect the ammunition together, where I was confined till near 5 o'clock.

240   *Marching, Fighting, Dying*

He passed through Salamanca again on 11 July.

> Halted at Salamanca. Went over the convent and forts with Lieutenant [John] Pascoe. Astonished at the strength of the works and the means the French had made use of to cut off all communication with the inner works, where we had made breaches. Parties were employed digging the shot from the ruins. A great many bodies were found that had perished in the flames, endeavouring to extinguish them.

Ensign Robert Garrett of the 2nd Foot recorded the dangers of the siege in a letter.

> Salamanca 17 June 1812
> During this day I had a canteen broken to pieces by a musket ball while in the act of drinking.

> Failed assault 28 June
> I have no time to give you chapter & verse now . . . suffice it to say that I am the only officer in the company who was not killed . . . I was slightly wounded in the leg but did not think it worthwhile to return my name as such, and besides had my cap completely cut to pieces with a grape shot, which took away a great part of my hair from the top of my head and broke the skin a little. The scabbard of my sword too was carried away by the same shower of grape that took my cap, so you see I had a narrow squeak for it; but a miss is as good as a mile . . . we found our ladders short by 6 or 8 feet, the wall being nearly 50 feet high . . . I had my cap knocked to pieces & my head cut, which is now nearly well, by a grape shot, & my leg slightly scratched by a musquet ball which took away part of my boot & overalls & shortly afterwards was knocked off the scaling ladder by a large beam or stone which was thrown on me from the fort & which stupefied me for some little time . . .

Even the lowly Pay Clerk Robert Duffield Cooke, with no business being near the front line, was desperate to tell of two close calls in a chipper letter to his father.

> Head Quarters, Madrid!!!! 19 August 1812
> I was in Salamanca at the taking of the forts and assure you that I am not telling fibs when I say the whistling of the shells and balls buzzing close to your ears has such an effect on one that I fancied I heard them three days after it was all over. Two narrowish escapes (real facts I must relate) 1st viz: I went one morning with a friend to a lady's house to look out of her garret window for the purpose of viewing the fort stormed

by the English. The window was occupied by the lady so I got out on the leads to give her room. The French were then throwing shells into the town, some of which buzzed so close I began to get quite warm. The lady laughed, of course, I could not be afraid. Presently a shell burst on the house opposite dispersing all round our heads, I began to sweat the lady smiled. I sat on. Presently a musket ball stuck in the framework of the window. At that minute, my friend inside, who was putting his spy glass to rights, let it drop and broke the glass. He then called me to walk with him to get it mended and I jumped inside with a good excuse. We had hardly got outside the door when a shell came, cleared the whole garret window away, killed a man servant and took both hands of the lady smack off. I intend buying the spy glass as a preserver.

The other close one was while gaping on at the top of the cathedral; balls delightfully buzzing as usual, one of them came and killed a Spaniard about a yard to my left. You may judge whether I walked or ran in.

Later that year, the Duke of Wellington badly underestimated the strength of Burgos Castle and he attempted to attack it with a pathetically small body of artillery. The weather was extremely wet and the mud and terrible conditions, coupled with a frustratingly difficult siege, a sense of hopelessness soon permeated throughout the army and very few were sorry when the decision was made to abandon the attempt. Lieutenant Hough was there and continued his diary of events. It is interesting that he immediately realized the strength of the French defences.

18 September
[Moved] on Burgos, where we drew up, almost within cannon shot of the fort & works, which are exceeding strong. The castle stands on a very steep hill, and is entirely surrounded with works, and on another steep hill to the left is a very strong redoubt, in which is a battery of 3 18 pounders, and several other pieces of ordnance of smaller calibre, the whole surrounded with ditches strongly palisaded and supported by loopholed works, from which they are capable of keeping up a very strong fire of musketry.

In the evening Lieutenant Pascoe & myself ventured into the city of Burgos & about 6 more British officers also went in; but when we were looking out for some things to purchase, an alarm was given that the garrison had made a sortie & that if we did not immediately go out at the other end of the town we should all be taken. In the bustle to get off one dropped his rice, another sugar, and as we went down one street the enemy came down the other. They gave us a volley, but thank God we were out of range, and we made the best of our way back to camp where we remained quiet for the night.

28th

Lieutenant Elgee and Major Arriaga[9] went to the batteries, mine going on. At 5 pm Captain [William] Power and myself relieved the above mentioned officers. We formed a communication this day between the two approaches, and the enemy threw a great many shells &c. over the walls on our working parties; 12 or 14 men of the line were wounded this night, but no casualty in the batteries. I got two F[rench] guns out of the hornwork this night; they were both spiked and unfit for service. I was much shocked this night, during the search for the guns; it being dark, we were obliged to feel our way very carefully, and seeing something very imperfectly I went to see if it was any part of a gun, but judge how disappointed I was, instead of stores, I laid hold of a dead Frenchman, and after recovering I found myself surrounded by dead bodies and in the dark trod on many others. Just after, I received a smart blow on my right ancle [sic] from a stone which was knocked off the trenches by a round shot from the castle.

4 October

Colonel Dickson and Lieutenant Elgee opened the batteries and made very excellent practice. Captain P[ower] and myself went in at ½ past 3 o'clock and opened with shrapnel and spherical about ½ past 4 o'clock to support the 24th Regiment that stormed about that time at two breaches one of which was made at the same hour and served as a signal to attack. Upon our men showing themselves at the top of the breach on the 1st line, the enemy retreated in great confusion to their 2nd, losing many killed and wounded and several prisoners, besides several that perished when the mine blew up. From the 2nd line and the guns and mortars &c. on and about the castle, a most tremendous fire was kept up, for upwards of an hour. The fire over our battery for 20 minutes was truly awful; we lost many killed and wounded and I had a most miraculous escape, by a grape shot passing through my cocked hat slightly touching my head, and killing a poor fellow who was standing in my rear (Bombardier Ridley), besides which I was struck several times with stones from the top of the battery; in short, we could

---

9. Major Sebastiáo José de Arriaga, Portuguese Artillery.

not expect to escape without being wounded. Our men established themselves on the 1st line and continued firing all night . . .

Lieutenant William Bragge of the 3rd Dragoons was much more succinct.

> Villayerna 3 miles from Burgos 18 October 1812
> . . . From the moment we first invested this cursed castle, the weather has proved particularly unfavourable to our operations, having scarcely ceased raining the whole time accompanied by occasional high winds and very severe nights, notwithstanding which our divisions of infantry still remain encamped and may truly to be said to resemble 'father pigs', not having any covering but very indifferent huts built of boughs and open at each end, without any straw, palliasses or things of that nature to lie on. You can easily conceive the state of such a camp on low ground after three weeks rain, which has almost filled our trenches with mud and water as well as the camp.

Lieutenant George Young of the 38th Foot summed up the failure at Burgos.

> Lamego, 10 December 1812
> You doubtless long before this have heard the reverse of fortune the army has met with since their advance to Burgos, of the long destructive and fruitless siege of the castle of that city, and our precipitate retreat from its neighbourhood, in all of which you may easily suppose suffered extremely through excess of marching and fatigue. To be sure we lay for a month in front of the town without marching, but if we did it rained nearly the whole of the time upon us, with nothing but the canopy of heaven for our covering. I think you will do us the justice to say, that was nearly as bad as marching. On the evening of the 19th of October the enemy pushed forward a large body of cavalry and infantry, with some artillery to reconnoitre our position in front of Burgos, which brought on some skirmishing in which the enemy were worsted and driven back. However the day following they showed such an immense superiority in number, particularly in cavalry, that it was found not safe to risk a battle, which of course obliged us to raise the siege. We marched all night, all the next day, and till 5 o'clock of the morning following without a halt, which tired us not a little . . .

The campaign of 1813 was mercifully less dominated by sieges, particularly once the French abandoned the dreaded fortress of Burgos and destroyed it in a huge explosion. Pamplona was only invested to starve the French out, therefore the only siege of the year was progressed at San Sebastian. Lieutenant James Crummer of the 28th Foot probably spoke for the majority when he voiced his dislike of all sieges.

> Camp near Gallisteo 16 May 1813
> We have a strong report that our division, the 4th and Light Division are to have the honour of striking our heads against the wall of Burgos, a service I do not admire so much as fighting in the field.

An unknown ensign of the 59th Foot wrote of volunteering for an exceptionally dangerous job and described the first unsuccessful storm.

> Before San Sebastian 8 August 1813
> I will tell you news which you will be surprised to hear, which is, they have appointed me Assistant Engineer during the siege, through my volunteering it when we first came. And I can assure you, we have had some hard work, and not only hard, but hot work also.
> On the morning we attempted to storm, it was the brigade of sappers, that I belonged to, carried the ladders to the breach, where the captain, commanding the brigade, was wounded; and not only he, but every engineer officer, on duty that night, except another and myself, was either killed or wounded; seven in all.
> I have been three times breaking ground, exposed to as hot a fire of musquetry, as the French advance could keep up, and once, completely driven out of a breast work, which I was throwing up over the main road, where I had all my men killed or wounded except three, out of a dozen; but thank Almighty God, it has not been my lot.
> Our advance work is about twenty yards from the French, so that of a still night we can hear them talk. I suppose you would like to hear something of the storm, or rather attempt to storm, which we made. It was to commence at break of day, and the signal was the springing of a mine which had been an old aqueduct we hit on the last parallel which ran under the ravelin or hornwork, and into this covert way. But we are afraid the French found it out, for it had not the desired effect.
> This was to be the signal at which the cacadores on the right of the trenches were to keep up a heavy fire, till our first brigade of the 5th Division came up to the breach. The first brigade was composed of the 1st, 9th and 38th Regiments, and the cacadores on the left were to rush on to where the mine was sprung, and where we expected to have breach; but when they got there, nothing but the palisades of the hornwork was gone; and they waited there calling for ladders to escalade; but no

ladders came. At last they were obliged to retreat, under heavy fire of musquetry and showers of grape; and poor fellows, they strewed the sands in numbers ere they reached the trenches.

In the mean time, the first brigade pushed on for the breach, under a heavy fire from the ramparts, of grape and small arms and, as they became near the breach, it was troubled by hand grenades.

Some of our gallant fellows got in, and were either killed or taken immediately, for they kept throwing stones and logs of firewood on them as they entered. The Royals, or 1st, lost 300 men and 15 officers. The 9th, 100 [men] and 3 officers. So ended our storming.

Major General Frederick Robinson wrote a succession of letters to his wife during the siege.

Camp before San Sebastian 23 July 1813

We have been besieging this place ten days, and this night it will be stormed. I have just received notice that my brigade is to be in the trenches tonight, but whether I am to be honoured with the advance or not, I cannot tell, but be that as it may, I hope I shall do my duty. I have a brave set of fellows under me, that will follow wherever I lead, ...

We are in hopes of having some rest if we succeed like good boys in taking the place. Our noble Lord is arrived, and if he places himself within view of the men they will fight like heroes. It is not easy to describe the enthusiasm of the Army about him, although he appears to harass them more than any army suffered before. Our whole division are nearly bare footed and the clothing torn to pieces, besides which they are constantly covered with mud from head to foot owing to their working in the trenches night and day in the most dreadful weather I ever remember. Still no complaint is heard and their only hope is that the town may not be allowed to capitulate *after all the trouble they have had*. They little think or care for the inhabitants, but you may form an idea of their situation, when I tell you we fire about 400 cannon shot & shells every hour.

San Sebastian 2 September 1813

At eleven o'clock I gave the word to advance, which was instantly obeyed with a shout that gave promise of success. The fire of grape and musquetry against us cannot be described, the strand and bottom of the breach was in five minutes covered with dead and wounded. Notwithstanding which, they gained the top and maintained it for three hours, when by the explosion of one of the enemy mines, a passage was opened into the town. In an instant the whole division as well as other troops charged into it and the French ran in crowds to the castle. In two hours more the town was completely ours. . . . The melancholy part of my story is yet to come. Out of 1,000 brave fellows who accomplished this extraordinary feat, with the addition of 200 more that came up some time after, seven hundred and forty together with fifty officers were killed & wounded on the breach and advancing to it. Among the rest *My Excellency* was laid sprawling in the mud by a ball through my beautiful face, which occasions my sitting as unnaturally upright as any boarding school Miss. Fortunately my teeth and jawbone are safe, but I shall have a nice little scar to remind me of San Sebastian for the remainder of my life . . .

San Sebastian 11 September 1813
    . . . The beautiful town of San Sebastian is no more, there are about ten houses left. It was the most beautiful, the most opulent and the happiest in this part of Spain . . . It contained twelve thousand inhabitants and every house was a good one, but most of them excellent. During the confusion what the fire spared, our men took, the plunder was immense. I went over it all yesterday and could have wept with grief & vexation at the sorrowful and wicked act. It was done by the French as soon as they saw that our people had gained the breach . . . I am nearly recovered from my wound, and begin to move my jaws at dinner time with their wonted activity, but the surgeon has been so very clever, that I fear I shall have but a very small scar to exhibit. Had the ball gone a hairs breadth nearer to my neck I should have slept with my fathers.

Lieutenant Colonel John Hunt of the 52nd Foot recorded events during the storming in his journal.

31 August [1813] San Sebastian
    Sir James Leith ordered me to move my men forward, he showed me the way, which although I then considered as not very fair, at a time when the failure of the others was anything but embarrassing and as my men were so scattered along the works, yet as soon as I supplied them with a little ammunition I ordered them to move on. With about 20 men I gained the breach & reached the top where, as I was examining it, I was struck on the breast with a spent ball, which however, only bruised. I endeavoured to prevail on the men below me to follow me, but finding the precipice too deep on the other side and the troops not

much inclined to follow, excepting my few brave companions of the 52nd, who were but a handful, I proposed to go to another breach which seemed more practicable and notwithstanding the constant fire of the enemy, which every moment, killed numbers, I succeeded in passing. On reaching the summit, I found myself only with about ten of my men, the rest including Captain R[obert] Campbell, Lieutenant [John] Harvest O'Connell 43rd &c were either killed or disabled. I however endeavoured to lead on the men of the other regiments underneath who were principally Portuguese & observing a part where I could descend into the town, I exerted myself to arouse the soldiers. At length while in the act of taking hold of the Colour of a Portuguese regiment with one hand and stepping over the crest of the breach I received a ball under my left knee which knocked me completely over and put an end to all further exertions on my part. Two of my men undertook to lead me off, and with the blessings of providence I was conveyed safe from farther injury to the convent where we had assembled in the morning.

Ensign the Honourable Orlando Bridgeman of the 1st Foot Guards was wounded in the final attack and soon after wrote a long account of the proceedings.

Oiartzun 2 September 1813

Thank God I am quite well; we stormed San Sebastian on the morning of the 31st ult & after a good deal of resistance carried the breach, I am slightly wounded on the left knee, but when you see that I write from this town, having ridden two leagues this morning, you cannot I am sure be uneasy. This morning I received a most kind note from General Stopford, inviting me to his house, but my wound is so slight that I mean to go to camp; poor [William] Burrard of our regiment was killed by my side about half an hour after we stormed, our loss has been severe.

His later account gives much greater detail.

Irun 7 September 1813

... the enemy were posted in the horn-work firing grape shot & musketry on our troops as they advanced & here our poor fellows began to tumble, we soon reached the breach & we then opened upon the enemy in our front. They also gave us a pretty warm reception, we were here between two fires, one in our front & the other on our flank, and notwithstanding a pretty heavy fire of musketry which we kept up,

& also all our batteries, the enemy stood their ground well. In about half an hour I was close to poor Burrard when he received a musket shot in his left groin, & [Captain Thomas] Barrow of the Coldstream & myself went to his assistance, almost the first words he said were 'I fear my wound is mortal for it is exactly the same as my poor brother received at Corunna'.[10] & 'get the enemy off the glacis for me'. This is a very singular circumstance for his brother actually died of the very same sort of wound; he endeavoured to stand but was not able, & we got a bier with four men to carry him to the hospital where he died at nine o'clock the next morning. As soon as he was gone we remounted the breach, and we about this time began to flag in ammunition, having fired all their own, & we were occupied by collecting it out of the dead men's pouches. About half an hour after this, I thought our men began to give way, indeed I could not wonder at it for the fire from the enemy was tremendous & our men were falling by dozens, but just at this time we saw to our great joy a brigade of our Portuguese coming to our assistance on the right of the breach, & notwithstanding the fire of grape from the enemy, they advanced in the most gallant style; this was everything to us, just as they got to the breach & were mounting it; I received a wound on my left knee, & as I was falling a large stone, I believe it was, struck me on the back, & I recollect no more, till I found myself at the bottom of the breach supported by two men. At that time I did not feel my knee, but only my back, & I thought I had been seriously wounded there for I could scarcely draw my breath, I however managed to get to the hospital, but was obliged to rest several times in the trenches, where the scenes I witnessed, as well as those after I arrived at the hospital, were more horrible than anything I had conceived. As soon as I arrived at the hospital I found that the pain in my back was occasioned by a severe blow, & I cannot conceive it to have been from anything but a stone for they were flying about almost as fast as the shot. The surgeon of the 1st Division dressed my knee, & assured me no bone was broke, & he recommended my going home & getting to bed. I consequently sent for my horse & with the assistance of my servant got home & got to bed; when I say home I mean to the ground we left in the morning & where all my baggage was; by five o'clock I was in bed . . .

---

10. His brother Ensign Paul Henry Burrard of the 1st Foot Guards, aide de camp to Sir John Moore, had been severely wounded at Corunna and died of his wounds on board HMS *Audacious* on 21 January 1809.

George Barlow of the 52nd Foot visited the town only a week after it had surrendered but while the castle was still holding out.

> Camp near Vera, 10 September 1813
> On the morning of the 2nd instant I obtained permission to take a trip of excursion to St Sebastian . . . On arriving about half way, the object of my journey might be discerned from afar, marked by a tremendous volume of smoke arising from the conflagrations of this unhappy city and so eager was I to discover the shortest route that upon attempting to cross a narrow arm of Passages [Pasajes] harbour at low water, where footsteps might be seen in the mud and three marks of direction, my mule was swamped up to his belly & there stuck. After being extricated from this plight I arrived safe enough at St Sebastian. You approach it by a very long and beautiful avenue of trees, which would make a very pretty promenade for any of our sea bathing places, the sands are extensive and the country round about delightful. It was necessary for me to pass close to the batteries at that time, in full volley; but my mule stood fire like a veteran. Being pretty well jaded by a journey of twenty miles in very mountainous roads; the city stands of a narrow neck of land running out into the sea and forming on either side two very picturesque bays, outside of which might be seen Sir George Collier's squadron at anchor. The castle forms a very striking object in the picture & together with the heavy bombardment would form one of the most beautiful panoramas you can imagine, partaking of which the ground moreover presents peculiar facilities.
> I took up my quarters with a brother officer in the Convent of St Bartholomew,[11] terribly ruined by our cannon, whilst approaches [were] approaching the suburbs, and on this occasion [now] converted into an hospital for our wounded. After putting up my mule, I went immediately into the town and passed over the breaches. It was the third day subsequent to the storm, but its melancholy victims might be seen strewed all over them and in their vicinity, English and French, German or Italian, promiscuously mixed and their numbers attesting the gallantry shown by either party during the combat. The main breach was a most gigantic one, very easy of access, but had most formidable defences within, was well traversed, so that on mounting you found yourself exposed from head to foot to a line of troops firing from behind parapets about twelve yards in rear, themselves being well protected & posted in ruined houses. A battery of six pieces from the castle played

---

11. The Convent of San Bartolome still stands on a hill dominating the city of San Sebastian.

terribly on the ramparts as soon as you gained their height. The streets were also well entrenched, deep pits cut and every precaution taken by a skilful foe to maintain his posts, their troops encouraged by former success, fought most obstinately & certainly with every advantage. But the assault of our people was irresistible,

As is customary amidst such scenes of carnage & disorder, various conflagrations quickly broke out in several parts of this unhappy town, already well sacked by the French garrison previous to our attack. All our attention, even on the third day, was directed to the carrying off the wounded, burying the dead & bombarding the castle. During this period, no attempts were made to arrest the flames, which on the contrary, feeding on the dry timber & nourished by a succession of brisk sea breezes raged with the utmost fury. On the day of my return from thence, I left the two principal streets and market place on fire from extremity to the other, whilst the houses were falling in every direction and I really think that scarcely one stone can be left standing on another.

Lieutenant Charles Crowe of the 27th Foot wrote extensively of his visit to San Sebastian some months after the siege.

5 October 1813

We ordered the baggage to take the direct road to Renteria [or Errenteria]. And leaving our rural abode about 8 o'clock made the best of our time to visit the ruins of the famed fortress of San Sebastian. . . . We reached the spot where our engineers first broke ground; which rising, did not, at first, require much labour to render the approaches safe. A large convent on the right had been transmuted into a fortress of considerable importance, as an advanced position. It was taken by [the] Portuguese; and very much was said about their gallant conduct on the occasion. Within a few days the French recaptured it; and deserved infinite praise for the boldness of the attempt and the bravery with which they retained it.

This convent, converted, rivetted our attention for some time, and we were surprised to see it still standing: we could not conjecture, why one brick was left on another, as our lines so entirely commanded its situation. In our progress we could, by the gabions still standing, mark the admirable position of our various batteries: all of which had a good command or range, until our lines reached the seashore. When our engineers advanced their approaches in rear of the convent they exhumed many coffins of French officers and placed them in their ramparts; which being now levelled, these coffins were exposed to the weather, more or less. Our regrets and indignation were much excited, that these coffins had not been placed in the trenches, and again buried. When we came in full view of the fortress, we noticed that the sea wall on the east had been carefully repaired; to effect which, the workmen had cleared away and made use of chief of the materials battered down from the awful breaches, on which our own immediate comrades had died, and by which our brave soldiers had reached the heights. This circumstance was a great disappointment to us! For we had fully resolved to have secured our steeds, and with a melancholy satisfaction passed up over the footsteps of our lost comrades; and searched out the spots where our much lamented friend Jack Harding & poor Kennion and other brave fellows had died!!! The town showed all the horrors of a bombardment: excepting the houses under the rock, on which the citadel is built, which our guns could not reach, not one remained entire. They had been uniform and handsome; with stone basements and had extensive and handsome balconies to the upper windows. The streets are parallel, and at right angles. We could not discover a lane or alley anywhere.

The ascent from the town to the citadel on the south side of the rock, was en barbette:[12] but the French built a parapet with flat loose stones, sufficiently high to secure all passes up and down. When ascending this road we arrived at the fatal south east angle commanding the main breach, from whence the besieged incessantly poured forth death and destruction on their assailants. This parapet originally had but one large gun; in consequence of our attack, however, it became a most important place, and the French, by cutting into the face of the rock, and other expedients, established three twenty-four pounders, on traversing carriages. These kept up such an unceasing fire, that their touch-holes, the size of this quill with which I am writing, were fused, like holes in a honey-comb; which admitted my four fingers! The centre gun was dismounted and burst, by one of our shots sticking in its muzzle. From this spot we had a full view of the breach and [were] well contented that our turn of duty had not forced us into it. I reflected upon it with acute feelings for had I been with the regiment, and

---

12. En barbette – a military term for an arrangement for cannon whereby they are mounted on high platforms or carriages so that they fire over a parapet rather than through embrasures. Therefore he means that the ascent was raised and with a parapet.

Harding availed himself of his office as acting Adjutant, I must have risked my life there. Approaching the castle we had a view of the north side of the rock furrowed by the shot and shells from our guns which had passed over the citadel: to which the garrison retired, after our troops had taken possession of the town; but next day surrendered. And well they might! Their ammunition was exhausted we found their flour magazine no longer proof against the weather and the few remaining bags were so mouldy that they could not be lifted.

On passing through the different apartments of the castle we were surprised to observe how remarkably thin the walls of the upper rooms were. We could distinctly perceive that our balls, from our batteries, and also from our ships in the bay, had passed directly through both walls although so elevated. Every room had from two to six perforations of this kind; excepting the donjon;[13] which being in the rock, had escaped. The 400 Portuguese taken prisoners by the French when they recaptured the convent, were confined in the upper part of the castle: sixty of whom were killed by our shots. Having attentively surveyed the fortifications collectively we were strongly inclined to the opinion, that the engineer who constructed these works, relied too much on the appeared strength of the conical shaped rock. For had it not been [for] the additions which the French made in various parts, the capture would not have cost us so dearly. It will be many years ere this town and fortress can be restored to their original grandeur and importance. On leaving San Sebastian we passed by the route along which poor Jack Harding and his gallant party must have advanced to their death beds.

San Sebastian was the last siege of the war, but the city of Bayonne was required to be cut off from all supplies, and the work was just as harrowing and in dreadful conditions: Lieutenant George Young of the 38th Foot wrote a few letters describing them.

Arcangues, 14 February 1814

On my landing I marched immediately to join the regiment and came up with them on the 24th of December near Bayonne. Nothing has occurred since my joining, nor do I think it likely for some time at least, while the weather continues in the very bad state it is at present. We are here about three weeks and I think we had but two or three

---

13. Donjon – the main tower or keep within the walls of a medieval castle or fortress.

days dry and then frosty. It is now while I write this pouring so that you could hardly see forty yards. The duty comes rather hard on our division; being in front we are nearly every other day on picquet close to Bayonne, so much so that we can hear the town clock strike the hour of a still night, and so close to the French sentinels that we could almost chuck a biscuit in their mouths and I daresay very thankful they would be to us to do so. We are amused listening to their bands of musick play and looking at them drilling their conscripts which they are constantly at; some of them take opportunities of coming over to us, they say they are tired of the harrying life they lead. . . heavy siege they had, and tell us there are many in Bayonne who wish us there very much. We receive every attention from the peasantry, they bring us everything to sell but charge rather immoderately.

Arcangues, 16 February 1814

We are here close to Bayonne and expect to attack it in two or three days . . . It [hole – is believed?] our division is to have the honour of taking [hole – it?]. The enemy are constantly employed in strengthening [hole – the defences?] the citadel is immensely strong and contains altogether a garrison of about six thousand men. There will be some rum work at it. Yet how vain will all their exertion be to defend it when attacked by Britons who know not but to conquer. San Sebastian's bloody journal will be a lesson to them, there they saw what British soldiers were capable of performing, there they saw that every fresh obstacle put in his way only inspired him with fresh courage and that he advanced to the attack with the determined resolution of burying himself in the ruins or become victorious. Men possessed of such hearts must be conquerors.

Perhaps Ensign John Blackman of the Coldstream Guards summed up siege work best.

Saturday 31 October, Camp near Tordesillas.

I do not recollect having ever heard my dear grandfather say whether he has ever been employed in a siege, but no doubt he is perfectly acquainted with the nature of that employment and I dare say will agree with me when I pronounce it the most harassing and unpleasant duty in the British service, arid attended with no small degree of danger, however, I thank God I am as well now as I was before the siege and have only to lament the death of my friends and companions in arms.

Perhaps not surprisingly, just like their accounts of battles, they were sparse on details of troop movements in general, but understandably concentrated on what actually happened to their own regiment and their own actions specifically, particularly if they were wounded or had some near misses. The emphasis was on their deeds and their survival and those of their friends.

Chapter 16

Wounds and Hospitals

Sickness in a foreign country, thousands of miles from home, caused great concern and frequent requests for updates litter their letters from family, but at least this sensitive information was within their own control. All officers wounded in battle were listed within the despatches sent home, unless they persuaded the surgeon to leave their light wounds off the list. Knowing that their wound had been listed and was certain to be printed in the *London Gazette*, those who could hurried letters of reassurance home. Reports of battles were read avidly at home and the names of the killed and wounded officers were scanned to ensure that no one they knew was listed there. This public announcement also led to a flurry of letters from concerned relatives and friends written to the principal family, seeking confirmation and to seek every known detail. To try to lessen this maelstrom of fear for their loved ones at home, wounded officers, if capable of doing so, would often scrawl a few sentences and ensure that it was posted as quickly as possible to calm family fears. If unable to do so, a good friend might well fulfil this office for them.

Regimental surgeons maintained small hospitals to cater for minor ailments and to provide initial medical services to the wounded. However, more serious cases were transferred to divisional or even general hospitals for more expert treatment. The establishment of these local hospitals are regularly mentioned and some even visited them to assess their quality, when most found that they were generally impressed with the facilities. The allocation of buildings to these hospitals did cause some difficulties for previous tenants, however. Lieutenant Hugh Mallett of the Royal Horse Artillery was driven out of his cantonment and billeted instead to make room for a Portuguese hospital.

> Lisbon 26 August 1810
> Since I last wrote we have been turned out of the convent, which is fitting up as an hospital for the reception of the sick Portuguese, who are to be sent down from the army: we are distributed about in billets . . .

Lieutenant James Crummer found Lisbon to be one huge hospital the following year.

Lisbon 26 June 1811
Lisbon is a most vile place, nothing but sick & wounded, it is a complete hospital altogether, every large airy building is filled with either the sick or the wounded . . .

Staff Surgeon George Morse was actually attached to the Portuguese Army from 1809 to 1814 and wrote to his wife explaining his responsibilities.

Salvaterra [de Magos] April [1810?]
My chief duty is to inspect the two Portuguese Hospitals, instruct the surgeons to keep the Hospital Accounts & to transact the whole business in the same way as that of an English Regimental Hospital, the duties of which you know I am well acquainted with. I have a little difficulty at first, because I cannot yet speak the language sufficiently correct as to enable me to hold a perfect conversation. I am now better acquainted with it & receive every assistance from Colonel Campbell[1] who is an Englishman, commands the brigade & is well acquainted with the language.

He wrote again a couple of months later, further explaining his duties, which apparently were not onerous.

Alanaemos [Estremoz?] 10 June 1810
I have very little to do. I have a brigade hospital with 2 surgeons & their assistants & have but very few sick . . . . In [their practice they?] have my confidence & I never interpose with my authority [unless I am asked on?] particular occasions & always in the arrangement of the [hospital?] which is conducted upon the same plan of English [hospitals, but?] they have not knowledge of medicines, but this I [willingly perform. What?] they can understand they will do, not that known by [Hospital surgeons?] which is so much the fashion in English hospitals, [but they benefit from?] more the goodness of his advice in most disorders is to do your [best] *'and to act boldly in the dark'*. I have not lost a man since I [arrived here?] originally (going on for three months) a circumstance almost [unheard of?] but is with much owing to my moving those diseases as [may be infectious and?] prevent them by making them [practise] cleanliness in their [wards that was not?] existing & regularity

---

1. Colonel Alexander Campbell of the York Light Infantry commanded a brigade in the 4th Division.

of dist[tribution] (good & spacious) which was unknown to them before & they seem grateful for it.

Ensign Orlando Bridgeman of the 1st Foot Guards accompanied his general on a round of regimental hospital inspections and was generally impressed, although he was clear to state that he was not talking of the general hospitals.

Vizeu Tuesday 6 April 1813
While I was at Mangualde I went with General Stopford round all the hospitals of his brigade & it really does one's heart good to see how perfectly comfortable the men are, I thought nothing could be so good as ours, but really nothing in England can be better than these, mind I am talking of the regimental, not the general hospitals.

He also explained that his servant had been in hospital so long that he would probably be forced to replace him.

Irun Saturday 13th November 1813
You will be sorry to hear that I begin to fear I must give up all idea of keeping my old servant, his health is so very bad, since he returned from Oporto, he has been to the hospital, I got him again only a few days ago & last night he was attacked with the rheumatism so violently, that he has been obliged to return to the hospital this morning; I am very sorry for it, as though he is rather slow, he is honesty itself & I flatter myself from his general conduct is attached to me; but what can I do? It is no use keeping a man, who is to be in the hospital three days out of four & the doctor thinks that he will never be able to stand the fatigues of this country, I therefore shall endeavour to get him sent to the second battalion in London, where he may recover his health. I have got another man who has an excellent character as a soldier, but is very raw

Band Master John Westcott of the 26th Foot saw the hospital at Coimbra and was quite impressed, but still talked of the dreadful consequences of war.

29th February 1812
We took a walk through the city for the purpose of taking a complete view of Coimbra . . . Fronting this bridge on the side of a hill, on the Estramadura side of the river stands the noble Convent of Francisco, which is appropriated at present for an hospital for the army, about four hundred soldiers are at present in this hospital sick and wounded . . . From this I went to see the college of Arts which is a very extensive

building, but at present appropriated as an hospital for the use of the army, it's of such an extent that at present it conveniently accommodates one thousand sick and wounded soldiers of the British army. I was shown over the whole building, through every ward of the hospital by an acquaintance of the 51st Regiment who was one of the ward masters of the hospital. Although such a number of sick in this hospital, every apartment was perfectly clean, we considered our walk through this building to be one of the most affecting scenes we ever beheld, to see one thousand brave soldiers, parts of every British regiment serving in Portugal lying on their sick beds and dying hourly, some through desperate wounds and others through different disorders – occasioned by the excessive fatigues of Portugal. Nine hundred Britons had been buried from the hospital alone, I was told by several of the ward masters that this number of men died within six months in the most deplorable state. Let any of the most hardened self-interested well-wishers of war, only take a tour through the hospitals of Portugal, after one of its sanguinary and fatiguing campaigns and then can it be possible after viewing thousands of their fellow creatures and mutilated countrymen, that any man calling himself a Christian could ever after be an advocate in the cause of war. To see thousands of the finest soldiers on the face of the earth dying in the most miserable state occasioned either by the sword, famine, long marches, or some other (of the innumerable) miseries attending on war . . .

Lieutenant Colonel George Bingham of the 53rd Foot also recorded the vast numbers of sick, particularly in the 40th Foot at Coimbra.

Camp near Abrantes 16 June 1809
A battalion of the 40th Regiment was put into our brigade, on our advance from Coimbra their strength was 750 on paper, . . . the effectives were 350, of whom about fifty were left in hospital at Coimbra when we left it. The 2nd battalion was attached to Cameron's Brigade could only muster forty-six rank and file.

He also blamed his superior, General George Clinton, for excessive parading and marching thereby causing much of his division's sickness.

Portalegre 18 April 1812
General Clinton . . . has no consideration for the soldier or indeed for anyone else; he does everything by the book, the end of which will be he will have his division in the book; it will be the hospital book.

Ensign John Blackman of the Coldstream Guards testified to the heavy workload of his friend Assistant Surgeon Thomas Maynard.

> 31 January 1813.
> There are a great number sick in hospital and Maynard is employed morning and night . . .

But despite their best efforts, fevers regularly broke out. Colonel John Keane wrote of the terrible ravages caused by the fevers amongst the wounded left at Badajoz and Salamanca.

> 28 September 1813 Salamanca
> . . . I am sorry to add they [wounded] are but too well stacked therewith & wounded officers alone amounts to nearly five hundred. The want of money has occasioned great distress amongst the poor fellows, several of them have died, from not being able to procure the common necessaries of life, others have only been saved, from parting with every article belonging to them for a very few dollars. A bad fever has attacked the hospitals here and at Badajoz and has carried off many many fine fellows, who were on the point of recovering worse wounds. Melancholy to relate, but still a truth, that several officers strong and hearty on passing these places, have been cursed with this disease and finished their journey in very few hours, not to the army, but to the grave.

Private John Bald of the 91st Foot wrote of the fever he contracted in Portugal.

> 15 November 1809
> I was very well in health all this time till the 8th of October 1808 – when] I took very bad of a blood flux. Then our army marched up to Spain and I was left behind in hospital along with many more of our army. Then I got better with many more, thanks be to God for it.

Other rheumatic fevers were more difficult to diagnose, Lieutenant George Barlow of the 52nd Foot set out his ailments to his uncle like a shopping list.

> Lisbon, 29 March 1811
> My dear uncle,
> In commencing the present, I must begin with informing you that I have duly weighed & most attentively considered *every cost of* what I now write, & you may rely therefore of the rigid exactness in the truth

of the following statement of my case. I write *the present* separate from my letter, in order that my aunt may not be uneasy, which she would be although there is no ground, it tends *for alarm*, destroy it as soon [as read] *my arm is quite well*, my eyes nearly so, though still a little weak, & I am told will keep apace in improvement with the strength of my body & leg. They are so strong, that I *never* wear a shade, excepting when a candle or some glaring light is brought near them. My hip was daily improving, till within this last week, when a rheumatism has flown into it & although that limb does not *improve*, I do not think it gets worse but is at a standstill. When I am in bed lying down, it gives me considerable pain, but *none* whilst I sit in my chair. The surgeon says that the whole of my frame sympathizes with the late inflammation of my eyes & lungs; for my cough was dreadful & lasted nearly a month. In consequence of the above there has been a slight swelling of the liver in my right side; it must have taken place some time back but escaped my notice until two days since when I stripped to wash my legs in some warm water. From the above circumstance & its giving me no pain, it can't be very bad. Upon Mr Cook examining it the next day, he accounted for it in the way I have just mentioned. Upon my requesting to know the real state of the case & my wish to know the danger if there was any, or its fullest extent. He adds that there can be no danger of the liver complaint, as I have always lived temperately & been healthy; and said as my leg & body acquired strength, it would resume its natural size. Adieu, I am well & in good spirits.

I went yesterday & appeared before the Medical Board, they recommend me to come home & I have a certificate from its president to that effect. I was lifted into a chaise & spent the day in driving to every part of Lisbon, commencing [with] the public buildings. Came home & eat [sic] for dinner half a chicken & two large soals [sic] & drank a bottle of good strong porter. You can hardly call me a *sick* man.

Band Master John Westcott of the 26th Foot suffered personally on the march, but did credit the surgeon's humanity to one of the sick men.

28 August 1811

In consequence of my weak state, not being quite recovered, the commanding officer ordered my knapsack to be carried by the sick cart, this was the first day's march, I had my knapsack carried in Portugal. The sick cart was always loaded, with knapsacks of the men who had taken ill on the road, sometimes on fatiguing marches, the cart was not sufficient for the sick, in that case the doctor of the regiment ordered the knapsacks of the men he considered the most weakly to be carried and the remainder had to carry them as well as they could, in such circumstances the doctor held a very unthankful post for it was not in his power to assist all at one time on the severe day's march of the 27th July Doctor Taylor gave his own mule to a musician who fell sick on the road and walked himself.

One action which did improve the health of the British soldiers significantly was the routine vaccination of all troops proceeding abroad for smallpox. As Lieutenant Colonel Bingham coolly recorded:

> Alegrete 17 May 1812
> On our arrival here, we found the place full of the smallpox. In my billet, there were four or five children ill with it . . . our men, who have been all vaccinated have stood it, without taking the infection.

Lieutenant James Gairdner of the 95th Rifles acknowledged this, stating that as the Portuguese troops were not vaccinated they couldn't always take up their billets.

> 28 May 1813
> Towards evening it began to rain very hard, the Portuguese having no tents, the 17th Portuguese Regiment was ordered into the village, but there being the small pox in it, our battalion were ordered to give up their tents to them and go into the town, which they did. I preferred remaining in camp as did most of the officers.

Surgeons sometimes had to forgo their own freedom to ensure the continued care of their patients, Assistant Surgeon William Whimper of the Coldstream Guards stayed to become a prisoner of war with his patients after the Battle of Talavera, but he did manage to escape.

> Lisbon, 19 January 1810
> I hasten, my dear Sir, to seize the very first moment of liberty . . . You have most probably heard, that after the Battle of Talavera, it fell to my lot to remain in that unhappy town with those unfortunates, the badness of whose wounds prevented them accompanying the army and that in consequence of this melancholy duty, I with twenty other surgeons became a prisoner. The nature of my situation then has I am sure fully pleaded my apology at being so long silent on your goodness. By great good fortune I received your favour and its enclosures the day before

circumstances, obliged me to make that attempt at an escape, which through the mercy of providence, has fully succeeded. As long as my services were required at Talavera, it was from the first my determination to stay there, but it was equally so not to leave it for France, unless I found it absolutely impracticable to take a different road. At first we were informed, that as the calls of humanity had thrown us into their power, the French would not consider us as prisoners of war, but no sooner could the Emperor Napoleon's orders be received on the subject, than our fate was changed.

Personal injuries also occurred away from the fighting, but caused just as serious wounds. Lieutenant Colonel Henry Murray of the 18th Hussars was one.

Palencia 2 July 1813

My dearest dear Emilykin,

Here I am still keeping quiet in bed, & getting my knee well, & I am much better even since yesterday as an abcess at the side of my knee which was very painful broke this morning & has relieved me much. My complete recovery will not however be for some weeks . . .

In case my first letter from Palencia has not reached you, the hurt in my knee was occasioned by Gabian's [his horse] slipping down on some rocks with me on coming out of the Esla . . .

However, the great majority of the letters were regarding wounds and providing reassurance to loved ones of their ultimate recovery. Private James Dilley of the 40th Foot wrote to his father regarding his wound at Badajoz in great detail, he also took the opportunity to report the wounding of a friend so that they could inform his family.

Galegos 5 November 1811

I suppose that you wonder at my long silence, in not sending to you before, but I received a very severe wond [sic] at the sege [sic] of Badajoz. A shot went in at my belly & it was cut out of my side, but by the blessing of God I am quite recovered & joyend [sic] the regiment again. I thought at one time that you would never hear from me anymore, for I suffered most dredfull [sic]. I was wounded on 5 May after a severe action which took place on that day, the French sallied out of the town in order to take our battery's but was repulsed by our picquets which I was on, the shots flid [sic] like hale [sic] on every side, which every man that was on the same duty with me was either kild [sic] or wounded. But thanks be to God I have tooked [sic] the first opportunity of sending to you, for I long to hear from you after so long time & I hope that you will send as soon as posably [*sic*] as I thought it my duty to send to you as soon posable, for I lay in hospital 4 months & had no opportunity of sending.

P.S. Jenkins was slightly wonded [*sic*] at the sege of Badajoz & he desires to be remembered to his friends.

Lieutenant George Barlow was wounded in the arm at Badajoz, but played it down to avoid worrying his aunt.

Camp before Badajoz, 7 April 1812

I am wounded in two places, first in the hip & second in the right arm by musket balls, the latter shattered the bone between the elbow & wrist, I am nevertheless doing as well as can be expected & the surgeons say that amputation will not be necessary for the latter, both balls were extracted last night & I propose going to Elvas as soon as my state of body will allow of moving.

On arrival at the hospital at Elvas, he had to admit that the wound was more serious than first thought.

Elvas, 22 April 1812

Upon examination it was found that both bones in the arm were broken, one was broke, the other shattered a good deal. The ball in my hip was soon taken out being simply a flesh wound; with that in my arm, two splinters of considerable size were extracted and since then ten or twelve more at various dressings, others the surgeons say are yet to make their appearance and add that it is lucky that the one bone is not shivered like the other, in that case I must have lost my limb.

He explained his wounds further to his uncle.

Estremoz, 4 May 1812

As I have told you before, my arm is found to be considerably more injured than was at first supposed; about two inches below the musket shot wound is a second of smaller dimensions, apparently made at the same moment by a slug, or as we call them, a musket-grape, which term I have explained in a former letter. The bone is also here broken and a splinter supposed to be near two inches long, shows itself. The direction has been ascertained, it is very firm and deeply seated, and an incision will it is supposed be required, once the aperture of the small wounds are not sufficiently large to admit of extraction. This operation cannot however be yet attempted.

 I have here again to repeat that there is not the slightest cause for any alarm on your part, thinking it proper at the same time to give you the real particulars of my case. The place in my thigh is doing remarkably well & as soon as the cloth works out, will soon be cured. I cannot however dissemble that the recovery of my arm will be far more slow[er]; owing chiefly to the above causes. I have for a time totally lost the use of my hand & fingers, besides three folds of my shirt, a bit of my jacket & also of my flannel waistcoat were carried in by the ball & the latter has only yet come out. None of the faculty have assured me of an earlier return to my duty than three or four months at soonest.

Having fully recovered and returned to his duties, he was writing home a year later confirming that he had been hit once again.

Vera, 11 November 1813
 By yesterday's returns you will see that I have again found a place among the list of the unlucky. I am pretty severely touched up but thank God that it was not worse. My left foot is a good deal shattered, a musket ball having entered close to the ankle and passing through the centre of the instep, came out underneath in the hollow of the same. The extent of the injury I have not as yet been able to ascertain, having as yet undergone a very cursory examination and am ignorant whether the above joint has sustained any injury, though I trust no material one. I suspect however that a bone which appears to bound the inside hollow of the foot has not been quite so fortunate as to escape from the above description. You may conceive there has been a severe smash among the small bones & sinews, which run along the top of the foot, this renders it a case of the most painful nature, which is in no small degree increased by the circumstance of my being obliged to *ride* with my foot dangling five or six miles from the field of action and bleeding very fast.

 Lieutenant Colonel Andrew Barnard of the 95th Rifles had been severely wounded at the Battle of Barossa, but you would not think it by his description of his wounds.

Isla 24 March 1811
 My wounds go on as well as possible, but as there are two apertures of some depth to fill up, it may be a little time before I shall be out of bed. Nothing however can be more healthy in appearance than they

are and there is a visible improvement daily. I have enjoyed the best of health possible during the whole of my confinement.

In 1813 he discussed his convalescence from a wound in the chest and gave regular updates.

> Farmhouse near Ascain, 12 November 1813
> Two lines from me will be more satisfactory than ten from another person. I therefore send an early despatch to tell you that I am going on as well as possible. I shall be moved into Vera this day. I cannot write a great deal as the action of my right arm is a little confined. You must make my excuses to many of my relations and friends to whom I could wish to have transmitted a little early and satisfactory intelligence. It is a great bore to be laid up at so interesting a moment but I trust my confinement will not be of a long duration.

> Vera 27 November 1813
> I have continued to mend daily since I wrote last. I am so far recovered that I had proposed moving this day to San Jean de Luz where I should have more society, which is always agreeable to a convalescent and this place is uncommonly dull . . I was on horseback on the fourteenth day after I received my wound, which is pretty well considering that it scratched the right lobe of my lungs. I cannot attempt to give you any news from this quarter which is now our hospital station . . .

> San Jean de Luz 9 December 1813
> My wounds are very nearly closed and I am acquiring strength very fast. I moved over to this place on the 28th and am situated as pleasantly as is possible, being in the midst not only of my Headquarters friends but also of my old friends the Guards.

His sister, Lady Anne, wrote back pleased to hear that he had not lost a limb and offering him recuperation in her house in London.

> Beaupark, Battle 2 December 1813
> Your safety and misfortune came so close together to me that I had half a day's fright before I was relieved by hearing that no limbs were lost, no bones broken and the ball had been extracted, that your doctor thought you would not remain long confined & that you was moved to headquarters . . . Let me propose to you as your headquarter No.21 Berkeley Square, where if you deem it expedient for health to be, you

shall have a couple of comfortable rooms on the ground floor to receive your world . . .

Though you may get tolerably well soon you cannot be in a state to duty and if you are not I submit it to you whether three months at home, might not be in all senses of the word a good measure.

The mother of the Freer boys, both officers in the 43rd Foot, received a double shock with the news that Lieutenants William and Edward Freer had both been wounded at the siege of Badajoz. Edward wrote initially.

Badajoz 14 April 1812

You will by this time have heard that William and myself are wounded, as Major Duffy wrote to Major Well's brother to inform you of the circumstance. I should have wrote also but did not know of the post going so soon as it did. William has lost his right arm but is getting on famously and intends writing you a few lines with his left. I am wounded through the testicles but it has not done my parts any material damage, so that I am in hopes of a speedy recovery, we have been here these last four days but expect soon to be removed to Elvas.

A handwritten note is attached from William, writing quite legibly for the first time with his left hand.

Thank God we are both doing as well as the nature of our wounds can possibly admit of. My right arm was amputated having had a musquet shot which shattered it above the elbow. I also had a slug in my backside which worked out the other night; from this place I have no pain. It is healing up. I have also a bruise on the knee from a stone with which they saluted us in the breach. A short time will bring me completely round, be assured we will not fail giving you an account of how we get on from time to time and with prayer for safety, believe me.

Lieutenant Charles Dawson wrote home regarding his recovery from a bad wound at Badajoz.

Elvas 16 April 1812

The ball being still in, occasions very severe pain, having as it is supposed, bruised the muscle of the leg and remaining near the nerve which it occasionally touches, it went in the inner part of the left leg, 6 inches below the knee and the leg is so swelled, the ball cannot be felt.

As usual he played down the severity of the wound.

> Elvas 29 April
> I am still being on my back, though on the outside of my bed, with my cloaths on, the slug still in the muscle of the leg which occasions great pain . . . . I observe I am returned severely wounded, you must pay no attention to it, as it is only a slight wound, though tedious.

Lieutenant James Gairdner of the 95th Rifles received three separate wounds at the storming of Badajoz.

> 8 [April]
> An hospital for the wounded being established in Badajoz I was removed there this afternoon and got into a very good house. Fitzmaurice who is wounded in the leg is also in the house, Johnston[2] who is wounded in the arm has another house but comes here to meals.

Lieutenant James Crummer of the 28th Foot wrote a hasty note following being wounded at Albuera and then transported to Lisbon.

> Elvas 22 May 1811
> My dear father
> . . . .ere this you have received the account of the action of Albuera in Spain on the 16 May, wherein your humble servant got at last a hit in the leg, just by the shin bone of a rifle ball, which though it had injured the bone a little will not signify, only confining me a little longer than my wish, however 'tis the fortune of war & fortunate that it is not a worse one.

> Lisbon 26 June 1811
> You should have heard from me much earlier but owing to my removal from Elvas & the long journey to Lisbon prevented my writing. I am now getting on very well and expect in the course of a month to procure leave of absence to Ireland, which will be no bad thing on my part and I know will be equally felt with joy by you and the family . . . the entire of the wounded are removed from Elvas to Lisbon . . .

---

2. First Lieutenant William Johnston served at Rolica, Vimiero, Bussaco, Fuentes d'Onoro, Ciudad Rodrigo, Badajoz and Toulouse. He was wounded at Badajoz as a volunteer on the storming party.

Major Thomas Brotherton of the 14th Light Dragoons wrote to his wife of his wound, which again is played down.

> Valladolid 28 July 1812
> I have only time to say that my wound at first thought severe, proves to be but slight. I was run through the body by a sword on the 18th, but I was with my regiment at the battle on the 22nd. I am recovering fast. I have not time to say more. Yours T W Brotherton

Ensign John Mills of the Coldstream Guards talked of lance wounds.

> Val de Ayres 2 October 1811
> I saw one man who had a lance through each arm and one through his body. He said he felt the lance enter him and turned his horse to the left or it would have gone through him.

Lieutenant Robert Garrett, now a lieutenant in the 7th Foot, gleefully wrote home to confirm that he had escaped amputation:

> Vitoria 1 August 1813
> I have only time to write one line to you to assure you that the wound I received on the 28th though a severe one is not dangerous. A musket ball entered my left arm at the back of my wrist & taking a direction upwards was extracted from the inside. The surgeons of the division at first wished to have taken my arm off, but I strongly opposed it. The wound is very painful. I have but this moment arrived here, having come about twenty leagues since I was wounded. This is the grand depot for wounded . . . Thank God however I have escaped amputation & that it is my left hand instead of my right.

Captain George Widdrington of the 34th Foot wrote to calm fears.

> Lisbon 13 May 1811
> I cannot miss the pacquet, that will sail for England tomorrow without sending you a few lines to assure you of my being in a fair way of recovering. My wound is considerably amended [sic] (but as yet) has not began to heal up. My health was never better and my spirits are more playful than they have been for many months . . .

On this occasion a family friend who was in the know also sought to forestall the news, having seen George's name listed in the Dispatch.

4 July

I have just received the confirmation of Lord Wellington's victory over the enemy on the 21st ultimo and as you must be anxious, I take the earliest opportunity to inform you that your son is safe, though it appears that he has been wounded. This information will enable you to break the matter to Mrs Widdrington before the list gets into circulation. I remain my dear Sir, very faithfully Colin Campbell.

Lieutenant Colonel William Gomm of the 9th Foot wrote home describing the wound received by his brother Henry at Sorauren, who was a lieutenant colonel in the 6th Foot, and reassuring them that he would soon recover.

Oyarzum 3 October 1813

Henry's wound is not yet closed, nor ought it till the cloth etc which the ball forced in before it have worked their way out. Part of the coat has already made its appearance and he is in anxious expectation of the shirt and waistcoat! In the meantime he suffers no pain and is only prevented from taking violent exercises. He eats stewed meats whenever he can get them and drinks more than you dare.

Just over two months later he was hurriedly writing home to assuage their fears as he was now on the wounded list himself.

Bidart 15 December 1813

It has been quite impossible for me to write you a line until this minute and I am afraid my letter will hardly be in time to keep pace with the despatch, which I am the more anxious it should do, as you will most probably learn that I have been slightly hurt in the scuffle and I wish you to be assured in the first instance from myself how very slightly it is. I cannot give you a stronger proof of it than by telling you that although I was struck early on the 9th, I was not only able to keep my place during the whole of that day, but to return to it on the two following days, which were much more trying ones . . . the musket ball, with whose progress I happened to interfere, passed through the fore part of my saddle and glanced off upon my left side below the hip bone and although it scarcely did more than cut the skin, it struck with some violence, for the honest marksman who fired it was not far off. Our loss has been severe, and to tell you the truth, I never have been exposed to so many risks as during the 10th and 11th.

The concern over foreign objects being carried into the wound – including dirty material from their own clothes and thereby causing severe infection or gangrene – was common Captain Charles Lennox, the Earl of March, of the 52nd Foot and aide de camp to the Duke of Wellington had not seen his cloth discs removed yet.

> Toulouse 17 April 1814
> I am very much obliged to you for your letters about my being wounded. I am now as well as ever I was, nearly not quite as strong & am obliged to take care of myself. A dangerous wound when once out of danger, particularly when in the body seldom leaves any bad effect. My wound is healing fast but I think it will open again some time or other when the cloth will come out, as the cloth of the jacket waistcoat, flannel waistcoat & shirt all went in. The ball will most likely never move as lead is very harmless.

Another one downplaying the seriousness of his wound was Captain George Miller of the 95th Rifles.

> Tarbes 8 April 1814
> I take the earliest opportunity of sending you a few lines, as I am afraid that you may perhaps be uneasy at seeing my name in the newspaper. You may however, be perfectly at ease on that score as I am getting on well, and in the course of a fortnight more expect to be quite recovered . . . The ball entered outside the thigh, a little below the groin and was extracted near the great artery.

More disconcerting for his brother was Lieutenant Colonel Alexander Gordon's presentiment.

> 23 September 1812
> A sort of presentiment that I shall be killed this campaign induces me to write my last wishes to you, which is to entreat you to pay my debts and to believe I ever was your most affectionate brother, Alex
> If you can take my servant into your family it would be kind. He is most faithful.

However, he did survive until Waterloo, although he did suffer a serious wound.

> Villaba near Pamplona 30 July [1813]
> I received a musket ball in my left arm which entered the fore part and came out under the elbow. It luckily has not touched the bone or

the artery though it went within a hair's whisker of it, which if it had cut I must have lost my arm. Although a severe wound I hope there is no danger and trust I shall be well in a month. It knocked me off my horse but I soon mounted again and although I lost a great quantity of blood [I] had it bound up and remained in the field till all was quiet.

Not everyone thought well of the medical department, however. Lieutenant William Swabey of the Royal Horse Artillery was one.

21 December 1812
But for the medical department, odious and detestable may their memory and their fate become, in proportion to the want of feeling they possess!

It can be clearly seen, that regimental hospitals were generally well organised, clean and healthy places. There was clearly a much lower regard for the general hospitals, although there is some evidence that they improved greatly towards the end of the war. Fevers were an ever constant problem and actually took far more men to an early grave than engagement with the enemy ever did. Despite, this, far less is written of fevers, although this might be because sufferers were far less likely to feel like setting down to writing a letter until they were well on the road to recovery.

If wounded in battle, their primary concern was to hastily send off a note following the engagement, clearly eager to calm the fears of their families who would read their names in the *London Gazette*. The threat of amputation or indeed subsequent death from complications meant that families would be desperate to know not only that they had survived but that they were recovering well. This was the motivation which drove the plethora of correspondence, giving quite detailed descriptions of their injuries and their long-term prognosis, a very understandable desire.

Chapter 17

The Ultimate Sacrifice

Death from fever or wounds was an ever-present threat to soldiers in the peninsula. It was also the cause of much fear and anguish for those family left at home. There was no system for announcing the deaths of rank-and-file soldiers, unless a letter home from a friend or their officer contained news of the death of a local lad, allowing the family to receive news of their loss. This, however, was far preferable to not knowing, loved ones spending the rest of their lives vainly praying for their return. As regards to officers, we have already seen that their deaths were listed in the *London Gazette*, leaving no doubt. But simply seeing your loved one's name printed in a newspaper was not a kind way to learn of their fate. Therefore fellow officers often wrote home with the dreadful news of the loss of a good friend, knowing that their family would pass on the sad news in a much more sympathetic way and hopefully before the *Gazette* was read. Sometimes they even wrote directly to the families concerned. Ensign John Blackman of the Coldstream Guards wrote of the death of his friend Ensign John Buckeridge at the siege of Burgos and confirming that he had contacted a friend, asking them to give the sad news to his family. He then mentioned further deaths and wounds.

> Saturday 31 October 1812, Camp near Tordesillas.
>
> First, then I must mention poor Buckeridge, he died nobly while doing his duty in the trenches, and I relieved him instantly in the very place where he received his death. I wrote concerning this unfortunate event to Mrs Swanton, requesting her to break it gently to the family. He was a most worthy fellow and I bitterly lament his loss. Captain Harvey, who commanded the company I am in, received his death by a musket shot in the advanced part of the trenches, a few days afterwards. He was a worthy officer. I was also in the trenches that day with some other officers, that evening about 4 o'clock we were intending to storm, in doing which, poor Burgess received his death and Captains Crofton and Walpole were wounded, I, myself escaped unhurt.

Lieutenant Colonel Henry Murray of the 18th Hussars wrote of the death of a close personal friend, Lieutenant Colonel Henry Cadogan of the 71st Foot.

Plasencia 6 July 1813

One event occurred at Vitoria most deeply afflicting to me & that that so many different letters from the army have mentioned that I am afraid there can be no doubt of it, poor Harry Cadogan's death. A few days before I sent for him to come & sit with me, he came to me in good spirits & pleasant as ever (though perhaps you have heard it, he was quite ruined by entering into a bond for a friend) . . . There is one circumstance that makes his remembrance particularly afflicting to me, that he was my friend & companion at the time I first became acquainted with you.

The death of Major George Widdrington of the 83rd Foot a few days after the Battle of Vitoria was reported to his father by his uncle Colonel Isaac Tinling of the 1st Foot Guards who was also serving in the peninsula.

Oporto 27 July 1813

Your letter of the 4th instant arrived by this day's post, which likewise brought me one from Captain Irwin of the 83rd Regiment dated Vitoria the 3rd. My feelings as a father unfit me (my dear brother) for the task of affording you and your family any consolation in the melancholy state of distress in which the Battle of Vitoria has plunged you and what can be said, but that in the present times, every family that has a friend or relation in the army must be prepared for what may happen and to look round us, how few there are in England who have not had cause for sorrow and for mourning. Believe me, I deeply and sincerely condole with you and your afflicted family on this trying occasion, which calls for all the fortitude the mind is capable of. The loss of your gallant son will be long and severely felt by us all; and with due submission to the will of God in the mode of such loss, we must endeavour to find some consolation.

I am assured by Captain Irwin that your son had the best medical attendance and that everything was done for him and it will be a comfort to you, to know that during his illness and in his last moments he had one of his most particular friends near him.

He enclosed an extract from Captain Irwin's letter, giving the circumstances of his death.

The 83rd Regiment was separated into wings in the attack of Vitoria, my friend [George] had the command of the left, which General Colville continued with. They advanced, led on by him, in the midst of a very galling fire which cost us near half of our men, and with them poor

Widdrington's mare had received two wounds of which she died before he was wounded; when he got a ball in his breast and was carried into a village near which we were engaged.

Before we went into action, we had agreed in case either was badly wounded, we would send a ring to the other. This I had not received, for although he had sent one, the soldier by some mistake never brought it me, till next day. Next morning however, I obtained leave and hurried to find him out. On my arrival I found him weak but with little pain, and his servant had sat up with him during the night. My poor friend expressed great satisfaction at seeing me. He continued weak but with great hopes of his recovery till the 28th when he became delirious. In which state (with intervals) he continued, till 8 o'clock in the *evening on the 30th of June*. His death was so easy that I could scarcely believe he had breathed his last. He seemed to be in a slumber which continued some minutes, when with a gentle sigh he departed this life and is gone, I hope, to enjoy the reward of his virtues. He was next day *interred with military honours in the garden of a convent in the city.* Irwin

First Lieutenant James Macleod of the Royal Artillery had the unenviable task of writing hastily home to inform his father of the death of his own brother Charles before the official papers arrived.

Elvas 9 April 1812

You will get these I hope before you hear any reports of the death of our dear lamented Charles even bad as I am sure my letters will be, they will be better than your feelings being shocked by being told or casually hearing it from a stranger. I have made an excuse to George for being half an hour away from him, but he has sent poor fellow to beg I will come to him. I assure you my dear father there is not the slightest danger of his not doing well, the leg is perfectly united & in a few days I hope to take him to . . . Lisbon.

Our poor Charles was carried from the breach by his own regiment, determined to carry the breach & at any rate save their wounded & among them they trusted to find their colonel. Dreadful was the contrary & possible the slaughter but they found even in the dark the body they loved so much & bore him to the camp. A third time with vengeance did they swear to revenge him & a third time were they obliged to give way, leaving the breach covered & the ditch full of their fine fellows 'twas an utter impossibility.

Major General Sir Charles Colville softened the news to his wife by talking of his own slight wound, before announcing the death of her nephew, Major William Nicholas, Royal Engineers who died of his wounds at Badajoz.

> 8 April 1812
>
> Badajoz has been a very dear purchase to us . . . I think myself very fortunate in having escaped in the assault with the loss of the upper joint of my third finger and a musket shot through the thick part of my thigh, which has most providentially kept clear of the bone . . .
>
> I exceedingly regret having to inform you, that there is hardly any possibility of the recovery of that very valuable young man and excellent officer, your nephew, Captain [sic] Nicholas of the Royal Engineers . . . I shall not write to my brother or any other friends by this opportunity, but leave you do to it for me.
>
> He was killed poor fellow, five minutes, I suppose after he had asked my opinion in the covered way if the scene was not the grandest that could be fancied, to which I naturally answered that were it possible to divest one's mind of the horrors consequent on it, it must be acknowledged such, particularly alluding to the uninterrupted blaze of light from the various explosions which made the works appear twice their proper height.

Lieutenant Charles Crowe of the 27th Foot wrote in his diary of the sadness at the last days of a fellow officer.

> 28 August 1813
>
> Our poor brother officer Lieutenant Phillip Gordon died this day; after most severe suffering from his wound received 21st June, by a musket ball, which broke the thigh so high up, that amputation at the hip joint was the only expedient. This arduous operation required greater skill than could be found in a new and hastily formed hospital station . . .

The following day he recorded his burial, which was watched by the local populace.

> We buried poor Gordon this day in a most respectable manner; we three, with crape on our arms and swords, followed as chief mourners; accompanied by all the officers of the division who were able to attend. The coffin was covered with black cloth, studded with brass nails. The ceremony attracted a vast concourse of inhabitants; who behaved with the utmost decorum, and evidently were much impressed by the

solemnity of the 'Funeral Service' although they did not comprehend a single word.

Lieutenant George Barlow of the 52nd Foot wrote of the solemnity of the funeral of General Robert Craufurd at Ciudad Rodrigo.

El Bodon, 28 January 1812

When I went into Rodrigo the day before yesterday, for the purpose of attending the funeral of General Craufurd. His remains were accompanied to their last home by all the officers of the division in procession, Lord Wellington & General Graham leading the train procession. The ball passed previously through his arm & then lodged in his chest, he lingered for three or four days & then died, leaving a wife and five children.

Lieutenant Colonel Sidney Beckwith of the 95th Rifles wrote to the father of Private Anthony Lampett to inform him of his son's death from fever.

Gallegos in Spain 14 May 1810

Sir, not having received an answer to my letter addressed to you some months ago, I am led to believe it did not reach you. I therefore consider it my duty to again to repeat to you, which I do with great regret, the information of the unfortunate death of your son Anthony Lampett, which took place at Elvas on Portugal on the 10th day of December 1809.

He had been ill of a complaint to which he told me, he had been formerly subjected, even in England, the dysentery. Every effort was made to keep him up till he could be conveyed to Lisbon, but unhappily he became too weak to bear the journey. Some days previous to the march of the army from the south of Portugal, he was extremely anxious to make his will and the foregoing one was executed by him in the presence of the surgeon of the regiment and the officer on duty. The original I keep, but fearful of the fate of the papers in the future movements of the army, it becomes advisable, I should transmit to you the foregoing copy duly certified according to the custom of the army. Regretting extremely to be the means of conveying such distressing intelligence.

Major Edward Cocks of the 16th Light Dragoons wrote home to announce the death of one of his men and to ask that his outstanding wages be paid to his poor widow.

15 March 1812

Trumpeter Gorse [a black man] died of a fever while I was in England, being absent I know nothing of his effects, but I have since got £4 13s 6d prize money due to him which I will be much obliged to you to remit to the widow.

Lieutenant James Crummer 28th Foot also wrote home on behalf of a soldier who had been sick, but whose wife had died on campaign.

Coria Spain 1 February 1813

In the act of writing this, a soldier of the name of Perfect who married a girl of the name of Welch of Ballyboy, who since fell a victim to the camp fever near Madrid came in and requested I would get my father to send to Mary Welch, his mother in law, five guineas for the use of his only child, which I promised to do and beg if convenient to ask my father to do. In the act of addressing me, tears rolled down his cheeks and completely stopped utterance, when I brought inadvertently to his mind the recollection of his departed wife. He is servant to Machan . . .

Edward Cocks wrote on another occasion of an odd incident regarding himself.

27 September Camp before Burgos

An odd incident occurred to me; it was represented one night in the trenches, apparently from authority which left no doubt, that I was killed. Next morning it was my turn for duty. The first groups I met were of other regiments. 'What news, lords?' say I. 'Nothing sir, but Major Cocks is killed'. One man actually argued the matter with me. A little further were my own men and some of my friends, condoling over my fate. The surprise of their faces was very whimsical and it [was] not a little gratifying to observe how one's death took.

He was in fact killed in the trenches on the night of 7/8 October.

Sometimes the losses occurred in very unfortunate circumstances. Captain James Gubbins of the 13th Light Dragoons wrote of the death of Lieutenant Samuel King of the same regiment.

22 November 1811

. . . the account came of the melancholy fate of poor Lieutenant King in a letter from Philippon, Governor of Badajoz, saying that Lieutenant King had accompanied Captain Margane with the flag of truce that brought in Captain Nixon and that a party of guerrillas were trying to cut them off, when Lieutenant King rode up to say they were English and explain the matter upon which a Spaniard, mistaking his motive, levelled his carbine and shot him dead and they also killed the French trumpeter's horse. The body of Lieutenant King was taken to Badajoz and buried by the French with military honours. Philippon reflected in his letter upon the English for sanctioning the guerrillas, or brigands as he called them.

Lieutenant Colonel Andrew Barnard of the 95th Rifles wrote to his sister Anne regarding the death of Colonel James Catlin Craufurd who had died of fever at Abrantes:

24 October 1810
Most sincerely do I feel for you, the melancholy intelligence was not communicated to me till last Saturday. General Graham who had received a report of it some time out of kindness to me concealed it still entertaining a hope that it would prove incorrect but more recent accounts confirmed it beyond a doubt, no circumstance can give me greater pain, independent of the near connection between us and the regard which I bore him on your account, I never knew any friend that I endeared more or any companion that I liked more. I will dwell no longer on a subject, on a future day we may derive a melancholy pleasure from the recapitulation of many circumstances which would now only tend to increase our grief. I know my dear Anne that you are possessed both of fortitude and good sense to a greater amount than most people and that though both must undergo severe trial the welfare of your young family will help you to exert them to the utmost.

We have a few rare examples of a letter from a rank-and-file soldier announcing the death of another. Privates George Stansfield of the 1st Regiment of Life Guards and Private Thomas Sutcliffe of the 2nd Life Guards wrote of the death of Private Henry Willis to his mother.[1] It is clear, however, that the lot of some rankers in the Life Guards was very different from the norm!

Viana, 3 September 1813
I take the liberty of writing these few lines to you which I hope you will excuse me, but I thought it my duty to inform you of the death of your son, Henry Willis being the only comrade he had when alive, who

---

1. These letters are published with the letters of Henry Willis.

have been comrades for this 14 years and I was very much surprised when I heard of his death. He died at a place called Bilbao, a sea port town, he was invalided for England on account of his leg being so very bad and he was sent into a hospital there and he caught a vilant fevour [*sic*]. He died in fits, he went in on the Thursday and died on the Sunday on the 28th of August. His things which he had has been sold by auction, but I know he had not many for he lost all he had the day after the Battle of Vitoria, that was the time he got his leg hurt again madam. I shall now give you account of his things here, his note of hand in his pocket book I know for 400 and 40 pounds and seven years interest besides more, but I forget them. There is likewise a box of clothing which he always promised to me if anything happened to him. The time he was in this cuntrey [*sic*] he always said to me before we engaged, if anything happens to me, take all I have got and what I have coming to me from the regiment and let my mother know of my death. These his words, he has repeted [*sic*] many a time, but little did I think of this when I parted with him at Logrono . . . The clothing I mentioned is left in London with the wife of Joseph Towers, he is now Quarter Master in the regiment and he owes Henry some money, but I cannot exactly say the sum, but I know he told me when he was at Salamanca but I think the amount is in his pocket book, but I understand the captain of the party has got it and he is going to give it to the commanding officer when he joins the regiment. There is more particulars I could let you know if I was in London, but I know they would not tell anyone but me. I believe he has left some writing, he said to me if I should be killed you go to such a place and they will tell you anything you want to know but forget the name, but I know the house and the person very well, for I have been there with him many a time. I have given you account of everything as far as I know at present and you may act as you think proper. Please to favour me with a letter and any further particular you want to know, I will do my best endeavour to do it. So I remain yours, George Stansfield, 1st Life Guards.

Thomas Sutcliffe of the 2nd Life Guards also wrote.

Logrono, 4 November 1813 North Spain
 In my letter to my Aunt Salt I mentioned that as soon as I could get to hear how Mr Willis were &c before his death, I would inform you of it. By his dying in an hospital very few things were to be found as those places are frequented by different persons that after a soldier's death his things are ransacked by the first that comes across them. However, his pocket book came to light in which was found a bill of

£440 on demand signed by Alice Willis, which is placed in the accounts of his regiment for security till you as his relations should send for it. He has about £12 pay coming to him also, besides several debts owing to him by several of his comrades. He left 2 watches & 2 suits of clothes besides linen at London, which ought to be looked after, they are at Quartermaster Towers, who I am informed also owes him £50, but I am not sure, as no receipts &c have yet been found. In my last to my aunt, I informed her how his death was occasioned, so I need not fill this letter up with what you are informed of. I am in good health and spirits & content with my station, which at present is interpreter of the Spanish language to our general, which frees me from a soldier's duty.

In a further letter Sutcliffe gives a little more detail.

Logrono, 19 December 1813
. . . You wish to know what day Mr Willis died on, upon my word I cannot truly inform you, as he died away from his regiment, separated from his comrades and in a General Hospital at Bilbao.[2] His fall from his horse was occasioned by passing a broken bridge on the 29th of June near Vitoria as we were pursuing the enemy. He had nearly been drowned, but through the exertions of his comrades he was extricated after losing most part of his clothes & he afterwards went to the Regimental Hospital at Logrono where I parted with him for the last time. He seemed greatly dejected, but his hopes of seeing home rather elated him. I have wrote to your mother stating that a bill of £400 odd upon his mother is in his colonel's hands, which is safe till sent for by her. He has about £15 pay due to him besides a number of debts due to him by several of his comrades.

Sergeant Thomas Clark of the 61st Foot wrote to the sister of Sergeant John Bennett, announcing his death.

Dundalk 23 October 1812
I am sorry that my duty compels me as a comrade to write to you upon a very unpleasant circumstance. I am sorry to say your brother Serjeant John Bennett was severely wounded on the evening of the 22nd July at

---

2. Surgeon John Hennen records that there was a high mortality rate at the infirmary at Bilbao during a severe outbreak of 'gas gangrene' in 1813. It seems likely that Henry may have succumbed during this outbreak.

the Battle of Sallamanca [*sic*], of which wound he died since in the town of Sallamanca. You may rely upon it, every care was taken of him but his wound was mortal, I have to lament a fine comrade in his loss, one who I have been with ever since the 28th of March at Gloucester and am sorry to say that he now l[y]ing in Sallamanca burying ground. And what the amount of his effects is, I cannot be certain, but you may obtain his rights by making application on oath that John was your brother before a magistrate and signed by the minister of the parish. Make the application to Greenwood & Cox, Craig Court, Charing Cross, London.

You would also much oblige me if you would undertake the unpleasant task of going to Mrs Guy's, No. 5 Gravel Street, near Lewins Mead, Bristol, and inform her that her son John Guy was unfortunately killed [*sic*] on the evening of the 22nd July about 8 o'clock, by a musket ball in the breast, he died instantly. He was a serjeant and paid our light company and his loss I greatly lament, having been with him so long. She may also apply to the same for his rights. . . . . Thank God I have escaped all and am well with the 2nd B[attalio]n in Ireland and would have wrote to you before had I known where be directed, as we always made bargain to write to each other's friends if either of us was kiled, so it came to my turn to write to you.

Passing over old battlefields, soldiers regularly write of seeing the bleached bones of numerous skeletons. Captain William Bragge of the 3rd Dragoons wrote of riding over the battlefield of Albuera.

8 April 1812
Passed the day on the fatal plain of Albuera, still white with the skeletons of last year's battle.

Lieutenant George Barlow of the 52nd Foot recorded his sadness on returning to the place where they had hastily buried Captain Henry Dawson, when he was killed instantly in a skirmish during the retreat to Portugal in 1812.

3 June 1813, Camp near Morales [de Toro] two leagues beyond Toro
I made an excursion round the environs of the place, which excited some interest and having seen the scene of a pretty smart skirmish between our division & the French advance on last year's retreat, we walked to the spot where one of our poor captains fell & discovered the identical tree but not the spot where during the affair he had been hastily interred. Bayonets [had been] the only tools for scraping a little hole and scarcely were his remains covered with a little loose earth.

After much difficulty his grave was discovered, but oh what a spectacle here presented itself of mortality in its most hideous form. The head of the chest lay in one place, the trunk in a second, the thighs in a third, and the lower jawbone compleat in a fourth, a dozen yards from the remainder of the sad relics. The latter I took in my hand, and by some very particular marks in the lower teeth I was one of the first who identified our unfortunate comrade, to make certainty till more sure, we picked up a ragged shirt & with a little difficulty found the name of the deceased in most legible characters, together with his overhauls & flannel waistcoat. Some wild animals had probably tore up the corpse & disarticulated it and mauled it. We designed therefore to re-inter with more cover, with feelings which you may well imagine, the sad remains of our friend whilst many reflections of the frail state of our nature and on the sad day which we also must sooner or later come pervaded every other and undoubtedly did mine.

The dreadful loss of a child was also laid bare in corresponding with friends and family. Mrs Martha Freer wrote to her son John, serving with the Royal Artillery at Gibraltar, of her grief for the loss of his brother Edward, killed on the attack on the Rhune Mountain while serving with the 43rd Foot. Her loss like many others was eased by their strong Christian beliefs.

29 December 1813
What comfort to my afflicted heart to know that the dear boy had fulfilled his [duty] and was prepared to stand before his maker with an unblemished character and with what pleasure do I look forward to be received into the bright mansion of peace.

In other letters, the grief of a sibling is laid wide open, such as Lieutenant Thomas Thompson of the 14th Light Dragoons in a letter to his wife, announcing the death of his brother Charles, a captain in the 1st Foot Guards, at the Battle of the Nive.

St Jean de Luz 22 Dec 1813
Thou has no rival now, Nancy. My poor good brother was killed on the 12th of this month, near Bidart. I rode today past the house where he is buried without knowing it. I only heard of his death yesterday . . . He was with the light infantry company opposed to the French infantry. The French were firing from behind cover within thirty yards and a sergeant cautioned him to kneel down and cover himself. He did so and in five minutes afterwards he was struck. The ball went in at his right

temple and out at the back of his head. He never moved after. He was buried in his clothes, with two more officers of the Guards [actually only Lt Colonel Coote Martin], behind the country house of the Mayor of Bidart [Villa Barrouillet] . . . He was buried with a little gold cross on, which he used to wear. I would take him up that I might see him again and get it from him; but there are two other officers with him. He must lie there till God calls us all.

However, it would seem that grief got the better of him as he wrote again on 23 December:

I have seen him again. I got some pioneers to uncover him. I knew him by the arched eyebrows and the dark chin. I took the little cross out of his breast and put a short note in pencil in its place. I cut some hair from his brows, where it turned up in what they call a 'calf lick' with the subtle knife. I send you a little, take care of it. The dust of the grave cleaves to it; but I have not removed it. It is mixed with grey hairs, like mine.

He lies in the garden of Monsieur Commamalle, on the right hand of the road from St Jean de Luz to Bayonne about five miles from St Jean de Luz. He is in a line northwest by compass from the house, at the distance of 80 yards from it; and six yards south east from a tree in the corner of the garden.

He is wounded in the breast as well as in the head. I think I have done to him, just as he would have done to me; and am content.

His wife had written previously a little colder at the news of the death of a nephew, Lieutenant Thomas Lindsay of the 83rd Foot in the *Gazette*.

Berkeley Square 11 July 1813
Alas my poor young nephew Tom Lindsay he has fallen I see and ended his short & harmless career, I hear he was a fine boy but never saw him but once.

Ensign Edmund Wheatley of the 5th Line Battalion KGL believed that all soldiers viewed death in the same way:

7 November 1813
All soldiers are predestinarians and if it is pre-ordained I should fall, I'll die with credit I hope . . . Llewellyn and myself have made our wills to each other, and he certainly will do me the last office of sending them.

The loss to families continued to haunt them for many years after the wars were over. Losses in terms of the overall population were roughly equal to those that Britain suffered in the First World War, with virtually every family being affected, although it must be admitted that this loss had occurred over 23 years of fighting rather than in four dreadful years. Some families were particularly affected, as shown in this letter by Maria Ramsay who was an aunt to the Ramsay boys, all four of whom died during the wars. Lieutenant John Ramsay Royal Navy had died of natural causes on the Leeward Station in 1807; Alexander died at the Battle of New Orleans in January 1815; Norman died commanding an artillery battery at Waterloo; and within two months the last brother, David, had died on the Jamaica Station (this news was yet to arrive).

> Boulogne sur Mer 16 September [1815] No. 412 sur le port
> ... it has been with difficulty that I have been able to console Major R[amsay] for the misfortunes, by death, which has taken place in his brother's family ... Isabella died at the age of seven, John died at the age of nineteen, some years ago and about a year since, in the month of October of a consumption, poor Katherine expired. Alexander fell in action, in the late affair before New Orleans in America and Norman was killed in the dreadful Battle of Waterloo on the 18th of June last. He had attained the rank of Major in the Horse Artillery, was an excellent character and officer, beloved by his commander & all who knew him. Thus he fell in his country's cause beloved & regretted, and we are all left to lament & deplore his loss. Had he lived, he would have been promoted and loaded with honours and his uncle & myself would not have been left to beg our bread in our old age, with our family.

Although people held a more fatalistic view of death in Georgian times and were more inured to the grief subsequent to the loss of children at a young age and generally had a greater acceptance of 'God's Will', the grief of such a loss was no less painful. Friends and family sought to soften the blow by pre-empting the announcement of a death in the *London Gazette* and offered whatever comfort they could. However, the loss was as raw as it ever has been and the fact that they would be buried in a foreign field, never to return home was accepted, but hurt none the less. Repatriation of the body was rarely an option for all but the wealthy; at best they were buried near the site of their demise, but many of their stripped bodies were simply left to be picked over by wild animals.

Conclusion

As has been clearly shown throughout this book, the level of communication with home was profuse and extremely diverse, but this should not be surprising in an era when virtually nothing could be achieved without written correspondence. However, the very proficient mail system meant that the regularity of the correspondence with family was high, so a letter could be received and replied to with some confidence within a month or six weeks, although as we have seen, the vagaries of the wind could play havoc with this.

This pretty regular correspondence encouraged both officers and ordinary soldiers to write frequently, giving them that all-important connection with home and their loved ones. Their letters cover the whole gamut of possible subjects, but of course, their main topics of conversation were with regard to their life on campaign and describing what they saw and did, to help their family understand both their trials and their experiences in such exotic lands.

Unsurprisingly therefore, the correspondence was very much centred on themselves, their friends, colleagues and at most the regiment. Only occasionally did they view the greater picture, to give their opinions on the war and how it was going, although it is also clear that their understanding of these greater events was severely limited to the opinions of their fellows, as discussed over dinner or at the fireside.

We have seen how the novelty of a passage at sea, with its novel working practices, the rigours of stormy weather and the threat of capture or shipwreck all both fascinated and challenged them. On arrival in Portugal or Spain the scenic views from the ship often flattered to deceive and their initial introduction to the peninsula via Lisbon or Corunna soon horrified and repulsed them. However, we have also seen that this initial shock often wore off and with time they became inured to the grime and the novelty of Portuguese and Spanish ways which soon became complacency. With a smattering of their languages, they soon began to enjoy themselves, taking in both the beauty of the stunning scenery and distracted by the dusky appeal of the local women.

Long marches in extreme heat and unsuitable clothing were commonplace given the size of the Iberian peninsula, but this could be endured without much comment, unless the commissariat failed. In these circumstances the marches became intolerable, causing many to fall out. The occasions when this occurred are legion and their letters are full of complaints at these times, but we must not make the mistake of regarding these occasions as the norm, as they were clearly not.

It is clear that sickness, particularly fevers, were prevalent within the army and that most suffered repeated bouts of these incapacitating diseases throughout the war. However, the general presumption that it was largely the rank and file who suffered, because they could not often afford to enhance their rations with local purchases and suffered greatly by being required to sleep out in all weathers with nothing but the night sky as their roof, is clearly shown to be wrong. Soldiers did often add to their rations by both legal and illegal means and in the inclement seasons they were regularly billeted in buildings to preserve their health until they were issued with tents in early 1813. Regimental hospitals appear to have generally been well managed but the general hospitals were better avoided at all costs.

Billets clearly varied in both size and quality depending on the available housing stock in the vicinity and we have seen how the soldiers often brought innovations from home to improve their comfort when quartered in any particular location for a considerable period, often to the horror of the locals.

Once over the initial culture shock, their view of the local populace mellowed markedly and some even grew to love the country more than their own homeland. Many fraternized with the local women, with many taking it much further, with a number making life-long commitments to these young ladies, but the threat of the stiletto remained a constant concern and such deaths were frequently reported.

In general they arrived with a good opinion of the 'Noble Spaniard' and a much less positive opinion of the 'Vile Portuguese', but this view did alter with personal experience, although there always remained a firm preference for the perceived Spanish physique and noble spirit over the Portuguese who were deemed more mean spirited. This view was not replicated with their soldiery; early positive hopes for the Spanish army were soon dashed and the soldiers of both countries were deemed little better than useless. However, with British officers helping to train them, the Portuguese infantry were soon seen as every bit the equal of the British soldier in all but siege operations, but this was not the view of their cavalry at any period. As to the Spanish, they were never viewed as equals but the improvement in their abilities was acknowledged; in fact the Spanish infantryman came to be seen as 'noble' but led by donkeys. Perhaps surprisingly, their positive view of the King's German Legion was also far from universal, the line infantry being seen as quite inferior to their cavalry and artillery which were universally admired.

We have also seen how they sought to fill the long periods of boredom and inactivity when there were no current operations, with hunting, riding and even acting helping to fill the void. Their attitude to corporal punishment was ambivalent; they regularly brought felons to court on lesser charges to keep it within the regiment, to avoid publicizing any signs of indiscipline to the top brass, but similarly in serious cases which required either capital punishment or more often the lash, there is little evidence that they thought it harsh or unwarranted and certainly show little inclination to see floggings end.

Their attitude to the French was singularly different to their view of the 'noble' Spanish or 'wily' Portuguese, who were still viewed as little better than savages. Despite the wanton terrorisation of the people and devastation of the country, the French individually were still seen as superior civilized beings, more on a par with themselves. This manifested itself in a courteous attitude to each other at all times away from the battlefield, more reminiscent of a far distant and undoubtedly partly mythological period, in the age of chivalry.

In their descriptions of the battles and sieges they took part in, they concentrated very much on their individual experience and those close to them, rarely venturing to mention anything beyond the regiment or at the very most the brigade. Their accounts are matter of fact, immediate and rarely even tinged with exaggeration or hyperbole. They are almost always straightforward narratives of their own trials without embellishment and without claims of great courage, meant to be seen by no one beyond their own close family and perhaps a few treasured friends. Their descriptions are, however, certainly more circumspect when writing to a female correspondent than to a male one, perhaps sparing them from the gory details.

As to their wounds, their primary concern was to inform their families of the situation themselves before they received the shock and anguish of seeing their names listed in the *London Gazette*, but with no immediate opportunity of establishing how serious the wound was. Indeed many lightly wounded soldiers specifically had themselves removed from the list of wounded to avoid such trauma at home. They simply wanted to reassure their families that their recovery was all but certain and that they were well and recovering rapidly.

Much the same stands for those who were killed in battle or succumbed eventually to wounds or fevers. There was no official system for writing to relatives regarding the loss of a loved one, but it was clearly normal policy for their comrades to write to the families of those who had been killed, in the hope of breaking the news before the official bulletin was published and, as has been seen, to give some consoling words regarding their last moments.

The evidence brought together in this book provides a very clear and consistent overview of all of this contemporary correspondence and establishes exactly how the soldiers viewed every aspect of their life while serving in Wellington's army during the Peninsular War. Some of these views are very different to those espoused by later memoir writers, as I have explained in the preface, and it is clear some 'established' views of life in the peninsula need to be reconsidered profoundly. It is hoped that this study will stimulate this debate.

I will leave the final words to Lieutenant Colonel Henry Murray of the 18th Hussars:

> Bordeaux 12 April 1814
>
> Here is an end of the business, an end to Bonaparte's visions of universal dominion, an end to war & repose to the world. What a field for moralising, what a field for prosing on the vanity of human nature & the power of providence to dissipate at a breath the deepest scheme of hitherto successful villainy & to vindicate her justice, but for my own part I shall not take the moralising field, *any more than the field of battle*.

Bibliography

Memoirs

Bald, Private John	*Journal of the Society for Army Historical Research* Vol. L No. 202 1972.
Barlow, Captain George	*A Light Infantryman with Wellington*, Gareth Glover, Warwick 2018.
Barnard, Lt Colonel Andrew	*Barnard Letters 1778-1824*, Anthony Powell, London 1828.
Bingham, Lt Colonel George	*Wellington's Lieutenant, Napoleon's Gaoler*, Gareth Glover, Barnsley 2004.
Blackman, Ensign John	*It all culminated at Hougoumont*, Gareth Glover, Huntingdon 2009.
Bragge, Captain William	*Peninsular Portrait 1811-14*, S. Cassels, London 1963.
Brooke, Major William	*Studies in the Napoleonic Wars*, Charles Oman, London 1929.
Brumwell, Lieutenant John	*Letters of a Weardale Soldier*, William Egglestone, University of Michigan 2012
Carter, Ensign John	*Ensign Carter's Journal 1812*, Gareth Glover, Huntingdon 2006.
Clark, Sergeant Thomas	*Waterloo Association Journal* Vol. 40 No. 2 Summer 2018, Ian Chard.
Cocks, Major Edward Charles	*Intelligence Officer in the Peninsula*, Julia Page, Tunbridge Wells 1986.
Colville, General Charles	*The Portrait of a General*, John Colville, Salisbury 1980.
Cooke, Robert Duffield	*The Letters of Robert Duffield Cooke 1811-14*, Gareth Glover, Huntingdon 2009.
Crompton, Lieutenant George	*Waterloo Association Journal* Vol. 32 No. 1 Spring 2010, Colin Yorke.
Crowe, Lieutenant Charles	*An Eloquent Soldier*, Gareth Glover, Barnsley 2011.

Dansey, Captain George	*The Letters of Captain George Dansey 88th Foot 1804-18*, Gareth Glover, Huntingdon 2007.
Dawson, Captain Charles	*'Every Implement of Destruction was used against us'*, Philip Abbott, London 2015.
Dawson, Captain Henry	*'Every Implement of Destruction was used against us'*, Philip Abbott, London 2015.
Dilley, Private James	*The Journal of the Waterloo Association* Vol. 36 No. 1 2014
Ewart, Captain John	*The Peninsular War Diary of Captain Ewart*, Gareth Glover, Huntingdon 2010.
Fitzgerald, Lieutenant Edward	*Journal of the Society for Army Historical Research* Vol. XLIV No. 178 1934.
Gairdner, Lieutenant James	*The American Sharpe*, Gareth Glover, Barnsley 2016.
Garrett, Lieutenant Robert	*Journal of the Society for Army Historical Research* Vol. XIII No. 49 1966.
Gomm, Captain William	*Letters and Journals of Field Marshal Sir William Maynard Gomm*, F C Carr-Gomm, London 1881.
Gordon, Major Alexander	*At Wellington's Right Hand*, Rory Muir, Army Records Society publication No. 21, Stroud 2003.
Griffiths, Major Edwin	*From Corunna to Waterloo*, Gareth Glover, Barnsley 2007.
Hill, Captain John	*Journal of the Society for Army Historical Research* Vol. LXVI No. 268 1988.
Hough, Lieutenant Henry	'Journal kept by Lieutenant Hough 1812-13', *Journal of the Royal United Service Institution* Vol. LXI, August & November 1916
Johnson, Aide de Camp Henry	*Journal of the Society for Army Historical Research* Vol. XLIII No. 174 1965.
Jones, Sergeant John Morris	'The Old Halbedier' by Eamonn O'Keefe in *The Journal of the Society for Army Historical Research* Vol. LXXXXV No. 381 2017 and subsequent.
Madden, Lieutenant Charles	*The Journal of the Royal United Service Institute*, Vol. LVIII 1914.
Maynard, Ass. Surgeon Thomas	*It all culminated at Hougoumont*, Gareth Glover, Huntingdon 2009.
Miller, Captain George	*The Making of a Rifles Officer*, Elizabeth Laidlaw, Edinburgh 2019.

Mills, Ensign John	*For King and Country*, Ian Fletcher, Staplehurst 1995.
Paget, Ensign Charles	*With Moore to Corunna*, Charles Esdaile & M Reed, Barnsley 2018.
Philips, Lieutenant Frederick	*From Corunna to Waterloo*, Gareth Glover, Barnsley 2007.
Pierrepoint, Captain Charles	*The Corunna Journal of Captain CA Pierrepoint AQMG*, Gareth Glover, Huntingdon 2005.
Robertson, Captain Duncan	*Journal of the Society for Army Historical Research* Vol. LXXX No. 324 2002.
Robinson, Maj. Gen. Frederick	'A Peninsular Brigadier', *Journal of the Society for Army Historical Research* Vol. XXXIV No. 140 1956.
Swabey Lieutenant William	*Diary of Campaigns in the Peninsula for the years 1811, 12, 13,* Col. F. Whinyates, Facsimile by Ken Trotman, London 1984.
Thompson, Lieutenant Thomas	*General T Perronet Thompson*, L.G. Johnson, London 1957.
Way, Major Gregory	*The Journal of the Waterloo Association* Vol. 39 No. 2 2017.
Westcott, Bandmaster John	*John Westcott's Journal of the Campaign in Portugal*, Gareth Glover, Huntingdon 2018.
Wheatley, Ensign Edmund	*The Wheatley Diary*, Christopher Hibbert, London 1964.
Whimper, Ass Surgeon William	'Assistant Surgeon William Whympeer, Coldstream Guards', David Rogers (ed.) *Waterloo Journal* Spring 2017.
Willis, Private Henry	*The Letters of Private Henry Willis*, Gareth Glover, Huntingdon 2017.
Woodberry, Lieutenant George	*With Wellington's Hussars in the Peninsula and Waterloo*, Gareth Glover & Colin Yorke, Barnsley 2018.
Woods, Lieutenant William	*Waterloo Association Journal* Vol. 26 No.3 Winter 2004 Timothy Cooke.
Young, Lieutenant George	*United Services Magazine* Vol. LI 1915–16.

Unpublished Letters/Memoirs (Soon to be published)

Ball, Lieutenant Benjamin	Hampshire Archives 20M62/11B.
Brown, Lieutenant George	Museum of the Oxford Soldier NARS861/4/6/1-26.

Coles, Lieutenant William   National Army Museum 1968-07-419.
Crummer, Lieutenant James   State Library of New South Wales ML MSS 821/2.
Duffy, Captain John   National Army Museum 1992-04-182.
Freer, Lieutenant William   Leicestershire Records Office 16D52 1/21.
Gubbins, Captain James   National Army Museum 2019-08-29.
Hamilton, Ensign John   National Army Museum 2002-09-179.
Hunt, Lt Colonel John   Museum of the Oxford Soldier SOFO 2195B.
Insley, Private John   National Army Museum 1974-09-12.
Keane, Colonel John   Private Collection.
Lennox, Captain Charles   Public Record Office of Northern Ireland Mic 573/10.
Macleod, Lt Colonel Charles   National Library of Scotland, MS15381.
Macleod, Lieutenant James   National Library of Scotland, MS15381.
Mallett, Lieutenant Hugh   Private Collection.
Mellish, Captain Henry   Nottingham University Archives Me 4 C 1.
Morse, Staff Surgeon George   National Army Museum 2005-09-188.
Murray, Lt Colonel Henry   Bangor University Archives Kinmel 1573 & National Army Museum 1974-06-34-9.

Oglander, Lieutenant Henry   Bodleian Library Ms Eng Misc c471.
Phillips, Gunner Andrew   National Army Museum 1980-09-9.
Ross, Sergeant William   National Army Museum 2018-12-33-1.
Rutherford, Ensign James   National Army Museum 1988-04-33.
Simonds, Sergeant William   National Army Museum 1997-04-51.
Smith, Private Richard   National Army Museum 2001-09-659.
Tylden, Lieutenant John   Kent Archives U771-C25.
Westcott, Captain George   Private Collection.
Widdrington, Captain George   Rice University Library MS139.
Woolger, Private George   National Army Museum 1999-09-54.

Other Published Works

Coss, Edward   *All for the King's Shilling*, University of Oklahoma Press, 2010.
Daly, Gavin   *The British Soldier in the Peninsular War*, Palgrave Macmillan, London 2013.
Haythornthwaite, Philip   *Wellington's Military Machine,* Guild Publishing, London 1989.
Rogers, Col. H.   *Wellington's Army*, Ian Allan, Shepperton 1979.

Index

1st Foot (Royals) 35, 244–5
1st Foot Guards 58, 68, 75, 81, 94, 95, 98, 116, 125, 138, 152, 157, 166, 183, 193, 247, 248n, 257, 273, 282
1st Life Guards 5, 42, 278–9
1st Portuguese Regiment 80
1st Royal Dragoons 77, 187
2nd Foot 40, 130, 144, 184, 225, 238, 240
2nd Life Guards 278–9
2nd Line KGL 47, 121
3rd Dragoons 16, 45, 54, 67, 82, 96, 111, 142, 165, 186, 215, 243, 281
3rd Dragoon Guards 117, 210
3rd Foot 115, 184, 210, 212
3rd Foot Guards 62, 78, 141, 161
4th Dragoons 21, 35, 56, 77, 87, 88, 95, 110, 113, 117, 179, 183, 188, 195, 208, 210, 215
4th Portuguese Cacadores 80
5th Dragoons 117
5th Line KGL 52, 84, 283
6th Foot 269
7th Foot 221, 268
7th Hussars 153
9th Foot 35, 139, 182, 244–5, 269
10th Hussars 38, 67, 84, 121, 123, 128, 140, 187, 199, 205, 209, 217
10th Portuguese Cacadores 80
11th Foot 80
11th Portuguese Cacadores 80
12th Portuguese Regiment 80

13th Light Dragoons 10, 130, 157, 182, 195, 209, 211, 237, 277
14th Light Dragoons 143, 190, 238, 268, 282
15th Hussars 8, 18, 25, 71, 72, 105, 107, 112, 143, 173, 202
16th Light Dragoons 36, 40, 59, 83, 88, 117, 128, 140, 182, 206, 216, 276
16th Portuguese Regiment 80
17th Portuguese Regiment 261
18th Hussars 3, 31, 32, 42, 68, 84, 86, 100, 123, 134, 140, 147, 159, 162, 175, 184, 187, 195, 197, 201, 216, 262, 272, 288
20th Foot 36, 140
24th Foot 242
24th Portuguese Regiment 78
26th Foot 4, 18, 27, 34, 39, 44, 49, 51, 56, 63, 114, 133, 215, 257, 260
27th Foot 41, 70, 101, 167, 174, 217, 250, 275
29th Foot 109, 205
30th Foot 35, 63, 133, 165, 232
31st Foot 173, 207
32nd Foot 4, 18, 167, 238
34th Foot 52, 61, 75, 87, 118, 138, 146, 214, 268
36th Foot 238
38th Foot 14, 35, 159, 230, 233, 243, 244, 252
39th Foot xiv, 1, 42, 43, 45, 158
40th Foot 47, 151, 160, 209, 258, 262

43rd Foot 25, 38, 49, 61, 72 76, 80, 87, 109, 118, 131, 135, 137, 150, 168n, 173, 198, 207, 208, 228–9, 247, 266, 282
45th Foot 168, 218
48th Foot 6, 20, 22, 29, 35, 111, 119, 191, 207, 210, 212, 213–15
51st Foot 258
52nd Foot 1, 4, 29, 34, 38, 48, 52, 62, 64, 70, 90, 97, 98, 99, 104, 110, 112, 114, 117, 124, 129, 139, 143, 145, 156, 164, 168n, 173, 180, 182, 185, 202, 203, 207, 209, 220, 221, 226, 228–9, 230, 231, 233, 234, 235, 246–7, 249, 259, 270, 276, 281
53rd Foot 27, 57, 61, 64, 66, 74, 82, 94, 95, 109, 122, 124, 130, 177, 179, 197, 258
59th Foot 244
60th Foot 44, 48, 93, 159, 160
61st Foot 197, 225, 280
66th Foot 210, 212, 213, 214
74th Foot 158, 218, 219, 237
77th Foot 4, 18, 49, 181
79th Foot 49, 55, 66, 114, 145
83rd Foot 273, 283
87th Foot 48, 60, 74, 96, 152, 158, 179
88th Foot 54, 82, 218–19
91st Foot 46, 206, 259
94th Foot 119n, 223
95th Foot 37, 44, 47, 69, 83, 84, 90, 99, 101, 106, 107, 125, 128, 129, 131, 134, 135, 136, 137, 152, 167, 168n, 183, 186, 187, 198, 203, 222, 227, 228–9, 232, 234, 261, 264, 267, 270, 276, 278

Abrantes 32, 53, 56, 58, 70, 75, 93, 109, 113, 115, 119, 144, 184, 190, 200, 258, 278

Albuera 30, 44, 69, 77, 183, 191, 209–15, 267, 281
Alcmene, HMS 4
Alcoentre 89
Almeida 33, 34, 35, 61, 63, 78, 118, 151, 225–6
Antelope, HMS 7, 11, 12
Arcangues 14, 222, 252–3
Arriaga, Sebastiao Jose de, Portuguese Artillery 242n
Astorga 75, 152, 205
Audacious, HMS 248n
Azambuja 30, 35, 119

Badajoz 48, 52, 53, 61, 75, 80, 81, 95–6, 124, 151, 156, 183, 189–90, 195, 209, 225, 232–8, 259, 262–3, 266–7, 275, 277–8
Bald, Private John, 91st Foot 46, 206, 259
Ball, Benjamin, 39th Foot 42, 45, 158
Barfleur, HMS 14
Barlow, George Ulrich, 52nd Foot 1, 4, 5, 9, 29, 34, 38, 45, 62, 64, 70, 90, 97, 104, 112, 118, 124, 127, 129, 131, 139, 143, 145, 164, 173, 185, 202, 220, 221, 226, 230, 233, 235, 249, 259, 263, 276, 281
Barnard, Andrew, 95th Foot 47, 83, 101, 106, 129, 134, 150, 152, 154, 156, 173, 198, 222, 227, 229, 264, 278
Barossa 264
Barrow, Thomas, Coldstream Guards 248
Baynes, Henry, RA 239
Bayonne 33, 160, 252–3, 283
Beckwith, Sidney, 95th Foot 276
Bedell, Walter, 95th Foot 229
Belem 5, 14, 21, 28, 49, 54, 110, 111, 167, 215

Index

Bennett, Sergeant John, 61st Foot 280
Beresford, Field Marshal William Carr 76, 188, 228
Bingham, George, 53rd Foot 27, 32, 57, 61, 64, 66, 74, 82, 94, 95, 99, 109, 122, 124, 130, 176, 179, 197, 201, 203, 258, 261
Blackman, John Lucie, Coldstream Guards 16, 29, 43, 44, 65, 93, 113, 154, 157, 253, 259, 272
Blake, General 75
Boggie, Surgeon John, 28th Foot 53
Bordeaux 160, 288
Bragge, William, 3rd Dragoons 16, 22, 45, 54, 67, 82, 96, 98, 111, 117, 119, 122, 142, 165, 186, 215, 243, 281
Bridgeman, Honourable Orlando, 1st Foot Guards 68, 81, 82, 94, 98, 125, 138, 144, 166, 185, 193, 247, 257
Brisbane, General Thomas 219
Brooke, William, 48th Foot 191
Brotherton, Thomas, 14th Light Dragoons 143, 190–1, 268
Brotherwood, Sergeant, 95th Foot 222
Buckeridge, John, Coldstream Guards 272
Burgos 66, 67, 81, 82, 123, 144, 145, 146, 155, 157, 169, 217, 241, 243–4, 272, 277
Burke, Richard, 45th Foot 168
Burrard, Paul, 1st Foot Guards 248r
Burrard, William, 1st Foot Guards 247
Bussaco 76, 78, 215–16, 267n

Cadiz 61, 81, 82, 185
Cadogan, Henry, 71st Foot 272–3
Calais 1
Campbell, Alexander, Royal York Light Infantry 256
Campbell, Robert, 52nd Foot 247

Carter, John, 30th Foot 63, 133, 165, 232
Castelo Branco 22, 30, 117, 144, 155, 165
Castelo de Vide 29
Celorico 40, 91, 97, 110, 116, 161, 164, 207
Church, James, 95th Foot 187
Ciudad Rodrigo 34, 47, 59, 137, 142, 167–8, 190, 207, 226–32, 237, 267n, 276
Clark, Sergeant Thomas, 61st Foot 280
Cochrane, Bombardier, RA 9
Cocks, Edward, 16th Light Dragoons & 79th Foot 66, 83, 88, 117, 128, 135, 140, 153, 155, 160, 182, 186, 216, 276, 277
Coimbra 34, 57, 80, 88, 89, 90, 91, 92, 112, 179, 230, 257, 258
Coldstream Guards, the 16, 29, 43, 52, 57, 65, 81, 83, 93, 105, 113, 122, 129, 139, 154, 157, 185, 199, 231, 253, 259, 261, 268, 272
Cole, General Lowry 188, 210
Coles, William Cowper, 40th Foot & 4th Dragoons 47, 56, 87, 113
Colville, Major General Sir Charles 88, 89, 122, 227, 232, 273, 275
Cooke, Robert Duffield, clerk 3, 8, 10, 23, 31, 54, 60, 115, 240
Corunna xiii, 8, 25–6, 36, 58, 75, 94–5, 112, 155, 205, 248, 285
Cottin, John, 10th Hussars 218
Cox, John, 95th Foot 229
Craufurd, General Robert 26, 48, 151–2, 229, 276
Crompton, George, 66th Foot 213
Crowe, Charles, 48th & 27th Foot 6, 20, 22, 29, 35, 41, 70, 72, 101, 111, 119, 120, 126, 167, 174, 189, 217, 250, 275

Crummer, James, 28th Foot 53, 57, 59, 69, 77, 81, 103, 128, 129, 133, 135, 146, 158, 160, 163, 244, 267, 277
Cuesta, General 75
Currie, James, 52nd Foot 220

Dansey, Charles, RA 54
Dansey, George, 88th Foot 54
Davis, John, Life Guards 221
Dawson, Charles, 52nd Foot 65, 124, 209, 231, 266
Dawson, Henry, 52nd Foot 52, 105, 139, 145, 155, 180, 207, 209, 231, 235, 281
D'Espana, Don Carlos 105
Dickson, Alexander, RA 242
Dilley, Private James, 40th Foot 151, 209, 262
Dobbs, Joseph, 52nd Foot 229
Duffy, John, 43rd Foot 49
Dundas, William, RA 228

El Bodon 134, 198, 227, 230, 231, 276
Elder, George, 52nd Foot 234
Elgee, William, RA 239, 242
Elvas 52, 53, 77, 80, 95, 149, 233, 263, 266–7, 274, 276
Ewart, John 48, 64, 90, 98, 99, 104, 114, 180, 182, 203, 228, 238

Falmouth xiii, 2, 3, 9, 155
Ferey, General 104
Fergusson, James, 43rd Foot 228, 229
Fitzclarence, George, 10th Hussars 199
Fitzgerald, Edward Fox, 10th Hussars 38, 67, 121, 123, 128, 140, 217
Fletcher, Sir Richard, RE 237
Framingham, Hoylett, RA 239
Franck, James, Inspector of Hospitals 51
Freer, Edward, 43rd Foot 150, 266, 282
Freer, John, RA 282

Freer, William, 43rd Foot 61–2, 118, 131, 150, 198, 208, 266
Fuenteguinaldo 47, 48, 134, 167, 231, 237
Fuentes d'Onoro 267n

Galegos 38, 151, 262
Gairdner, James, 95th Foot 37, 44, 69, 99, 106, 107, 125, 128, 129, 131, 132, 136, 167, 183, 186, 203, 222, 232, 234, 261, 267
Garrett, Robert, 2nd Foot 40, 130, 144, 184, 225, 240, 268
Gomm, Captain William, 9th Foot 76, 139, 147, 182, 269
Gordon, Alexander, 3rd Foot Guards 62, 78, 141–2, 149, 155, 157, 161, 168, 270
Gordon, Philip, 27th Foot 275
Gore, Honourable Charles, 43rd Foot 137
Gore, Captain Saunders, 94th Foot 199–200
Gorse, Trumpeter, 16th Light Dragoons 277
Graham, General Sir Thomas 130, 147, 172, 224, 228, 238, 276, 278
Griffiths, Edwin, 15th Hussars 18, 25, 71, 72, 105, 107, 115
Gubbins, Captain James, 13th Light Dragoons 10, 130, 182, 195, 237, 277
Gurwood, John, 52nd Foot 228–9
Guy, Sergeant John, 61st Foot 281

Hamilton, General John 233
Hamilton, John, 2nd Line KGL 47, 121
Hennen, Surgeon John 280n
Hill, John, 23rd Foot 212
Hill, General Rowland 71, 129, 135

Hobkirk, Samuel, 95th Foot 137
Holcombe, Harcourt, RA 228
Hope, General John 222
Hopwood, John, 95th Foot 222–3
Hough, Henry, RA 6, 32, 65, 111, 113, 122, 197, 239–40, 241
Hunt, John, 52nd Foot 177, 246

Insley, Private John, Royal Dragoons 77, 187
Irun 144, 247, 257
Irwin, Frederick, 83rd Foot 273
Irwin, Staff Surgeon Henry 51

Johnson, Henry, aide de camp 67, 137, 140, 145, 147, 166, 169, 237
Johnston, William, 95th Foot 267
Jones, Private John Morris, 39th Foot 1, 11, 43
Jones, William, 52nd Foot 228
Junot, General 23, 74

Keane, John, 60th Foot 48, 93, 142, 159, 259
Kennion, Volunteer George, 27th Foot 251
Kent, John, 95th Foot 135
King, Samuel, 13th Light Dragoons 277–8

Labastide 106
Lampett, Private Anthony, 95th Foot 276
Leach, Jonathan, 95th Foot xiv, 128
Leiria 94
Lennox, Charles, Earl of March, 52nd Foot 156, 157, 221, 270
Lindsay, Thomas, 83rd Foot 283
Lloyd, Captain, 10th Hussars 187
Luz 20, 32, 68, 86, 120, 162, 165, 167, 195

Mackinnon, General Henry 229
Macleod, Charles, 43rd Foot 80
Macleod, James, RA 227, 233, 274
Madden, Charles, 4th Dragoons 21, 36, 56, 77, 88, 95, 110, 118, 179–80, 183, 188, 195, 208, 210
Madrid 99, 143, 145, 240
Mallett, Hugh, RA 89, 110, 193, 255
Martin, Samuel Coote, 1st Foot Guards 283
Massena, Marshal 79, 123, 215
Maynard, Thomas, Coldstream Guards 43, 105, 199, 259
Mellish, Henry, 87th Foot 48, 56, 60, 74, 75, 96, 152, 158, 179
Merida 60, 61, 96, 118, 195, 238
Michell, Edward, RA 239
Miller, George, 95th Foot 84, 270
Mills, John, Coldstream Guards 32, 52, 57, 81, 83, 93, 122, 129, 130, 139, 185, 231, 268
Mitchell, Samuel, 95th Foot 228–9
Morse, Staff Surgeon George 146, 148, 149, 256
Mortier, Marshal 188
Mulcaster, Edmund, RE 228
Murray, Henry, 18th Hussars 84, 147–8, 159, 162, 176, 184, 197, 262, 272, 288

Napier, George, 52nd Foot 228–9
Napier, William, 43rd Foot xii, 173
Nave de Haver 35, 84
Newland, Robert, RHA 200
Nicholas, William, RE 275
Nisa 30, 40
Nive 282
Nivelle, the 139, 222

O'Connell, John, 43rd Foot 247
Oglander, Henry, 43rd Foot 109

Oporto 27, 54, 60, 62, 74, 94, 166, 205, 257, 273
Orthez 107

Packe, Henry, 1st Foot Guards 58, 75, 95, 116, 152, 157
Paget, Charles, 52nd Foot 110
Palencia 82, 98, 144, 147, 197, 262
Pamplona 33, 147, 149, 174, 175, 177, 187, 196, 200, 220, 243, 270
Pascoe, John, RA 240, 241
Patterson, Cooke Tylden, 43rd Foot 137, 229
Peacocke, Major General Warren 49
Philippon, General Armand 189–90, 277–8
Phillips, Gunner Andrew, RA 60
Philips, Frederick, 15th Hussars 8, 25, 143
Picton, General Sir Thomas 194, 218
Pierrepoint, Charles, 20th Foot 36–7
Pinhel 49, 76, 87, 118, 122
Plasencia 84, 184, 273
Pompee, HMS 4, 5, 9
Portalegre 45, 77, 158, 258
Power, William, 28th Foot 53
Power, William, RA 242

Ramsay, Norman, RHA 284
Robertson, Duncan, 88th Foot 82, 218
Robinson, Major General Frederick 33, 38, 68, 145, 164, 183, 245
Ross, George, RE 228
Ross, Sergeant William, 74th Foot 158, 237
Russell, Francis, 7th Foot 221
Rutherford, James, 94th Foot 223

Sabugal 35, 45
Sacavem 32, 112, 162
Sahagun 36

Salamanca 37, 45, 53, 59, 66, 81, 93, 97, 104, 182, 185, 238, 240, 259, 279
San Sebastian xiii, 145, 164, 183, 244–52, 253
Santarem 33, 39, 66, 199
Saunders, Albert, 88th Foot 220
Setubal 87, 113
Silveira, General 74
Simonds *see* Sergeant Smith, 7th Hussars
Skelton, Thomas, RE 228
Skerrett, General John 221
Slade, General John 215
Smith, Private Richard, 3rd Foot 115, 184
Smith, Sergeant William, 7th Hussars 153
Soult, Marshal Jean-de-Dieu 60, 77, 175
Spedding, Carlisle, 4th Dragoons 215
Spencer, Lord Charles, 95th Foot 137
St Jean de Luz 106, 125, 127, 199, 282, 283
Stansfield, Private George, 1st Life Guards 278
Stewart, General William 214
Stopford, Major General Edward 172, 247, 257
Sutcliffe, Private Thomas, 2nd Life Guards 278–80
Swabey, William, RHA 278, 279–80

Talavera 37, 52, 59, 60, 75, 96, 179, 206–07, 261–2
Tarbes 54, 190, 270
Thompson, Charles, 1st Foot Guards 282–3
Thompson, Thomas, 14th Light Dragoons 282
Thrasian, HMS 6

Tinling, Colonel Isaac, 1st Foot
  Guards 273
Tomar 38, 42, 158
Tordesillas 43, 157, 253, 272
Toro 97, 125, 217, 281
Torres Vedras 14n, 79, 87, 180, 181
Toulouse 72, 107. 143, 267n, 270
Towers, Quartermaster Joseph,
  1st Life Guards 279, 280
Trant, General Nicholas 166
Tylden, John Maxwell, 43rd Foot 25,
  38, 72, 76, 87

Uniacke, John, 95th Foot 229

Vera 44, 45, 83, 132, 185, 186, 221,
  249, 264, 265
Vila Franca 28, 30, 34
Vila Velha 40
Viseu 157
Viseu Militia, the 78
Vitoria 38, 42, 71, 82, 98, 123, 126,
  143, 173, 175, 176, 199, 202, 218,
  220–1, 268, 273, 279, 280

Walpole, John, Coldstream Guards 272
Way, Gregory, 29th Foot 109, 205
Webster, James Wedderburn, 10th
  Light Dragoons 205
Weeks, Driver William, RA 94

Westcott, George, 77th Foot 181
Westcott, Band Master John, 26th Foot
  4, 8, 14, 18, 27, 33, 39, 44, 49, 51,
  55, 63, 78, 80, 114, 164, 168, 170–1,
  189, 215, 225, 257, 260
Wheatley, Edmund, 5th Line KGL 52,
  84, 283
Whimper, Assistant Surgeon,
  Coldstream Guards 261
Widdrington, George, 34th Foot &
  83rd Foot 52, 61, 75, 87, 118, 138,
  146, 149, 268, 273–4
Willis, Private Henry, 1st Life
  Guards 5, 42, 143, 221, 278–80
Woodberry, George, 18th Hussars
  3, 10, 19, 31, 32, 33, 42, 68, 71,
  86, 100, 120, 123, 125, 134, 140,
  141, 162, 163, 165, 167, 169, 173,
  175–6, 187, 188, 195, 198–9, 200,
  201, 204, 216
Woods, William, 48th Foot 213
Woolger, George, 16th Light
  Dragoons 36, 38, 40, 59, 206
Worcester, Lord 71, 134

Young, George, 38th Foot 14, 35, 159,
  230, 233, 243, 252

Zafra 208